GIRL FRIENDLY SCHOOLING

GIRL FRIENDLY SCHOOLING

Edited by
Judith Whyte
Rosemary Deem
Lesley Kant
Maureen Cruickshank

Routledge

First published in 1985 by
Methuen & Co. Ltd
Reprinted 1989 by Routledge
11 New Fetter Lane, London
EC4P 4EE

© 1985 J. Whyte, R. Deem,
L. Kant and M. Cruickshank.

Photoset by
Rowland Phototypesetting Ltd
Bury St Edmunds, Suffolk
Printed in Great Britain by
Richard Clay (The Chaucer
Press) Ltd, Bungay, Suffolk

*British Library Cataloguing in
Publication Data*

Girl friendly schooling.
  1. Sex discrimination in
  education — Great Britain
  2. Educational
  equalization — Great Britain
  I. Whyte, Judith
  376'.941   LC2052

ISBN 0-415-04944-X

Contents

Notes on contributors

Carol Adams is currently Inspector for Equal Opportunities for the Inner London Education Authority, where she works with teachers in primary and secondary schools and colleges of further education. Her previous work includes co-authoring *The Gender Trap* series and publishing several books for schools on women's history. She has been involved in organizing in-service training in equal opportunities for the past five years.

Tessa Blackstone is Deputy Education Officer (Resources) at the Inner London Education Authority. Previously she was Professor of Education Administration at the University of London Institute of Education and before that a member of the Central Policy Review Staff in the Cabinet Office.

Andrew Cant is in the Schools Branch of Manchester LEA. He has been closely involved in the development of the LEA's policy on sex stereotyping and has worked with teachers on various anti-sexist initiatives.

Lynda Carr is the Equal Opportunities Commission's Principal Education Officer. Prior to joining the Commission in 1979, she worked as a comprehensive school teacher, adult education tutor and educational administrator.

Maureen Cruickshank became Principal of Beauchamp College (1200 students aged 14 to 18) in 1981 after 5 years as Vice Principal in another Leicestershire college. She has also taught in a girls' boarding school, an inner-city primary and 3 other comprehensive schools.

Hilda Davidson has spent 34 years teaching in a variety of schools. Over the last five years she has researched the position of girls and women in secondary education.

Rosemary Deem is a lecturer in the School of Education at the Open University. Her publications include *Women and Schooling* (1978) and *Co-education Reconsidered* (1984). She has also been a County Councillor and school governor.

Lesley Kant taught in London comprehensives before moving into teacher training. At the Schools Council she worked on examinations and assessment developments such as pupil profiles and examination reform, and co-ordinated the equal opportunities programme. She is currently working as a Senior Secondary Adviser with Norfolk LEA and is the co-author of *Jobs for the Girls*, a Schools Council publication on girls' career opportunities, and *A Working Start* (forthcoming, SCDC).

Val Millman Between 1981 and 1983, Val Millman was seconded from her teaching post to the Schools Council to set up an Equal Opportunities Information Centre and co-ordinate the Sex Role Differentiation project. Her present appointment is as a teacher-adviser with Coventry LEA on a three-year equal opportunities project.

Patrick Orr is an HMI based in the Midlands. Amongst other responsibilities, he has for some years been interested in sex-related under-achievement in education, and the ways in which schools can influence the aspirations and achievements of girls and boys.

John Pratt is Director of Institutional Studies at North East London Polytechnic. He has undertaken numerous research studies of educational policy and its consequences and writes extensively on education, equal opportunities and other policy issues.

Margaret Spear taught chemistry and biology for some years in a variety of schools. More recently she has pursued her concern over girls' reluctance to study science by researching into teachers' attitudes and expectations.

Hazel Taylor has been Adviser for Equal Opportunities in Brent since 1982. She works with teachers from nurseries to Further

Education, and across the curriculum, on the issue of gender equality. This chapter is for Stephen her 16-year-old son who was killed in the week it was written.

Jenny Headlam Wells is a Senior Lecturer at Humberside College of Higher Education. She is a member of Humberside's Working Party on Equal Opportunities and Sex Discrimination and is currently supervising a research project on girls' option choices and exam performance.

Judith Whyte is a Senior Lecturer at Manchester Polytechnic, from where she co-directed the GIST (Girls Into Science and Technology) Project. She has written *Beyond the Wendy House* (Longmans, 1983) on sex stereotyping in primary schools, and *Girls Into Science and Technology* (Routledge & Kegan Paul, in press). Her current research and teaching interests include educational innovation and evaluation, and women in educational management.

Helene Witcher has worked with the Equal Opportunities Commission and a variety of groups in Scotland active in anti-sexist education. She completed an M.Ed. on anti-sexist strategies for infant teachers in 1984 and currently works in multicultural education in Central region.

Lyn Yates works in the School of Education, La Trobe University (Melbourne). Her research is concerned with general theories and movements of practice related to non-sexist education, and she is involved in various associations concerned with women and education in Australia.

Glossary

AMMA	Assistant Masters and Mistresses Association
APU	Assessment of Performance Unit
ASE	Association for Science Education
BEC	Business Education Council (since October 1983 merged with TEC as BTEC)
BRUSEC	Brunswick Secondary Education Committee
CDT	Craft, design and technology
CPVE	Certificate of Pre-Vocational Education
CRE	Commission for Racial Equality
CSE	Certificate of Secondary Education
DES	Department of Education and Science
EEC	European Economic Community
EOC	Equal Opportunities Commission
ESN	Educationally sub-normal
GIST	Girls Into Science and Technology (project)
HMI	Her Majesty's Inspector/Inspectorate
ILEA	Inner London Education Authority
INSET	In-service education and training
IPN	Institut für die Pädagogik der Naturwissenschaften (Institute for Science Education)
LAP	Lower Attainers Project
LEA	Local Education Authority
MEP	Microelectronics Education Programme

MSC	Manpower Services Commission
NAS/UWT	National Association of Schoolmasters/Union of Women Teachers
NATFHE	National Association of Teachers in Further and Higher Education
NUT	National Union of Teachers
PE	Physical Education
RSA	Royal Society of Arts
SCDC	School Curriculum Development Committee
SCRE	Scottish Council for Research in Education
SDA	Sex Discrimination Act
SSCR	Secondary Science Curriculum Review (project)
SSRC	Social Science Research Council (now ESRC: Economic and Social Research Council)
TEAC	Transition Education Advisory Committee (Australia)
TEC	Technician Education Council (since October 1983 merged with BEC as BTEC)
TES	Times Educational Supplement
TVEI	Technical and Vocational Education Initiative
YOP	Youth Opportunities Scheme
YTS	Youth Training Scheme
WNC	Women's National Commission

Tessa Blackstone

Preface

As little as two decades ago the subject of girls' education and the particular problems that girls face in achieving their potential was not on the agenda. It was not given much consideration. It was not perceived as a problem. Where people were aware of the differences between boys' and girls' experiences of school, they accepted these differences with little or no concern. Most people were unaware of the more subtle differences that existed then as now.

The re-emergence of feminism in the late 1960s and the subsequent struggle to obtain improved opportunities for women has changed this. From being not just a neglected issue but a non-existent issue, it is now a subject of concern for many people with responsibility for providing education and for parents. However, in spite of the fact that many people are interested in how girls perform at school and what they do when they leave school, compared with boys, many myths exist about the subject. For this reason I greatly welcome this book, for among other things it helps to dispel some of these myths.

The most important myth that needs exposing is that girls under-achieve at school. An analysis of a wide range of measures of achievement reveals this to be quite untrue. Girls, in fact, perform remarkably well. Given that less than a hundred years ago campaigners for reform had to fight to gain acceptance of the idea that girls had an equal right with boys to secondary education, the success of girls has in some ways been remarkable. But, as I shall show, it has not yet been complete.

In primary schools girls do better on average in most standardized tests of attainment. This is notably true in nearly all areas involving language skills, although it is less true of tests involving numerical or mathematical skills. In the days of selection at 11 it was necessary to standardize the eleven-plus examination results differently for boys and for girls in order to avoid a substantially higher proportion of girls than boys 'passing'. At the secondary stage girls also do better in school leaving examinations. In both GCE 'O' levels and CSE exams they obtain higher grades than their male peers. Moreover, the gap that used to exist at 'A' level, where fewer girls were entered and those who were took fewer subjects than boys, has now been virtually eliminated. It is only in the physical sciences and to some extent mathematics that there is still cause for concern about the performance of girls in relation to boys. The problem in physics and chemistry is not that girls do badly when they take these subjects but that they opt out of them altogether in such large numbers. Thus, if schools are unfriendly to girls, this does not seem to prevent them from doing well. However, we cannot conclude from this that all is well and that there are no problems.

First there is the science problem to which I have just referred. Girls are willing to study biology but when presented with a choice tend to be reluctant to study physics and chemistry. Several of the chapters in this book examine this issue and some of them describe ways in which girls can be encouraged to take science subjects. A number of local education authorities (LEAs) are now taking initiatives and it is to be hoped that more will follow suit. The Equal Opportunities Commission (EOC) has helped to draw attention to the problem by making 1984 Women into Science and Engineering year. The immediate success of its campaign was obvious, including extensive newspaper coverage, although it is too early to say what kind of lasting effects it may have had.

Important as the issue of the rejection of the physical sciences is, there is a second and in my view more important problem, which also may be more intractable. This is that girls' choices of careers do not reflect their educational success. Girls at all levels of ability tend to select from a narrower range of occupations than boys. Moreover, their post-school destinations do not match their qualifications. At the top end of the ability range this is illustrated by the fact that although girls have caught up with boys in the 'A' level stakes, only 40 per cent of undergraduates are women. While this represents a considerable improvement over the last twenty years, this disparity should not still exist. Among 16-year-old school leavers the evidence also indicates that girls are more likely to enter a restricted range of low status jobs where opportunities for further training are limited. It appears that girls' aspirations are limited in relation to their qualifications.

While parents' attitudes and stereotyping in the wider society undoubtedly play an important role, girls' experience of the educational system seems to reinforce these stereotypes rather than challenge them. If we are to avoid under-achievement in terms of career choice it is vitally important for schools to intervene to raise girls' apparently depressed aspirations. A number of chapters in this book consider teachers' attitudes towards the issue of sex equality. The findings of empirical research on this question reveal that teachers are often equivocal in their views. While they tend to back equal opportunities in education, they may be less committed to equal opportunities in relation to future careers. Moreover, women teachers' behaviour in respect of their own careers seems likely to reinforce their pupils' attitudes towards their future. Fewer women teachers apply for promotion than their male counterparts. This leads to a major imbalance in the proportion of women teachers who become heads and who occupy other senior positions in schools. Thus the role models for girls are not as positive as they might be.

Women teachers in positions of responsibility may help. However, the most important task is to widen girls' horizons about what opportunities are available to them in relation to the qualifications they already have and those which they have the potential to achieve. This requires both general improvements in careers counselling and specific initiatives to encourage girls to consider occupations which have traditionally been dominated by men. New approaches need trying out. Such innovations need monitoring. Those that are successful need disseminating to teachers through in-service training programmes.

It is through in-service training that we are most likely to make the teaching profession aware of where we need to intervene to create equal opportunities for girls. This book provides material for use on in-service courses. It also provides valuable information and ideas for the continuing research needed to increase our understanding of the subtle processes at work in the educational system which may contribute to inequality between the sexes. I hope that both the EOC and research funding organizations will continue to support studies of this kind.

List of unpublished conference papers

The Girl Friendly Schooling conference was held at Didsbury School of Education, Manchester Polytechnic in September 1984. Over 100 people took part, and a total of fifty-one papers were presented to the conference. Much as we would have liked to, for reasons of space it has been impossible to include every contribution in this volume, and so the additional thirty-seven papers are listed below. Copies are held at the Information Office, Equal Opportunities Commission, Overseas House, Quay Street, Manchester.

Is schooling unfriendly to girls? Analysis and critique of contemporary schooling.

Janet Hough Deprivation of necessary skills
Norma Lumb How far does a pupil's experience of schooling in the early years in secondary school differ according to sex?
Oliver Leaman 'Sit quietly and watch the boys play': for how much longer?
Margaret Crossman Girl talk/teacher pupil interaction
Janet White The writing on the wall: beginning or end of a girl's career?
Margaret Bird Curriculum innovation: attitudes towards sex role differentiation

Interventions to make schooling more girl friendly

Gill Rhydderch Half the class: strategies for single sex teaching groups in mixed schools

Dr John Taylor and *B. B. Waldon* (untitled) Report of policy and interventions in the Manchester LEA

Daryl Agnew Anti-sexist initiatives within Sheffield LEA

Gaby Weiner Feminist education and equal opportunities: unity or discord?

Janie Whyld Anti-sexist teaching strategies with boys

Patsy Mackintosh Oxford Equal Opportunities in Education: a network for change

Barry Everley Strategies for changing beginning teachers' attitudes

Implications

Dr Miriam David Teaching the work of motherhood formally and informally

Catharine Valabregue (France) Countering sexist assumptions: the French experience

Janet Smith (IFAPLAN, Germany) International perspectives: affirmative action and policy responses in Germany, France, Denmark

Dr Geoff Chivers Comparative international study of strategies to encourage girls into science and technology

Isabel Romao (Portugal) Equal opportunities policies in Portugal

What makes schooling unfriendly to girls?

Editors' introduction

Gender inequality in schooling is now a respectable issue; it is debated in the media and taken seriously by national policy makers, some local education authorities, and a growing number of schools. For those who have been working for ten years or more in the area, this is heartening. But wider interest in the issue of sex differentiation at school puts the onus on us to go beyond a critique of schooling, to offer practical and realistic recommendations which can be taken up at national, local authority and school level. This is the task which we set ourselves in organizing the conference on Girl Friendly Schooling, of which this volume is one outcome. Many more papers than could be published in one volume were prepared for the conference; those we have selected we consider to be of particular relevance and interest to practitioners and policy makers as well as readers and researchers with a wider interest in non-sexist education.

As the chapter by Patrick Orr indicates, much of the debate about gender inequality at school has centred on the demarcation of secondary school subject choices by sex, especially the shortfall of girls in science and technology. This gap between the sexes in secondary school subjects in the later years, and in the jobs they are qualified to enter, is not closing fast, despite policies designed to bring about change.

Some people might have hoped that computers and information technology, with their contemporary image, would appeal equally to girls and boys. This has not proved to be the case. Girls form less than 30 per cent of those who take 'O' level computer studies and less than a fifth of 'A' level passes in computer science.

The reasons appear to be home as well as school based. A survey carried out by Acorn Computers found that of all households owning microcomputers, boys were thirteen times more likely than girls to be using them. Thus far more boys are likely to be familiar with the procedures for using and designing simple programmes. This finding is not surprising when it is considered that certain manufacturers have deliberately aimed their advertising in the home computer market at boys and men.

In schools, computers are usually physically and organizationally located in maths and science departments, already male dominated. Where they are in short supply, i.e., in most schools, boys hog computers as they do other scarce resources, refusing to give girls a turn so that they soon give up and go away.

There is evidence that women are moving into employment associated with computers and information technology, but they appear to be taking the least skilled, less well paid jobs. The implication is that as schoolboys develop a familiarity with the principles of computing, men will increasingly dominate the development of high technology while women work in operational roles where quality of work and job satisfaction are minimal.

Part I of this volume highlights important determinants of the gender spectrum of school subjects. The beliefs of adults about girls' and boys' future lives are especially significant, since they often contain stereotyped views about the sexes. This is despite changes which have already occurred over the last forty years in the lives of men and women in British society.

The study by Margaret Spear strongly suggests that teachers of physical science and craft, design and technology are actively discouraging girls from studying their subjects. This discouragement seems to be based on beliefs that girls are inherently less competent in these areas, and assumptions that female careers are of less importance than male employment because women's primary adult role will be that of wife and mother.

These two beliefs need to be undermined. As Tessa Blackstone's preface and the first chapter of this book indicate, girls are not under-achieving at school, and the idea that they are less able scientists or technologists is based more on their past absence from these areas than on any real estimate of their potential.

John Pratt's large survey of teacher attitudes indicates that teachers of science and technology have the most stereotyped views. Professional commitment to equal opportunities is apparently superficial and subject to the countervailing pressure of powerfully conventional assumptions held by largely male teachers of traditionally masculine subjects. The exceptions among male teachers are those who have been trained in social studies: perhaps a pointer for the educational needs of today's schoolboys.

When we consider that the new TVEI (Technical and Vocational Education Initiative; for a glossary of terms used in this book, see page x) programmes are often technologically oriented, relate to a gender segregated labour market, and are frequently staffed by men with a technical background, we should not be surprised that the commitment to avoidance of sex stereotyping in TVEI projects has proved difficult to meet. The division of the school world by sex is so powerful and pervasive that good intentions, broad policies or superficial reorganization are inadequate tools for change. Val Millman's report on the new vocationalism and some recent efforts to reduce the effects of sex stereotyping show that specific well-planned awareness-raising exercises, careful monitoring and review, and a willingness to experiment radically with the formal and hidden curriculum, are necessary if the new vocationalism is not simply to reinforce and exacerbate existing gender inequalities.

Sex bias in schools: national perspectives

Sex differentiation in schools: the current situation

In recent years there has been a clear commitment in government policy statements to the need to promote equal opportunities in schools and to encourage girls, in particular, in those areas of the curriculum where there is evidence of sex-related separation or under-achievement. The extent of this separation and under-achievement is now well documented and a proliferation of research activities has done much to explain its nature and genesis. There is, however, less clarity about what can or should be done to improve the situation.

Since the early 1970s equal opportunities for both boys and girls in schools have been implemented largely through equal access policies, associated with the Sex Discrimination Act of 1975. In terms of the letter of the law, there are probably relatively few cases where the Act is not observed, and teachers, by and large, are convinced that they are promoting equal opportunities in schools. However, statistics concerning subject take-up and examination entries in secondary schools do not suggest any rapid movement by boys or girls into most of the subject areas which for them are often regarded as 'non-traditional'. The most obvious changes have been in the physical sciences: between 1976 and 1983, for example, the numbers of girls taking CSE and 'O' level in chemistry and physics doubled and the numbers taking 'A' level also rose rapidly. This improvement took place from a relatively low base, however: in physics, although not in chemistry, the increase in terms of absolute numbers was greater for boys than for girls. In physics at CSE and 'O' level the number of girls rose from 28,500 to 69,400 and of boys from 139,080 to 204,180. In chemistry at CSE and 'O' level, the increase for girls was from 40,060 to 86,830 and for boys 86,000 to 124,510. At 'A' level in physics, the number of girls rose from 5400 to 8870 and of boys from 24,300 to 31,850. In chemistry at 'A' level, the increase for girls was from 7400 to 13,140 and for boys from 18,000 to 23,160 (DES 1976, 1983).

There are some encouraging signs for girls in this situation: the growth in numbers of girls taking chemistry has been quite marked, and there are some signs of acceleration in both physics and chemistry. Nevertheless, the contrast between the numbers of boys and girls remains acute, particularly in physics.

When, on the other hand, the numbers taking and passing public examinations in all subjects are taken into account, girls do better than boys. They now outnumber boys in examinations in all categories except the group taking and passing three or more 'A' levels: here boys remain slightly ahead of girls, but the gap is narrowing. The movement by girls towards equality has so far been mainly associated with the pursuit of examination success, rather than with wider subject choices and the benefits in educational, training and employment prospects that such choices can bring.

National initiatives

The continuing traditional nature of curricular choice highlights the difference between the provision and the take-up of equal opportunities. Many would argue that real progress in reducing sex differentiation in schools can only be made through directly interventionist strategies on a national scale including bold curricular reform. The fact that the education system in England is locally administered remains, whatever its other strengths, a major constraint in these matters. Nevertheless, various recent government initiatives do have important implications for our thinking about the education of girls and for the reduction of sex bias in the curriculum.

In 1981, a Department of Education and Science (DES) publication, *The School Curriculum*, outlined government policy for the curriculum and made several statements concerning equal opportunities. The document pointed out: 'The equal treatment of men and women embodied in our law needs to be supported in the curriculum', and 'It is essential to ensure that equal opportunities are genuinely available to both boys and girls.' It also emphasized the need for girls and boys to avoid closing career avenues by making inappropriate option choices, and the desirability of following a balanced science curriculum up to the age of 16. The importance, during the primary years, of a secure grounding in science and technology was underlined. Since the publication of this document, government Circulars 6/81, 8/83 and 3/84 have invited schools and governing bodies to review their aims and objectives for the curriculum, and have asked local education authorities to make returns to the DES concerning their curricular policies in the light of the suggestions made in *The School Curriculum*. There have been references in other DES publications to the need to eliminate sex differentiation in science and technology. For example, the consultative document *Science Education in Schools* (DES 1982) suggested:

> Throughout the period of compulsory secondary education every school, with the support of its LEA, should adopt the policy of giving all pupils a broad science programme which . . . gives genuinely equal curricular opportunities in science to boys and girls.

At the North of England Education Conference in Sheffield in January 1984, the Secretary of State announced that there should be a nationally agreed framework for the 5–16 curriculum and nationally agreed objectives for its various components; and that all pupils should have a curriculum that is broad, balanced, relevant and suitably differentiated to take account of different aptitudes and abilities. This policy statement may lead to a more positive approach in attempts to reduce sex differentiation in schools.

Since the North of England speech the DES has published a short statement on *The organization and content of the 5–16 curriculum* (DES 1984b). Although this document makes no specific reference to equal opportunities, it includes, as starting points for discussion, some suggestions which have obvious pertinence for the reduction of sex differentiation. It refers, for example, to the need to introduce all pupils in the primary phase to science, computers, and to work leading up to some experience of design, technology and problem-solving. More ambitiously, it suggests that craft, design and technology might become part of the programme for all pupils during the secondary years to the age of 16. The document also points out: 'Pupils suffer a particular loss of subsequent opportunity if at the end of year three (in the secondary school) they cease to study any important element of a broad science curriculum.'

Discussion of the curriculum and of curricular aims and objectives has not, of course, been restricted to these government initiatives. It is usual practice now for schools to draw up aims for the curriculum, and usual also to express these aims in terms of the qualities pupils should develop. There have also been various attempts to describe the curriculum on the basis of the knowledge, skills, attitudes and concepts which pupils can be expected to acquire – the HMI 'areas of experience' constitute one of the better known 'checklists' of this sort. These cross-curricular explorations have not, however, led to widespread discussion of sex differentiation at school level. It appears often to be assumed that differences in choice and performance between boys and girls are societal in origin and therefore largely beyond a school's control. Such a response pays scant attention to the interrelationship which must exist between schools and society: each contributes to the other. Schools have a responsibility to attempt to reduce sex differentiation in the curriculum, so that girls and boys are adequately prepared for the changing and increasingly uncertain circumstances of domestic and working life.

The Secretary of State gave clear recognition of this responsibility in a recent speech to the Girls' Schools Association, when he pointed out that: 'Girls' education must reflect the fact that most women will be working for much of their lives, and that many may be the sole or principal breadwinner for a family.' In the general debate on the curriculum, however, the question has not yet been afforded the centrality it demands, although this may change as the implications of recent government policy statements – notably those made in the North of England Conference speech – become clearer.

There is already a measure of agreement that schools should ensure the provision of a broad and balanced curriculum for all pupils. It is important, however, to recognize that 'breadth and balance' implies the need to remove unprofitable sex differentiation. That is no easy remit. Attempts to remove sex bias from the curriculum by organizational means appear often to postpone the problem rather than eliminate it. For example, rotational arrangements in craft subjects in the early secondary years have had little effect on options, where girls and boys continue to make traditional choices. Even in those secondary schools which manage, often in the face of considerable organizational difficulties, to introduce an extended core curriculum up to the age of 16, it is difficult to find firm indications of an effect on subject choice or employment aspirations beyond that stage. Nevertheless, it can be argued that pupils at the age of 16 make choices with a fuller knowledge of the implications than is possible at the usual age for options, and that by postponing choice in those subjects where there is unhelpful sex differentiation, schools could make a considerable advance towards meeting their responsibility to reduce sex bias.

There is a growing recognition that sex bias in schools should be a focus in training programmes for teachers, but the extent to which this takes place is difficult to judge as the issue is sometimes approached within other contexts, such as courses concerned with science or computer education. Gender issues are considered in some initial training courses, but few institutions have developed co-ordinated approaches to the subject. Government statements on teacher training provide some guidance. For example, DES Circular 3/84, which outlines the procedures and criteria for the approval of teacher training courses, points out:

> Students should be prepared . . . to teach the full range of pupils with their diversity of ability, behaviour, social background and ethnic origins. They will need to learn how to respond flexibly to such diversity and to guard against preconceptions based on the race or sex of pupils.

A small number of DES regional in-service training courses for teachers have been held in recent years on different aspects of sex-typing and the inclusion of a course on 'Promoting Equal Opportunities in Schools' in the DES national short course programme gives recognition to the importance of the subject.

The Equal Opportunities Commission and the Schools Council have played a considerable role in bringing together working groups of teachers, advisers and administrators to devise approaches which may be used to reduce sex differentiation in schools. They have produced publications on primary school methods and on the organization and teaching of science, mathematics, craft, design and technology, and home economics. The newly formed School Curriculum Development Committee is also considering ways in which sex differentiation in the curriculum can be reduced. Her Majesty's Inspectorate (HMI) have published a discussion document *Girls and Science* (DES 1980), and are currently carrying out a survey on the teaching of modern languages to boys which it is hoped will be published. It is likely that impending government and HMI publications on the curriculum will include further references to sex differentiation and to the importance of working towards a shared curriculum as a long-term objective. There is, in fact, little shortage of published advice on such gender issues from government and other national bodies.

The Technical and Vocational Education Initiative (TVEI) is the most significant government financed 'special project' to include a central reference to sex-typing. TVEI, which was introduced in 14 LEAs as a pilot scheme in 1983 and extended to a further 45 LEAs from September 1984, provides Manpower Services Commission funding for a wide variety of schemes intended to develop new approaches to technical and vocational education for 14–18 year-olds. An important criterion is that the schemes would as far as possible avoid sex-typing; it is also stated that young people of both sexes should normally be educated together. The MSC has reinforced this requirement by asking for 'measurable responses' to the criterion. This is proving difficult to meet, particularly in schemes whose initial design relies heavily on curricular structures which reflect the traditional sex-based preferences of pupils. Furthermore it is unfortunate, perhaps, that men have formed the great majority of staff appointed to run the schemes. However, some schemes are being reviewed and adjusted to meet the demands of the criterion more effectively.

The Certificate of Pre-vocational Education (CPVE), for which courses are currently being devised, will provide certification at 17+, in the main for young people of lower ability. One of the declared aims of the Joint Board for Pre-vocational Education, in their consultative document on CPVE, is to 'promote equality of opportunity'. Sex-typing has often been evident in pre-vocational education at this stage, but it is too early to assess the effect of CPVE in this context, as the courses are at present at the pilot stage.

More is now known of the sorts of development which will be necessary within schools and local education authorities if girls are to be adequately prepared for a wider range of opportunities in mathematics, science and technology. National surveys and government sponsored publications have played a part in generating this information. For example, the results of Assessment of Performance Unit (APU) tests have shown how differences in performance between boys and girls in mathematics and science can be detected quite clearly at 11, and that the differences discernible at 11 set the pattern for what happens at 15. The APU has also found a correlation between pupils' attitudes to subjects and their performance in them. More crucially, perhaps, it has found that, in some aspects of science, the better performance of boys seems to some extent to reflect the fact that boys of 15 have, on average, studied more science than girls (DES 1984a).

Such findings are important in the light of government decisions to introduce computers into primary schools and to support the improvement of science teaching at this level. HMI, in their survey *Primary Education in England* (DES 1978), recommended the introduction of craft, design and technology for boys and girls at an early age:

> The comparative neglect of three-dimensional construction is disappointing. Opportunities should be provided for . . . both boys and girls to undertake some work with wood and other resistant materials and to learn to handle tools and techniques associated with them.

Slow progress is being made in primary schools, through a broadening of the curriculum to include elements of science, technology and computer appreciation. Evidence suggests, however, that unless there is informed and sensitive intervention by the teacher, boys are likely to take the dominant role in all these activities, both inside and outside the classroom. There is room for further research into ways in which teachers can be helped to avoid such inequities. We also need to know more about the ways in which girls' confidence in mathematics can be maintained. The Cockcroft Committee, in their report on the teaching of mathematics in schools (Cockcroft 1982), recommended that discussion should be an essential part of all mathematics teaching. The report also suggested that girls in particular need to undertake extended discussion in order to clarify their ideas and understanding and that plenty of verbal interaction is essential if they are to learn mathematics satisfactorily.

Attempts to bring girls and craft, design and technology (CDT) together at the secondary stage are often unproductive. Nevertheless, girls will respond well to the problem-solving, design and technological aspects of CDT, particularly when the personal and humanitarian relevance of the work is made clear. The recently published DES document *The organization and content of the 5–16 curriculum* (DES 1984b) suggests:

> A possible objective might be that throughout the five-year period all pupils should have in their programme this subject (CDT) which requires them to study and solve problems involving the use of materials and which entails some element of designing and making things.

Much remains to be done before such an objective can be realized. However, the document points out that 'Some contribution may be available from teachers of other subjects, with appropriate support, including teachers of art and design.' Improvements might also be made to some of the arrangements which exist at present in schools. For example, girls are often discouraged from taking CDT by timetabling which requires choices of craft subjects to be made at too early a stage.

Work is being done by the Microelectronics Education Programme (MEP) to promote the involvement of girls in computer education. Efforts are being made to avoid sex-typing, both in the

courses and in the development of teaching materials. Additionally, two projects under MEP are assessing the reaction of girls to
materials which have been developed to give children an awareness of information technology. The aims of these projects are,
first, to see whether girls react differently from boys to the
materials, and, second, to use this information in the development of further materials.

A survey by HMI in 1978 of a number of schools which were
more than usually successful in encouraging girls (and boys) to
take physics and chemistry (DES 1980) found 'strong indications'
that the content of the science curriculum, the ways in which
subjects were organized and taught, and particularly the careers
guidance programme, could do much to influence girls' choice of
subjects in the fourth and fifth years. There are implications here
for the content of science examination courses; and levels of
staffing and laboratory provision would need to be improved in
many schools if the number of girls taking physical sciences
increased sharply. A firm recommendation in *The School Curriculum* (DES 1981) is for a balanced science curriculum for all pupils up
to the age of 16. The Association for Science Education is
committed to the same aim (ASE 1979), and the Secondary
Science Curriculum Review, with the help of some government
funding, is investigating ways in which this might be achieved.
Extensive consultation and co-operation will be required to find
ways round problems of staffing, accommodation, curricular structure and syllabus content, before such an aim can be realized
nationally.

Despite the reduced recruitment to teaching in recent years, the
proportions of men and women entering the profession have
remained approximately the same. More than twice as many
women as men qualify as teachers each year. There is some
evidence of slow change in the distribution of men and women
within the profession as a whole, with more men than used to be
the case choosing to teach young children. Some attempts have
been made to increase the number of women teaching craft,
design and technology in secondary schools, but there are prima-
facie difficulties in this respect because of the low overall recruitment to CDT teaching. Concern is growing at the under-
representation of women in positions of authority in schools, and

the consequent lack of role models for girls. For example, although women make up almost half of all teachers in maintained secondary schools, fewer than one in six secondary head teachers is a woman. By contrast, ten years ago one-quarter of secondary headships were held by women. The decline may to some extent be due to the reduction in the number of girls' schools: in 1960 there were 1300 maintained girls' schools and today (1985) there are just under 400, providing for 15 per cent of girls in maintained secondary schools. Although the decrease in the number of women head teachers appears to have stopped, it is necessary to ask why so few women achieve headships or indeed senior positions in mixed schools. There is room for further research in this area. Sir Keith Joseph, in his speech to the Girls' Schools Association in 1983, suggested the need to 'reflect on the methods by which we select head teachers' and he hoped that the reflection 'would embrace the question as to whether our present methods are fair as between the sexes'.

Local education authority initiatives

There is an increase in the number of local authorities issuing policy statements concerning the promotion of equal opportunities. Naturally, these statements vary considerably in quality and even more in effectiveness. The best recognize the complexity of the problems to be faced, allow for long-term strategies in meeting them, and set up sound methods for the gathering and dissemination of information concerning the performance, aspirations and choices of boys and girls. Equal opportunities is a major feature of policy in a small number of LEAs, and in most of these it is part of a larger programme concerned also with racial discrimination and under-achievement among working-class children. However, most authorities provide relatively little practical support for reducing sex differentiation in schools; the issue is seen as one of a large number of causes arguing for priority treatment in the allocation of resources.

Full-time advisers in equal opportunities have been appointed in two authorities and several others have designated teacher advisers or teacher co-ordinators to work full-time in this area. A larger number have advisers, often women, who are asked to take responsibility for equal opportunities in addition to their phase or subject responsibility. In the majority of cases there is resistance to appointing extra staff to work in this field, for a variety of reasons. For example, it may be felt that promoting equal opportunities is best seen as a cross-curricular responsibility which should be shared.

Although there has been some growth in in-service training dealing with sex bias in schools, provision remains uneven, even on the fundamental issue of raising awareness among teaching staff. Considerable progress might be made if the question were treated as a major theme in courses dealing with such matters as careers education and school organization.

Early experience is important in shaping girls' attitudes to science, and much work is being done by LEAs to support the development of primary school science. There have also been initiatives designed to increase the involvement of girls in physical sciences at the secondary stage. Most authorities have sought to promote the growth of technology and computer education in schools, but few have given special consideration to the needs of girls in this context. The Women's Engineering Society has recently argued that too much emphasis on technology and computer studies as isolated subjects in schools could put girls off science and engineering, and that there is a need for computing and technology to permeate the whole curriculum, especially in non-science, non-mathematical topics. Technology and computer studies are heavily dominated by boys in the option years. Firm and informed guidance from local authorities in developing the cross-curricular applications of computers and technology could do much to promote the involvement of girls in these areas.

As a result of LEA initiatives in many instances, growing numbers of schools are developing personal, social and moral education courses for all pupils, particularly in the fourth and fifth secondary years. These courses are sometimes used to introduce topics such as home management and family care, and to provide opportunities to discuss the changing roles of men and women in society. Although potentially useful, the courses can be difficult to sustain unless the subject-matter is convincingly related to the pupils' immediate interests. Also, the fact that these courses are not examined sometimes reduces their status in pupils' eyes.

Many authorities are attempting to develop home economics as an area of study which is seen to be appropriate for both boys and girls, and which can gain esteem with employers because of the opportunities it offers for co-operative planning and problem-solving. The emphasis is on home economics as a means of developing the knowledge and skills people require in managing resources – money, time, energy and materials – in relation to the needs of people, whether in the family or the community. Such initiatives may, in the long term, help to establish the desirability of a broader curriculum for many boys in the later secondary years: it can be argued, for example, that many boys lack experience in the personal and caring areas of the curriculum.

It is often assumed that there is no particular advantage to girls or boys in single-sex education, at least as far as achievement is concerned, and some recent investigations – notably those carried out by the Inner London Education Authority (ILEA) and the National Children's Bureau, into examination results – have supported this view (ILEA 1982) (Steedman 1983). It is probably true that many single-sex schools have a tendency to reinforce the traditional aspirations of boys and girls. However, there is also some evidence that single-sex schools may help boys and girls to separate subjects from gender and that girls in girls' schools are likely to have a more positive attitude to 'male' subjects (Ormerod 1975). Nevertheless, in very few instances have accommodation and staffing been upgraded to facilitate the introduction of non-traditional subjects in single-sex schools.

A few local authorities have devised schemes to improve the career patterns of women (and men) who leave teaching temporarily because of family responsibilities; in this context there have been some useful experiments in job-sharing. It is also possible for local education authority employers to encourage women to seek management posts in schools by, for example, providing women-only training courses allowed under section 48 of the Sex Discrimination Act. However, co-ordinated action at various levels is probably necessary if much change is to be achieved in the distribution of posts of responsibility among men and women in schools. At least one local authority has already sought ways of securing better promotion prospects for women. Some positive results have been achieved.

School based initiatives

A better understanding is needed of the difficulties which face teachers who wish to help boys and girls overcome their well-documented unwillingness to transcend the discriminatory practices of our culture. It has been argued that there are limits to what can be achieved through classroom interaction, given the complexity of the problem (Deem 1980). Boys and girls develop firm ideas about their respective life roles at a very early age, but there is no reason to suppose that schools cannot effect some change in attitudes and aspirations. In a different context, the work done by Rutter *et al.* (1979), for example, has shown that schools can have a substantial influence in modifying the effects of disadvantage.

Some work is being done in nursery and primary schools, particularly in the ILEA, to attempt to reduce the effects of sex-typing. There are schools where teachers try to help young children move beyond the behaviour patterns associated with their sex – where, for example, girls are given extra help in construction activities, and girls and boys are encouraged to adopt non-traditional roles in their play. There are also schools where attempts are made to monitor teaching approaches and materials for sex bias, and where equal opportunities is a regular focus for staff discussion. This is not generally the case, however. There is a particular need for greater understanding of latent discrimination in schools – the 'hidden curriculum' – and of the differential treatment boys and girls appear often to receive in the classroom.

Attempts to reduce sex differentiation have been more noticeable in secondary schools. At departmental level in many schools efforts are made to foster the interest and involvement of girls, through improved teaching methods and syllabus content. Such work is most frequently done in science departments. There are also schools which seek to mitigate the effects of sex bias by such means as skilful timetabling, carefully structured option schemes and appropriate guidance, for parents as well as pupils, when choices have to be made. Very few schools are able to reach towards the ideal situation, however, where work in individual subjects is underpinned by a 'whole school policy' for reducing sex differentiation – a policy co-ordinated by the head and senior members of staff and supported by parents and teachers.

Some schools have sought to improve the quality of careers education and guidance for girls; and some are aware of the need to encourage girls to broaden their aspirations, as a means of preparing more effectively for changing patterns in training and employment. It is not easy, however, for a school to mount the sort of programme of combined careers education and guidance which would be likely to help girls in significant numbers first to identify and then to make non-traditional curricular and career choices. The issues involved are complex. Such a programme would require careful co-ordination across the curriculum and would need, in many instances, to be capable of influencing the views of parents as well as pupils. Close liaison with the LEA Careers Service would also be necessary, so as to ensure that the programme was realistically related to training and employment opportunities, both locally and nationally.

An evaluation of the ways in which the curriculum is mediated to boys and girls should, however, be an important aspect of curriculum review in schools. As Education Survey 21 *Curricular Differences for Boys and Girls* (DES 1975) points out:

> If all secondary schools were to carry out an analysis of both content and organisation of the curriculum from the first year onwards and to ensure that choices made later were based, as nearly as practicable, on a real equality of access to experience, to information and to guidance, that would be one step towards eradicating prejudices about the roles of men and women which frustrate individual development and cause a wastage of talent a country can ill afford.

Some of the more successful initiatives in promoting girls' opportunities appear to be in girls' schools with informed and committed heads and senior management. A few such schools have overcome problems of staffing and accommodation so as to provide the full curriculum available in a mixed school. However, single-sex schools now cater for only a small proportion of all the girls in maintained secondary schools: the main developments will therefore necessarily be in mixed schools.

There are still large numbers of schools where there is very little understanding of the issues involved, and where staff are not aware of their own school's position in relation to a developing national picture. During one recent inspection HMI were told that records of subject choices by sex were not kept as this would be discriminatory. In another school neither the senior staff nor the science department was really conscious of the fact that boys outnumbered girls in physics by ten to one. It is still the case in the majority of schools that many male teachers, in particular, have little genuine interest in positive action to promote equal opportunities. Changes in attitude are needed on the part of many teachers, but such changes may be difficult to achieve with a largely static teaching force. A priority should be, therefore, to provide in-service training, so that teachers can be helped to understand the subtle processes that lead to undue differentiation by sex among boys and girls during the school years and afterwards in training and employment.

Conclusion

It may not be easy for schools to recognize more fully their responsibility to promote equal opportunities, at a time when the sheer weight of demand for curriculum development could limit the attention paid to this issue. Schools are being asked to undertake the difficult task of preparing boys and girls for a world where patterns of employment are likely to become more fragmented for many people, and where men and women may need increasingly to share domestic responsibilities. The possibility of such changes has not yet greatly modified the assumption made by some employers, and indeed some parents, that men and women should be concentrated in separate areas of training and employment. It is difficult for schools to prepare pupils for flexibility in aspirations when the world of work is still heavily stereotyped. If progress is to be made there will have to be closer consultation on this issue between schools, parents and employers. Both government and local authorities have a role in promoting such co-operation.

Over the last ten years, the number and range of initiatives to reduce sex differentiation in schools have increased at government, local authority and school levels. However, it is open to question whether this increase will lead to an early or major shift in the aspirations and expectations of the majority of boys and girls in schools. Schools are not the only influence on children, and sex differentiation in the curriculum has its roots in deeply entrenched social structures and predispositions: although there are improvements, progress is likely to be very gradual. This rate of change suggests the need for more ambitious and co-ordinated intervention, but it also underlines the difficulty of achieving such co-ordination in a decentralized education system. Nevertheless, recent government policy initiatives possibly give some cause for optimism about future developments in relation to the curriculum. There appears also to be a growing acceptance of the need to reduce the sex-related contrasts that exist in many aspects of the educational experience of boys and girls.

References

Association for Science Education (ASE) 1979. *Alternatives for Science Education: A Consultative Document* ASE.

Cockcroft, W. H. (Chairman) (1982) *Mathematics Counts: A Report of the Committee of Inquiry into the Teaching of Mathematics in Schools,* HMSO, London.

Deem R. (ed.) (1980) *Schooling for Women's Work,* Routledge & Kegan Paul, London.

DES (Department of Education and Science) (1975) *Education Survey 21. Curricular Differences for Boys and Girls,* HMSO, London.

—— (1976) *Statistics of Education,* HMSO, London.

—— (1978) *Primary Education in England: A Survey by* HM *Inspectors of Schools,* HMSO, London.

—— (1980) *Girls and Science.* HMI *matters for Discussion 13,* HMSO, London.

—— (1981) *Circular 6: The School Curriculum,* HMSO, London.

—— (1982) *Science Education in Schools: A Consultative Document,* HMSO, London.

—— (1983) *Statistics of Education,* HMSO, London.

—— (1983) *Circular 8: The School Curriculum*, HMSO, London.

—— (1984a) *Assessment of Performance Unit: Science Age 15 Report Number 2*, DES, London.

—— (1984b) *Organisation and Content of the 5–16 Curriculum*, HMSO, London.

—— (1984c) *Circular 3: Initial Teacher Training: Approval of Courses*, HMSO, London.

EOC (Equal Opportunities Commission) (1983) *Girls and Girls' Only Schools: A Review of the Evidence*, EOC, Manchester.

ILEA (Inner London Education Authority) (1982) *Sex Differences in Educational Achievement: ILEA Research and Statistics Report 823/82*. London.

Ormerod, M. B. (1975) 'Subject preference and choice in co-educational and single sex secondary schools', *British Journal of Educational Psychology*, 45, November, 257–67.

Rutter, M., Maughan, B., Mortimore, P. and Ouston, J. (1979) *Fifteen Thousand Hours: Secondary Schools and Their Effects on Children*, Open Books, London.

Steedman, J. (1983) *Examination Results in Mixed and Single-Sex Schools: Findings from the National Child Development Study*, EOC, Manchester.

Two   John Pratt

The attitudes of teachers

Schools cannot become more girl friendly unless teachers work to make them so. At present the two sexes are channelled into separate life routes with distinct styles of socio-personal development geared towards work and careers rigidly demarcated by gender. Will teachers be prepared to make the necessary changes in their attitudes and practices for the reduction of such stereotyping?

In 1982, my colleagues and I completed a major research study for the Equal Opportunities Commission (Pratt, Bloomfield and Seale 1984) on curricular differences in secondary schools. It was the first survey since the HMI report of 1975 (DES 1975) of the national picture of subject take-up and it showed that the pattern had changed little over the period, notwithstanding the passing of the Sex Discrimination Act in 1975. We investigated a number of factors that might contribute to these findings, one of which was the attitudes of teachers.[1] This chapter summarizes the results of our survey of attitudes of over 850 teachers in fifty secondary schools in England and Wales.[2] The sample had roughly equal numbers of men and women covering twenty-nine different subjects, though in some subjects such as crafts, teachers of one sex dominate. English and maths constituted the two largest proportions (13 and 10 per cent of responses respectively). We had a high proportion of staff on scale 3 and 4 posts (24 and 26 per cent) and a noticeably high proportion of men in higher scale posts.

Table 2.1 Score T: agreement with EOC policy on good equal opportunities practice; by sex of respondent

	28–49	50–58	59–65	66–74	75–117	Number
Females	24.3	24.3	18.1	18.6	14.7	
	86	86	64	66	52	354
Males	15.2	17.0	17.8	22.9	27.2	
	77	86	90	116	138	507
Totals	18.9	20.0	17.9	21.1	22.1	
Base	163	172	154	182	190	861

The survey offered teachers a series of twenty-eight statements
about equal opportunities to which they were invited to indicate
their degree of agreement or disagreement. We aggregated their
responses to all the statements into a score T.[3] The theoretical
range of score T was from 28 to 140 with lower scores indicating a
sympathetic attitude to equal opportunity. Just under 60 per cent
of teachers scored 65 or less – indicating that a majority were
sympathetic. Males were more likely than females to be opposed to
equal opportunities practices and 27 per cent were strongly
opposed (Table 2.1).[4]

Fifty per cent of males' responses indicated opposition to equal
opportunities, with 27 per cent in the most negative category,
compared with 33 and 15 per cent of female responses. The impact
of sex on responses is, however, not as dramatic as the effect of
subject specialism. Table 2.2 shows score T for each of the main
groups of subject teachers and shows that teachers of English and
social studies (the latter mostly male) were most in favour of equal
opportunity, while teachers of maths, physical sciences, and
technical crafts (all mainly male) and languages were least in
favour. This distribution of responses by sex and subject group was
broadly maintained in responses to specific statements throughout
our survey.

We examined responses to individual statements in detail,
which cannot all be presented here. A number of important
features of teachers' views emerged from these analyses. Two of
the most important concerned teachers' basic beliefs about equal
opportunities, and the contrast between their commitment to
equal opportunities principles and to actions to implement them.

Table 2.2   Score T by subject

Subject	28–49	50–58	59–66	67–74	75–117	Number
English	33.0	27.2	17.5	8.7	13.6	103
Maths	5.3	19.7	18.4	30.3	26.3	76
Social Studies	34.0	18.0	12.0	20.0	16.0	50
PE	10.4	14.6	20.8	18.8	35.4	48
History	24.1	17.2	24.1	12.1	22.4	58
Geography	20.4	18.5	25.9	13.0	22.2	54
Physical Science	7.5	12.0	25.4	17.9	37.3	67
Biology	17.5	22.5	20.0	27.5	12.5	40
Domestic and Secretarial	12.7	14.6	25.5	27.3	20.0	55
Technical Studies	7.8	21.6	25.5	19.6	25.5	51
French and German	8.3	21.7	26.7	20.0	23.3	60
Others	25.2	23.4	18.0	12.6	20.7	111

Basic beliefs

Two statements were concerned with basic beliefs about equal opportunities:

STATEMENT 24: Innate psychological differences between the sexes are largely responsible for the different subject and career choices of boys and girls.

STATEMENT 14: The educational system treats girls less favourably than boys.

The response was at best equivocal; nearly half the sample disagreed with both statements but there was a disturbing number of teachers in the unsure/uncommitted category and a high proportion accepting that there are 'natural' reasons for differences.

	Agree		*Unsure/*	*Disagree*		
Statement	*Strongly*	*Mildly*	*uncommitted*	*Strongly*	*Mildly*	*Number*
24	8.5	28.5	16.4	16.5	30.2	849
14	11.5	27.2	15.0	24.7	21.6	846

On the other hand, fewer than half believed that the system treats pupils equally. There were relatively few differences between the sexes in their responses, though more females agreed with statement 14.

When we extended our analysis to the subject specialism of teachers we found the patterns which characterized most of the rest of the responses. Teachers of domestic, secretarial and technical craft subjects tended to show least agreement with the idea of equal opportunities; biology teachers were mostly sympathetic, physical scientists generally most unsure or uncommitted and teachers of English and social studies most committed to equal opportunities.

Encouragement to equal opportunity

Four statements in our survey were concerned with the extent to which schools and teachers should encourage equal opportunities:

STATEMENT 1: Schools should set an example in reducing sex discrimination.

STATEMENT 7: I am generally sympathetic to teachers and educationists trying to encourage equal opportunities between the sexes.

STATEMENT 20: Teachers should encourage equal opportunities between the sexes even when there is no parental support for this policy.

STATEMENT 16: I am particularly interested in encouraging equality between the sexes in my teaching.

Responses were as follows:

	Agree		Unsure/	Disagree		
Statement	Strongly	Mildly	uncommitted	Strongly	Mildly	Number
1	60.6	32.0	4.4	2.0	1.1	848
7	68.0	25.0	3.8	1.6	1.5	851
20	51.4	34.9	8.5	3.1	2.1	847
16	41.9	30.6	21.0	4.2	2.2	849

ʎority of teachers were in agreement with commit-
/th the school and the teacher to promote equal
es. Over 90 per cent agreed with statements 1 and 7,
faced with issues of implementation there was uncer-
ʎong some teachers. A sixth would not commit them-
sɛ. /action without support from parents; over a quarter were
unsure, uncommitted or disagreed with encouraging equality in
their own teaching. In all responses, female teachers showed more
commitment than males to equal opportunities. Teachers of
English and social studies agreed most strongly with the statements; maths, PE, physical science, domestic and vocational and
craft teachers showed least agreement with them (though the
percentage of agreement was still 80 per cent or more in all cases
for the first two statements and at least 60 per cent even for
statement 16).[5]

Stereotyped subjects

Three further statements highlighted the gulf between teachers'
recognition of problems of equal opportunity and the implementation of a solution to them. These statements sought to establish
teachers' attitudes towards the stereotyping of subjects and the
role of teachers in this process.

STATEMENT 4: It would be a good thing if pupils did not regard
certain school subjects as 'girls' subjects' and others as 'boys'
subjects'.
STATEMENT 5: Teachers generally tend to support pupils' existing
ideas about what subjects and jobs are appropriate for each sex.
STATEMENT 17: The teaching profession tends to give pupils the
impression that some subjects are more appropriate for one sex
than for the other.

| | Agree | | Unsure/ | Disagree | | |
Statement	Strongly	Mildly	uncommitted	Strongly	Mildly	Number
4	73.3	19.9	1.5	2.1	3.2	851
5	7.2	47.0	15.9	8.1	21.9	851
17	16.5	55.2	10.7	5.3	12.3	852

Strong and nearly complete agreement that subjects should not be stereotyped is matched in statement 4 with mild but convincing majority agreement that teachers in practice support and encourage stereotyping of subjects by pupils. There were few differences in the views of male and female teachers on those statements, though fewer male teachers than female strongly agreed with statement 4.

Least support for statement 4 came from PE, craft and domestic and secretarial teachers, although even so only 12 per cent of the latter were in favour of pupils identifying boys' and girls' subjects. An unusual agreement between social studies and craft teachers occurred in response to statement 5, when they showed most positive agreement that teachers tend to support pupils' views on stereotyping of subjects and jobs, though probably for different reasons. Craft teachers also joined social studies and English teachers in showing most agreement with statement 17 – that the teaching profession gives stereotyped impressions about subjects to pupils.

Other responses

Our examination of responses to statements about particular subjects showed the now familiar pattern of agreement with principle but less commitment to action.

The great majority of teachers agreed that careers education should look critically at sex roles and encourage non-traditional take-up of subjects or careers, but once again the more positive statement drew diminished agreement and enhanced numbers were unsure or opposed. Examination of subject groups demonstrated that male dominated groups were most unsure/uncommitted. We examined technical and physical science teachers' responses in relation to compulsory physical science and preference for boys when technical subjects are oversubscribed. Physical science teachers were much in favour of compulsory physical science; technical staff much in favour of reservation of their subject for boys. A high proportion of technical teachers supported the view of physical science teachers on compulsory physical science, but physical science teachers did not reciprocate for reservation of technical subjects to boys.

A large majority of teachers agreed that girls should be encouraged to choose technical and scientific subjects. There was more support for encouragement to science than technical subjects; and boys were convincingly but less emphatically to be encouraged to choose child care and home economics. A majority also rejected statements that such encouragement was misguided; a high incidence of unsure/uncommitted responses to these statements suggested that teachers are in need of more access to and support from policy formulation.

We compared the responses to statements on encouragement to choose non-traditional subjects with those on encouragement to choose non-traditional careers. We concluded that teachers were lacklustre in their agreement with the latter and that the observed intractability of pupil preference for traditional careers is in part the result of inadequately formulated policy on the role of careers education in subject choice decisions. Responses to other statements in our survey showed that a large majority of teachers believe in mixed playground areas and similar punishments for boys and girls. Teachers believe that too much emphasis is placed on a need of separating boys and girls for PE, but they firmly believe that physical differences demand some separation. A majority of teachers also believe there should be more teachers of subjects thought non-traditional for their sex; but there was a high unsure/uncommitted response. We took these responses to indicate that the value of non-traditional role models is familiar but unproven ground for teachers.

Statements on the role of parents provided the most united and positive response. Working lives and higher education, and parental stress on planning future working lives, were emphatically agreed to be appropriate for both boys and girls. Domestic and secretarial subject teachers were most positive; technical teachers were most likely to differentiate, though only a tiny minority among that group. We noted that the strength of opinion should not distract attention from the small minority who demonstrated agreement with a strongly discriminatory practice.

Teachers and the idea of 'neutrality'

The teachers in our attitude survey were invited to comment on any of the statements or the survey in general. A number did so, and their comments illuminate some of the reasons for their responses to the statements, particularly the thinking underlying the responses of the minority of teachers who are not in favour of positive equality of opportunity policies. Several teachers advocated a view (which we also encountered in case study schools) that equal opportunities is irrelevant; for example:

> Most teachers are too busy getting on with the job of teaching to bother too much about most of the issues raised here. (In the attitude scale statements.)

> Overall the educational system is neutral.

In support of this view, some teachers distinguished between 'educational' values and the values implied by the scales – especially in the statements which used the word 'encouragement'. For example:

> Pupils should not be 'encouraged' in any particular direction, they should be advised of their capabilities and career opportunities.

> The emphasis must be on the right of the individual to make a choice. It is the school's task to provide the background and information which will enable the individual to make an enlightened choice.

But the 'background and information' are not neutral: a number of responses identified undesirable influences:

> I agree wholeheartedly with positive discrimination as a long-term aim in education, but I worry about short-term job prospects with our less than radical employers.

> Education has to reflect society to some extent and likely future prospects of either sex must be taken into consideration.

But these views can be translated into discriminatory practice:

> Schools have to prepare pupils for work in society as it is. Some

boys *need* restricted workshop space more (than girls) at present, desirable as it (equal access) may be in future for equality.

In practice I would not like boys to be excluded from traditional male subjects which may lead them to a career in order to make room for girls. . . . Equally I would not like girls to be excluded from needlework, typewriting, etc. as these subjects may be of greater use in life to girls.

For other teachers, the issue of equality had to be positively resisted:

Many of the questions (i.e. attitude scale statements) suggest that we should deliberately draw students' attention to possible sex discrimination in schools. If a school is conducted in a climate of *assumed* equality, whether regarding sex or race, there should be no occasion to make a self-conscious and overt attempt to gear one's teaching towards this view. To do so might suggest that there could or should be an alternative view thus sowing seeds of discord where none originally existed.

Some teachers disagreed with 'neutrality' and took it upon themselves openly to declare their interest and influence. Others pointed to the influence of the environment in shaping the views – and, therefore, choices – of pupils:

Biological imperatives indicate that (a) women are less likely to be able to pursue a continuous career, and (b) that the children of those who do may, in some cases, lose thereby, judging by the pupils I teach. On the other hand, in a higher socio-economic bracket, they seem likely to benefit. Thus one cannot generalise on the benefits of careers for women.

One correspondent was quite clear on the role of the school:

A lot of sexism is evident not in direct teaching but in general organisation – i.e. boys carry, girls mark off medical lists, girls staple things, put raffle tickets in bins, fetch the head's dinner . . .

Clearly all this is irrelevant for those who agree with the correspondent who in one sentence asked for a survey of parental attitude and roles in the home, and in the next wrote in response to the statement on football and cricket for girls: 'Isn't there still a flavour of the absurd about this? Will we advocate boxing for girls next?'

Conclusions

These results point to a number of conclusions disturbing for those committed to equal opportunities policies in schools. But it is worth stating the positive first, which is that a majority of teachers are broadly sympathetic to equal opportunities in school. However, nearly half of teachers appear to be, overall, unsympathetic towards equality of opportunity. Moreover, they show marked disparity of attitudes depending upon the subject they teach, suggesting that pupils will receive conflicting impressions on this issue. While it is perhaps unsurprising that teachers of traditionally stereotyped subjects such as the physical sciences and crafts show least sympathy to equal opportunity, the lack of sympathy of teachers of 'core' subjects such as maths and PE is a matter of concern since practically every pupil follows these subjects until leaving age. The attitudes of maths teachers suggest that girls' reluctance to study that subject, and by association physical sciences, is unlikely to be recognized as a matter of concern by these teachers. Similarly, in stereotyped option subjects pupils are mainly taught by teachers who are unlikely to wish to redress disparities in take-up.

Our more detailed analysis of individual statements also revealed disappointing results. While it is clear that a majority of teachers are in favour of equal opportunities in principle, they show a markedly lower commitment to practices which positively encourage equality. Thus a majority of teachers in all subject groups is in favour of pupils making non-traditional choices, but less sure about positive actions to encourage this. They are particularly unsure about encouraging pupils to make non-traditional career choices. The relatively high proportion of teachers who were unsure about or thought that efforts to encourage non-traditional choice were misguided suggests that many schools are acting without a firm foundation of commitment or even a clear idea from teachers about the validity of the policy.

This impression of uncertainty, at least in a large minority of teachers, is confirmed by the comments many offered during the survey. A number of teachers are hostile to the idea of promoting equality of opportunity, on the grounds that they and the educational system are or should be somehow 'neutral'. We reject this view; the teacher shapes the environment, indeed is part of it, as well as operating within it. The attempt to maintain 'neutrality' means simply allowing the many and powerful pressures on pupils to follow traditional educational and career patterns to operate untrammelled upon them. It is surely a task of education to enable pupils to consider, question and confront these pressures and only then to decide whether or not they wish to make traditional or non-traditional choices. The teachers who pointed to the pervasiveness and power of the external environment are right only in the sense that they – and pupils – need to know of its existence. By accepting its power the teachers are making decisions for the pupils – the antithesis of education.

Every cloud has a silver lining. Our survey also offered some helpful findings. Many teachers recognize that pupils bring stereotypes with them into school and that teachers sometimes accept or even encourage these, even if they believe them to be inappropriate. Many teachers were unhappy at the dissonance between their beliefs and their practices.

All this suggests that we should be wary of excessive criticism of teachers. They face many pressures in schools and the injection of equality of opportunity as an issue may well seem like yet another bright idea from the government or the education office that will die like most others, or a further demand on a profession that feels itself already at breaking-point just surviving the school day.

It suggests to us, however, that many teachers were looking for a lead on equality of opportunity, and that they could be helped towards a more widespread positive attitude towards it. We have added to the demands made of teachers: that they should take responsibility for the role they play in shaping the views of pupils and influencing choice. The additional burden of work implied by this requires support and guidance. There is clearly a task for committed teachers to engage their colleagues in this kind of debate. For many teachers the wider issues of changed curriculum, equal opportunity and reconciliation of conflicting demands will imply structured assistance. This demands time for in-service training so that teachers may explore the new issues; it demands advice from policy-making and supervising bodies; and it argues for the establishment of channels of communication which effectively disseminate ideas and initiatives.

Notes

1. We would emphasize the importance of considering our findings on teachers' attitudes in conjunction with our wider analysis.
2. The major day-to-day work on this study was undertaken by John Bloomfield and Clive Seale and I would wish to acknowledge their contribution to this chapter.
3. As with all surveys of this kind there is some danger of misinterpretation of statements by respondents, though we have no evidence of this from our respondents. Our general conclusions rely on responses to the statements as a whole, as does score T.
4. These figures are broadly comparable with findings reported in the *Times Educational Supplement*, 24 September 1984, showing 56 per cent of all teachers agreeing that every school should have a declared policy to combat sexist attitudes in the classroom.
5. It has been commented that Statement 16 could be interpreted as referring not to being fair to each sex but to teaching specifically about sex equality as might happen in a social studies class. This seems to us unlikely in the context of the study and, as noted above, our general conclusions do not rely on this single statement.

References

DES (1975) *Education Survey 21; Curricular Differences for Boys and Girls*, HMSO, London.

Pratt, J., Bloomfield, J. and Seale, C. (1984) *Option Choice: A Question of Equal Opportunity*, NFER-Nelson, Slough.

Three   Margaret Goddard Spear

Teachers' attitudes towards girls and technology

Introduction

The importance of technology education has been stressed repeatedly in recent government publications. A paper on the school curriculum produced by the Department of Education and Science in 1981 attached special importance to craft, design and technology (CDT) as part of the preparation for living and working in our technological society. In 1982, a report from Her Majesty's Inspectorate (HMI) recommended that technology merits a place in the curriculum of all pupils up to the age of 16.

The Equal Opportunities Commission (1983) has emphasized that CDT is as relevant for girls as it is for boys: 'This is not simply because of the value of any specific practical skills which may have been learned, but rather because of the general skills and attitudes which are found in CDT and which may be transferred to working and day-to-day living in adulthood.'

The report also draws attention to the under-representation of girls in a range of subjects that are essential for a wide variety of careers, training opportunities and further education courses.

Pupils' decisions about whether to take technical and technological subjects are influenced by a number of factors, including the advice and encouragement offered by teachers (EOC 1983; Nash, Allsop and Woolnough 1984). The small number of girls taking CSE and 'O' level examinations in CDT suggests that they may not be receiving sufficient encouragement and support from their teachers. Indeed, some writers report that girls are actively discouraged from studying technical and technological subjects (Chivers and Marshall 1983; EOC 1983; Newton 1981).

Most comments concerning teachers' attitudes towards girls wanting to study technology have been provided by pupils. Few investigations have asked teachers directly for their opinions and attitudes. This chapter describes the replies given by secondary teachers to a number of questions relating to the appropriateness of technology education for girls. These replies were received from four separate groups of teachers, each group being involved in a different investigation. All four investigations enquired into various aspects of teachers' beliefs about different school subjects and different categories of pupils, but only those questions from each investigation that refer to the appropriateness of technology education for girls are reported below.

The teachers

Four groups of secondary school teachers provided the data reported in this paper. The teachers all taught in mixed comprehensive schools located throughout the southern half of England. The schools were initially contacted by sending a letter to either the head teacher or head of science. Questionnaires were subsequently sent to those schools that expressed interest in the investigation and willingness to volunteer staff as subjects. Details of those teachers who returned questionnaires in each investigation are outlined below.

INVESTIGATION 1. Sixty-seven teachers (30 men and 37 women) from three schools. They taught a wide range of subjects.

INVESTIGATION 2. Thirty-six teachers (16 men and 20 women) from a single school. Again, the teachers taught an assortment of subjects.

INVESTIGATION 3. Sixty-seven science teachers from nine schools. Forty-four of the teachers were men and 22 were women. (One respondent's sex was unspecified.)

INVESTIGATION 4. Forty-five science teachers (35 men and 10 women) from six schools.

The importance of technology to boys and girls

In the first investigation, teachers of all subjects were asked about their beliefs concerning the importance of technical subjects to the general education of pupils. The question was asked twice, the first time with reference to the general education of boys, the second time with reference to the general education of girls. The teachers indicated their replies on 4-point scales, ranging from 'very important' (score 4) to 'not at all important' (score 1).

The replies showed that the teachers believed that technical education was of greater importance to boys than to girls (Table 3.1). Forty-nine per cent of the teachers rated technical subjects as being very important to boys' general education. A similar rating for girls was given by only 24 per cent of the teachers. On the other hand, 30 per cent of the teachers indicated that technical subjects are not very important to girls' general education, but less than 2 per cent gave a similar response for boys.

Besides comparing percentage responses, the mean ratings[1] (or average ratings) given to boys and to girls can also be compared. These were calculated by assigning the scores shown in Table 3.1 to the replies in the various categories. The mean rating for boys was 3.48 and for girls it was 2.91. These values further emphasize that the teachers judged technical education to be of greater importance to boys than to girls.

The question asked in the first investigation referred to a rather abstract concept, the general education of pupils. It gave teachers the opportunity to express a theoretical view about the comparative importance of technical education for boys and for girls. In

Table 3.1 The importance of technical subjects to pupils' general education as judged by secondary teachers of all subjects (Percentage responses shown, N = 67)

Importance Scale	Very (4)	Fairly (3)	Not very (2)	Not at all (1)
Boys	49.3	49.3	1.4	0
Girls	23.9	44.8	29.9	1.4

Table 3.2 The importance of qualifications in technical subjects for pupils' future lives as judged by secondary teachers of all subjects (Percentage responses shown, N = 35)

Importance Scale	Very (4)	Fairly (3)	Not very (2)	Not at all (1)
Boys	60.0	40.0	0	0
Girls	25.7	34.3	37.1	2.9

contrast, the second investigation enquired into teachers' actual views on the topic. Teachers were asked how important they thought CSE/'O' level qualifications in technical subjects would be to pupils in their future lives. Again the question appeared twice, the first time referring to girls and the second time to boys. The same 4-point rating scale was used.

Replies were received from another group of teachers of all subjects. They showed that the teachers again considered technical education to be of greater importance to boys than to girls (Table 3.2). Mean ratings of 3.60 and 2.83 were given to boys and girls respectively.

In the third investigation, a group of science teachers were given the second question. The views of science teachers are particularly crucial since science teachers can be involved in the introduction of technology into the curriculum (Allsop and Woolnough 1981). The replies received from the science teachers indicated that they too believed that technical education was more important for boys than for girls (Table 3.3). The mean rating for boys was 3.61 and for girls it was 2.60.

Statistical tests can help to determine the significance of the differences between the mean ratings reported above for boys and

Table 3.3 The importance of qualifications in technical subjects for pupils' future lives as judged by secondary science teachers (Percentage responses shown, N = 62)

Importance Scale	Very (4)	Fairly (3)	Not very (2)	Not at all (1)
Boys	62.9	35.5	1.6	0
Girls	14.5	37.1	41.9	6.5

for girls. Application of the T test produced T values of 6.83, 5.63 and 9.53 for the three studies. These values indicate that the possibility of such large differences between the mean ratings of boys and girls having occurred by chance is less than 1 in 1000. The differences are judged to be statistically significant. A statistically significant result suggests that some difference does exist, but gives no indication of the size of that difference. However, the effect size (ES) index 'd'[2] does provide a convenient measure of the magnitude of a difference. Hence d values allow the educational significance of a result to be assessed. The d values for studies 1 to 3 were 0.85, 1.10 and 1.47. All of these values can be described as 'large' (Cohen 1977).

Consideration of the mean ratings and d values associated with Tables 3.1 to 3.3 reveals that teachers' responses varied according to the context of the question and the teacher's subject speciality. Teachers expressed more sex-differentiated views when they were asked a specific question about the importance of technical subjects to pupils' future lives, than when they were asked an abstract question. This implies that when teachers consider real conditions their views about technical subjects are more sex biased than when they consider hypothetical conditions. This gives some cause for concern since it is teachers' actual views that are more likely to influence their advice and behaviour towards boys and girls wanting to study technology. Of even greater concern is the finding that science teachers' replies to the second question were more sex differentiated than were the replies received from teachers of various subjects.

Attitudes towards women's role in society

Little is known about the types of occupations and life styles that teachers envisage for their pupils. Some pointers emerged when, in the fourth investigation, a group of science teachers were asked to complete an 'Attitude to Female Role' questionnaire (Slade and Jenner 1978). This questionnaire consists of twenty-five items, but only those items that refer to women's careers and to women's competence at technical activities are reported here. The teachers recorded their responses to the items on 4-point scales, ranging from 'strongly disagree' to 'strongly agree'. An undecided category was not included.

Details of the replies received for the items specified above appear in Table 3.4. Briefly, only 51 per cent of the science teachers agreed that women are as good as men at complicated technical matters. Moreover, considerable doubt was expressed about the importance of women's careers. Forty-two per cent agreed that a woman's career is *not* as important as a man's. There was more than a slight feeling that women should be occupied with domestic activities. Eighteen per cent agreed that women's most important job is to look after the comforts of men and

Table 3.4 Science teachers' responses to selected items from the 'Attitude to Female Role' questionnaire (Percentage figures shown, N = 45)

	Strongly disagree	Mildly disagree	Mildly agree	Strongly agree
1. Women are as good as men at complicated technical matters.	2.2	46.7	24.4	26.7
2. A woman's career is *not* as important as a man's.	42.1	15.6	35.6	6.7
3. Women's most important job is to look after the comforts of men and children.	57.9	24.4	13.3	4.4
4. Women should only have children if they are prepared to give up their jobs to look after them until they are old enough to go to school.	6.7	22.2	26.7	44.4
5. The saying 'a woman's place is in the home' is generally correct.	44.4	26.7	26.7	2.2

children, and 29 per cent thought that a woman's place is in the home. Many respondents viewed child care as the sole responsibility of the mother: 71 per cent agreed that women should only have children if they are prepared to give up their job to look after them until they are old enough to go to school.

The influence of teachers

Many science teachers believe that qualifications in technical subjects will be unimportant to girls in their future lives. This belief is presumably linked with the view that a girl's career is relatively unimportant, since she will soon marry and then devote her time to caring for her husband and children. If this is coupled with the view, held by many teachers, that girls are weak at technical subjects, then it is hardly surprising that some teachers do not actively encourage girls to opt for technology and that some even positively discourage them.

Among other factors, the advice and encouragement offered by teachers is known to influence pupils' decisions to study technology (Nash *et al.* 1984). Since many girls are likely to be hesitant about entering a male dominated subject, any opposition or discouragement from teachers will tend to dampen their interest and deter them from choosing or continuing the subject.

Teacher influence could operate to help persuade girls to study technology rather than deter them. If teachers actively encouraged girls and stressed the importance of qualifications in technology for further education and employment, then more girls would consider technology as a viable subject option. Such changes in teacher behaviour would emerge if teachers' attitudes and beliefs changed.

It is important that attempts are made to change teachers' attitudes so as to improve the recruitment of girls to technology. More research into the problem is required, possibly using affirmative action strategies (Kelly, Whyte and Smail 1984). Teachers need to be made aware of their own attitudes and beliefs, and the effects of their attitudes and expectations upon their pupils, especially girls.

With improved attitudes towards girls and technology, and a

commitment positively to encourage girls into technology, teachers can alter the usual trend of girls' under-representation in the subject. A report by Vlemmiks (1983) describes the steps that he took to ensure that girls joined his newly formed technology club. The outcome was most heartening. After a year, there were more girls than boys in the club.

In contrast, teachers who continue to hold sex stereotyped attitudes and beliefs are likely to convey these sentiments to their pupils. Even if such teachers do not actively discourage girls from studying technology, the girls will probably still perceive that technology is not an appropriate subject for them. The likely outcome is that the girls will reject technology, thus unnecessarily restricting their career aspirations and prospects.

Notes

1. Mean ratings were calculated by the usual method used to obtain an average, i.e., the sum of the teachers' ratings divided by the number of teachers.
2. Values of d were calculated by subtracting the girls' mean rating from the boys' mean rating and then dividing by the standard deviation of the whole sample.

References

Allsop, T. and Woolnough, B. (1981) 'A technological flavour' *Times Educational Supplement*, 18 Sept.

Chivers, G. and Marshall, P. (1983) 'Attitudes and experiences of some young British women entering engineering education and training courses', paper presented at Girls and Science and Technology Conference, Oslo, Sept.

Cohen, J. (1977) *Statistical Power Analysis for the Behavioral Sciences*, Academic Press, New York.

DES (Department of Education and Science) (1981) *Circular 6: The School Curriculum*, HMSO, London.

EOC (Equal Opportunities Commission) (1983), *Equal Opportunities in Craft, Design and Technology*, EOC, Manchester.

HMI (1982), *Technology in Schools*, HMSO, London.

Kelly, A., Whyte, J. and Smail, B. (1984), *Girls into Science and*

Technology: Final Report, GIST, Department of Sociology, University of Manchester.

Nash, M., Allsop, T., and Woolnough, B. (1984), 'Factors affecting pupil uptake of technology at 14+' *Research in Science and Technological Education*, 2, (1), 5–19.

Newton, P. (1981), 'Who says girls can't be engineers?' in Kelly, A. (ed.) *The Missing Half: Girls and Science Education*, Manchester University Press, Manchester.

Slade, P. and Jenner, F. A. (1978), 'Questionnaire measuring attitudes to females' social roles' *Psychological Reports*, 43, 351–4.

Vlemmiks, J. (1983), 'Girls in the Technology Club' *School Technology*, 17, (2), 10–11.

Four   Val Millman

The new vocationalism in secondary schools: its influence on girls

WHAT'S NEW ABOUT THE NEW

VOCATIONALISM?

Introduction

In a talk given to social science teachers at their Association's national conference in September 1983, Professor Tomlinson, then Chief Education Officer for Cheshire, referred to the new vocationalism as the 'suppressed agenda' of education since the 1944 Education Act.

It is indeed true that the concept of vocationalism has underpinned significant developments in our post-war education system. While further education has remained the major educational interface with the workplace, a heavy emphasis on industrial relevance surrounded the expansion of the polytechnics in the 1960s. The Beloe Report of 1959, which preceded the establishment of the CSE examination, argued that secondary school syllabuses should also stress practical and industrial elements, even if their inclusion meant problems in traditional forms of assessment.

As educational provision expanded in the 1960s, and a spirit of optimism abounded among teachers, new teaching methods and fresh approaches to validation and certification were developed in an attempt to integrate practical with more academic approaches to learning. But these have largely failed to achieve credibility with employers, higher education institutions or the general public. The school curriculum has continued to be dominated by the demands of the GCE 'O'/'A' level system, designed to meet the academic needs of only a minority of pupils. Despite strenuous attempts by teachers to 'make it relevant' to the remaining majority, many pupils and parents have remained unconvinced.

THE GREAT DEBATE

In the mid-1970s, the Great Debate led by the Callaghan government focused public attention on tangible gaps in the education system. Such educational debate was welcomed but, coming, not coincidentally, at a time of increasing youth unemployment, it resulted in a narrow analysis of educational problems. This analysis held that young people remained unemployed because schools had failed to equip them with the skills and attitudes required by employers. Youth unemployment was being posed as an educational problem and, as such, demanded a response from local education authorities (LEAs) and educational institutions.

During the late 1970s a variety of responses began to take shape. Vocationally orientated exams and work experience became an established part of many secondary school curricula. Employers were encouraged to become more closely involved in the activities of local schools. A distinct change of emphasis crept into the liberal curriculum of the 1960s and early 1970s.

THE INFLUENCE OF THE MANPOWER SERVICES COMMISSION (MSC)

Meanwhile, the influence of the MSC, originally established in 1974 to reform industrial training, was extending dramatically. MSC-funded post-school training schemes for unemployed young people, initially launched on an ad hoc basis, evolved through the Youth Opportunity Programme (YOP) to the Youth Training Scheme (YTS) which purports to prepare school leavers, through 'high quality training', for the projected economic recovery and a new kind of economy.

The roots of the 'new vocationalism' were therefore put down some time before the emergence of two government-funded projects for school-age pupils – namely the Low Attainers Project (LAP) and the Technical and Vocational Education Initiative (TVEI), funded by the Department of Education and Science (DES) and the MSC respectively. Both were launched in 1983, and both signify the most powerful statement to date of the new priority to be given to vocational education in our state school system.

This chapter does not attempt to debate the correctness or otherwise of such educational priorities *except in so far as they affect girls*. By examining the implementation of LAP and TVEI pilot projects, and by looking critically at the relationship between policy and practice, it is hoped that we can respond to the 'new vocationalism' in ways that benefit girls, and draw lessons from our experience that will help to inform the development of future 'girl friendly' strategies in our schools.

The shape of the new vocationalism: two government-funded projects

Low attainers project (LAP)

In September 1983 central government allocated a total of £2 million to thirteen 3-year LEA projects designed to provide more effective education for low-attaining pupils, especially in their last two years of compulsory schooling. The curriculum strategies explored by LEAs have varied widely in size, organization, philosophy and content. Many authorities have built on existing developments in their own areas and each has chosen to stress different aspects of the themes identified by Sir Keith Joseph in his initial announcement of the government initiative as follows:

- investigations into new forms of co-operation between schools and further education
- an expansion of work experience schemes
- activities built around practical projects in the community with full participation by local employers

- an investment in the in-service training of teachers
- investigations into assessment and recording of pupils' achievements
- a use of residential experience
- new approaches to parental involvement.

The majority of LEAS spent part of their first year planning, designing and piloting new courses for low-attaining pupils. In contrast, Coventry LEA released over 800 fourth-year pupils from all its comprehensive and special schools for one day a week's 'occupational experience' at a local training centre, aiming to introduce a greater degree of experiential learning into the pupils' school-based curriculum (see pages 52–9).

PUPIL SELECTION AND COURSE CONSTRUCTION

Not all LEAS have involved all their secondary schools in the project. Nottingham's project is based in four schools, with a further thirty-one involved in disseminating project resources and activities. Many LEAS have used the additional finance to enable individual schools to extend initiatives already being piloted. Most schools have worked out their own ground-rules for pupil selection and course development: while some have identified a discrete target group from the 'bottom 40%' to follow a full-time two-year course, others have inserted a Low Attainers course into the standard fourth-year option package.

Christ's Hospital School, Lincoln 'undertook no special testing' to identify pupils. The LAP course was presented to pupils as 'part of the normal option process and one or two high-fliers and particular problem children who might be a danger in a workshop were gently steered away' (Venning 1984). In year one of the course, sixty-two pupils spent one day a week at Lincoln College of Technology studying engineering, construction, commerce or catering. For the remainder of the week they did CSE courses, maths and communications components of the City and Guilds Foundation Course and practical projects in the local community. During their second year pupils spent three days a week at college following vocational courses: 'Inevitably children tend to justify their preferences on the grounds that they should make it easier to get jobs – in spite of strenuous efforts by teachers not to sell the course on this basis' (Venning 1984). FE college staff also work closely with the pupils on other aspects of the course such as residential experience and the setting up and running of a mini-company.

The majority of alternative curriculum strategies explored by LEAS have been based on practical rather than text-book orientated activities. In most cases work-related experience has formed the core of these activities although there are some examples of out-of-school activities designed to help pupils develop personal, social and leisure skills. In all cases the aim has been to identify curriculum strategies that will increase motivation and attainment among the 'bottom 40%'.

These strategies have all been evaluated at both LEA and national level, the latter programme being carried out by the National Foundation for Educational Research (NFER) which is due to make its final report in March 1987. It will be interesting to see to what extent equal opportunities has featured in these evaluations and contributed to the recommendations which will come out of the DES to be disseminated to LEAS. It will also be instructive to those of us involved in mounting short-term projects to see how many LEAS have succeeded in sustaining their initiatives beyond the period of DES funding.

Technical and vocational education initiative (TVEI)

The MSC launched TVEI in the same year as the DES launched LAP, but with 3.5 times the funding and amid lavish publicity. In contrast with the normal annual expenditure on each 14–18 year-old of between £1200 and £1600, this project enabled pilot LEAS to spend between £3500 and £4000 on each TVEI youngster, enabling Devon, for example, to achieve a pupil–teacher ratio of 10:1. Mr David Young, then chairman of the MSC, said at the outset that TVEI was aimed at producing 'more skilled youngsters', adding 'I hope that the schemes we set up will act as a catalyst to increase the pace of change.' But beyond that he offered no long-term perspective and no indication of expected outcome. He saw

the pilot courses . . . being directed mainly at young people in the middle and lower ability ranges, leading on from pre-vocational courses taking up perhaps 30% of the timetable before 16, to wholly vocational courses leading to recognised qualifications beyond that age. Local employers . . . will be involved in planning courses, which could include a sandwich element beyond 16. (O'Connor 1982)

LEAS were invited to submit proposals for four-year pilot courses catering for about 250 fourth-year pupils in the scheme's first year. In March 1983, 14 of the 66 proposals were recommended for acceptance by the MSC's TVEI steering group, and meetings with the selected LEAS took place to draw up contractual agreements.

EXTENSION OF PILOT PROJECTS

Three months later, before the first-round projects had even got off the ground, Sir Keith Joseph wrote to the Chairman of the Association of County Councils (ACC),

that many LEAS who had put a great deal of work into preparing their bids could not be offered a place in the programme. Against this background, and in view of the importance which the government attaches to technical and vocational educa- tion, the Secretary of State for Employment has today written to the Chairman of the MSC inviting the Commission to put forward proposals for extending the initiative by additional 5-year projects to start in September 1984 on the basis of the criteria adopted for those projects already agreed. (WNC 1984)

Subsequently, a further forty LEAS had their proposals accepted to start in September 1984; by this time over half of all LEAS were involved in TVEI and more were to follow at a later date.

PUPIL SELECTION AND COURSE CONSTRUCTION

Within the framework of aims clearly spelt out by the MSC,[1] substantial differences emerged between the fourteen first-round projects – differences emerging from variations in educational philosophy, local employment markets and existing provision for technical and vocational education. For the majority of LEAS, however, TVEI signalled a more radical departure from previous practices than the Low Attainers Project, demanding a rapid and high degree of innovation from schools involved. For this reason many mistakes were made, and most pilot projects decided to make significant changes to their programmes for their second year's intake.

Although the total number of TVEI students approximates 250 in each LEA's yearly intake, the number of schools involved varies from authority to authority. Pupil selection criteria also vary, although the majority of participants opt for TVEI as part of their standard option package. TVEI pupils generally follow modular courses in their first year for about a third of their school week, continuing with mainstream CSE/'O' level courses for the remainder of their timetable. By the end of their four-year course, pupils will have one or more qualifications which will include TEC/BEC, RSA and City and Guilds Certificates, GCE 'O'/'A' levels, CSE and an LEA record of achievement.

While some TVEI packages are heavily technologically orientated, e.g. Hertfordshire, others have broader vocational content with substantial 'general education' components and periods of residential experience. Most courses are school-based but some pupils attend off-site work experience at workplaces, in specially equipped studios or in mobile units. Some LEAs have been determined to integrate TVEI pupils as much as possible with others and ensure that all pupils benefit from new equipment purchased for TVEI. In some ways, integration has been easier to achieve than in the LAP project where money was allocated specifically for low attainers.

The impact of the new vocationalism on LEAs, schools, teachers, pupils and parents

Despite clear differences in the stated aims of the two government-funded projects, and despite the unequal status that differential funding conferred, there are strong similarities in many curricular strategies adopted by funded LEAs. These are strategies which have work-related experience at their core and which leave teachers in little doubt that the new vocationalism is rapidly becoming established in schools.

The speed with which both these schemes were introduced left little time for detailed consultation with LEAs and teachers' unions. Some Labour-controlled authorities, disagreeing with their underlying political and economic analysis, declined to submit proposals. Others, faced with the prospect of reduced central government funding and ratecapping, decided to bid for the money in the belief that they would be able to retain control over the projects despite their MSC funding. The LEAs themselves faced a mixed reaction from teachers, many of whom were worried by the potential divisive effects on pupils of both projects and the narrowing of the curriculum implicit in TVEI. At their annual conference in 1983, the National Union of Teachers (NUT), opposing the extension of pilot projects until new criteria were agreed, resolved that 'work experience must be used as a practical basis for learning and not as vocational preparation for jobs which do not exist'. (NUT 1983)

While the new schemes brought the possibility of promotion for teachers specializing in technical and vocational curricular areas, for those working in the arts and humanities LAP and TVEI also brought further disruption without reward and a reminder of their declining status. Nearly all LEAs were now faced with expenditure cuts and falling rolls, and setting up new schemes at a time of school closures, mergers and redeployment was a source of confusion to teachers, parents and pupils. Despite consultation at 'option choice time' parents and pupils remained vague about the organization and content of schemes. Many were concerned lest pupils would be cut off from the mainstream curriculum or would not have access to recognized qualifications. But in most cases they were convinced that the vocational components of the courses would help their children to 'get a job' and nearly all courses were eventually oversubscribed.

HOW GIRL FRIENDLY IS THE NEW VOCATIONALISM?

An example from the low attainers project

Year one: identification of problem areas

In the summer term of 1983, 21 comprehensive and 9 special schools were asked to submit to Coventry LEA numbers of fourth-

year low-attaining pupils selected for the fourth-year course beginning in September. Although there was little selection in special
schools, with nearly all their pupils following the course, in
comprehensive schools the pupils chosen were those to whom the
individual school programme was most suited. In some cases,
school programmes were based in remedial departments; in others
they were shaped around City and Guilds examination courses.
For some pupils it meant being withdrawn from the mainstream
curriculum for the majority of their timetable; for others it
represented an additional subject in their standard option choice
package. But from this highly diversified range of selection criteria
emerged a common pattern of gender imbalance. Very few schools
had chosen equal numbers of boys and girls, five mixed comprehensives weighing very heavily in favour of boys, one sending no
girls at all. Such imbalances resulted in boys outnumbering girls by
2:1 on the first year of the project.

Pupils were asked to choose four 'occupational experiences' in
their first year, to be undertaken at a local occupational experience centre on one day a week (for the remainder of the week
they followed school-based courses). Table 4.1 represents the

Table 4.1 Initial LAP placements of girls and boys in 1983

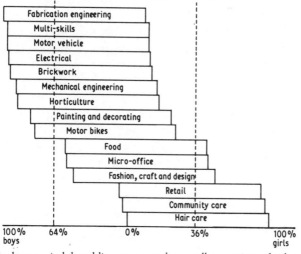

Note: The long vertical dotted lines represent the overall proportions of girls and boys
on this year of the project.
Source DES Special Project: A Report on Equal Opportunities, Coventry LEA 1984

proportion of girls and boys opting for each area. It shows that only three areas – fashion, craft and design; food; and micro-office – were not sex stereotyped (i.e.: their numbers reflected the proportion of girls and boys on the project). Three areas dominated by girls – retail, hair care and community care – were seen as stereotypically female areas; nine areas dominated by boys were seen as stereotypically male areas. It is possible that the male bias of the occupational experience programme initially discouraged schools from selecting more girls for the project. But even after allowing for the imbalance of girls and boys selected, LAP girls had a narrower range of areas to choose from than LAP boys. And over the course of the year the majority of pupils of both sexes restricted their experiences to occupational areas traditionally considered to be appropriate to their sex.

MALE DOMINATION: SEX STEREOTYPED OCCUPATIONAL CHOICE

The first year of the project proved exceptionally successful in meeting many of the project's objectives. Girls and boys who had truanted from school in their third year attended the Occupational Experience Centre regularly and showed greater motivation towards their work back at school. Many teachers were introducing more practical components into their school-based curriculum. But the male dominated nature of the project detracted from such successes in specific ways, posing questions which needed to be answered from early in the project's first year. School teachers needed to consider the reasons for such imbalance in pupil selection – was it really the case that only half as many girls as boys would benefit from a special programme to boost their attainment? And what effect did this have on the girls who found themselves in a minority in school and workshop groups? Occupational Experience Centre instructors and project staff needed to examine curriculum content and workshop ethos – was it really beneficial to either sex to work in an environment so heavily dominated by male interests and skills, and to restrict their experiences to areas with which many of them were already familiar?

SEEKING SOLUTIONS

During the first year of the programme, the project teacher with designated responsibility for equal opportunities co-ordinated a series of meetings and activities designed to examine these questions in some depth. By observing pupil behaviour in the workshops and on the site of the Centre, and by using personal record-keeping sessions back in school to locate individual interests and influences, teachers began to identify patterns of experience which were common to the girls and boys in their schools. They became particularly concerned that the low level of confidence displayed by many 'low attaining' girls might be reinforced by the male dominated ethos of the site and by the narrow range of occupational experiences girls were choosing to follow. But girls who *did* branch out into non-traditional areas often felt isolated and dominated by boys' interests, and unable to develop new skills at their own pace (Millman 1984). Sometimes the instructors unintentionally compounded this by holding different expectations of girls and boys, irrespective of individual aptitude. On occasions, a wider selection of tools, e.g., screwdrivers, would have enabled girls to succeed at tasks where physical strength was at a premium. It rapidly became clear that changes needed to be made to the programme on offer at the Occupational Experience Centre if pupils were to be encouraged to develop interests and skills irrespective of sex. Changes were needed not only in the formal curriculum of the workshop areas but in the hidden curriculum of the site itself; a few girls had complained of sexual harassment by boys, and it was felt that there was insufficient support for some girls from ethnic minorities who were not familiar with working in mixed settings.

Increased staff awareness during the first year went some way towards providing the extra support required by girls. Where pupils were isolated in non-traditional areas, groups were re-organized to ensure a minimum of three members of the same sex in any one group of fifteen. Staff realized that more substantive structural changes would be needed in the second year if sex stereotyping was to be seriously challenged and a more balanced programme followed by all pupils. It was recognized that the traditional occupational families on which the programme had been based had unintentionally led to stereotyped choice by both sexes. Not only did names of occupational areas need to be changed but a curriculum needed to be developed which appealed equally to both sexes. This was not easy to achieve in work areas which had already been established, staffed and equipped. But the setting up of the following new areas provided the opportunity for radical curriculum review:

a) the addition of home maintenance and printing, artwork and graphics to the fourth-year programme;
b) the compulsory pairing of some occupational experience areas in the fifth-year programme in an attempt to broaden pupils' experiences (see Table 4.2)

Year two: testing solutions

Prior to the selection of fourth-year pupils for year two of the project (the previous fourth year was to proceed to the fifth-year programme already described), schools were asked to review their selection criteria and counselling procedures. Early estimates of numbers indicated a greatly improved gender balance. Final figures, however, showed an overall decrease of 1 per cent in the

Table 4.2   Fifth-year choices made by girls and boys in 1984

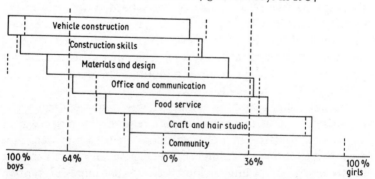

Note: The long vertical dotted lines represent the overall proportions of girls and boys on this year of the project. The short vertical dotted lines represent the proportions of girls and boys who chose related areas in their fourth year. These offer an indication of where there has been a move towards more or less stereotyped choices.
Source DES Special Project: A Report on Equal Opportunities, Coventry LEA 1984

Table 4.3   Percentages of girls and boys selected in 1983 and 1984

Type of school	% Female		% Male	
	1983	1984	1983	1984
Co-ed comprehensives	38	31	62	69
Single sex comprehensives	38	38	62	62
Co-ed specials	37	52	63	48
Single sex specials	–	–	100	100
TOTAL (Comps and specials)	36	35	64	65

Source DES Special Project: A Report on Equal Opportunities, Coventry LEA 1984

proportion of girls selected by comprehensive schools (see Table 4.3, above). This was disappointing and clearly limited the progress that could be made towards equal opportunities on the project. Ways of ensuring that this imbalance does not recur in future years are currently being examined.

Looking more closely at the figures for individual schools, it was clear that some teachers had gone to considerable lengths to achieve a better gender balance and a broader range of occupational choices. Table 4.4 indicates some shift in sex stereotyping in certain areas; the overall pattern, however, remained the same in the second year. Exceptions were painting and decorating which moved from being stereotypically male in 1983 to being the least stereotyped area – home decorating – in 1984, and printing, artwork and graphics, which proved to be non-stereotyped.

Home maintenance, however, despite its new emphasis on DIY jobs around the home, failed to appeal to the girls in the way that had been hoped. Table 4.2 (p. 56) has shown that greater success was achieved in some of the fifth-year sections, despite the persistence of the overall stereotyped pattern. A significantly higher number of boys chose community care in the fifth year than in the fourth year, probably as a result of the boys themselves talking to their friends about their success on the fourth-year course:

Patrick had a 7-year-old nephew who he thought was very spoilt. In his fourth year Patrick chose community care as well

Table 4.4   Fourth-year choices made by girls and boys in 1984

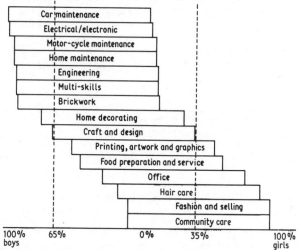

Note: The long vertical dotted lines represent the overall proportions of girls and boys on the second year of the project.
Source DES Special Project: A Report on Equal Opportunities, Coventry LEA 1984

as painting and decorating, motor bikes and food because he couldn't believe 'all kids could be like this'.

At the beginning both his friends and his parents were surprised at his choice:

MUM: How many other boys have chosen it?

PATRICK: Don't know – quite a few.

MUM: Don't you think it's a bit girlish?

PATRICK's friends laughed at him calling him 'a big queer, a big pooftah'.

PATRICK enjoyed the course 'doing different things each time, seeing the kids laugh and enjoy themselves!' He said, 'It sounds a lazy job but it's hard running after them when they're outside.' His mother and aunt now trust him to look after his nephew and a number of his friends have chosen to do community care.

(DES 1984)

Similarly, a higher proportion of girls chose materials and design in the fifth year compared with related fourth-year courses. Here it is likely that curriculum changes succeeded in appealing to the girls' interests:

The Materials and Design course will lead you to making a number of indoor and outdoor items for use by playgroups, schools and community projects. The course starts with an introduction to the materials to be used which include wood, soft fabrics, plastic and metal.

The first items you will make will cover the basic skills that you will need to cut, join and shape materials. You will then be able to use these skills to complete other larger tasks, including toys and games, climbing frames, floor jigsaws and toddler trucks. You will also be able to design and complete your own items and when you have finished your job you will have the opportunity to deliver it to the playgroup or project. (DES 1984)

The evidence so far is that both these courses have met the expectations of boys and girls respectively and it therefore seems likely that numbers making non-traditional choices in these areas will continue to grow. It is to be hoped that these successes will instigate change in other work areas and in the attitudes of all those who contribute to such courses. While it is true that only limited progress towards equal opportunities can be achieved in a short-term project, particularly where the experiential learning programme has been based on traditional occupational families, progress can be made, not least in the area of teacher and instructor awareness and attitudes. The direct involvement of project staff in analysing problems of gender imbalance and seeking solutions is likely to have repercussions beyond the confines of the project on the organization and curriculum of the schools themselves.

An overview of TVEI: policy and practice

Policy

Although LEAS receiving DES funding for the Low Attainers Project were not specifically required to ensure the provision of equal opportunities policies on the MSC Youth Opportunity Prog-meet in TVEI programmes. The MSC stated (1984) that 'Equal opportunities should be available to young people of both sexes and they should normally be educated together on courses within

each project. Care should be taken to avoid sex stereotyping.'
Trade union pressure had previously resulted in the MSC publicly
committing its Youth Training Schemes to equal opportunities. In
March 1983, the MSC chairman was eager to confirm that all LEAS
shortlisted for first-round TVEI money 'expressed a positive commitment to this objective', and, a year later, Mr Tom King,
Secretary of State for Employment, assured delegates to the
Women's National Commission conference that 'the government
was helping to increase opportunities for girls and women through
the Technical and Vocational Education Initiative.'

WNC/EOC INTERVENTIONS

National bodies such as the Women's National Commission
(WNC) and the Equal Opportunities Commission (EOC) were
concerned to see that policy was put into practice. Experience of
equal opportunities policies on the MSC Youth Opportunity Programmes had not given much room for optimism, and it was clear
from the outset that, without adequate safeguards, the vocational
nature of TVEI would bring about segregated, sex-stereotyped
programmes for pupils. Prior to selection of first-round LEAS the
WNC spelt out to the MSC chairman its own interpretation of good
'equal opportunities' practice. Despite this, and despite fairly
equal numbers of girls and boys participating over the fourteen
LEAS, the structure of most pilot programmes was blatantly sex
stereotyped. Prior to selection of second-round LEAS, the EOC and
WNC again asked the MSC to provide more 'detailed central
guidance' that would commit local authorities firmly and specifically to equal opportunities.

Although the MSC was keen to receive advice and support from
both the WNC and EOC it was adamant that it must avoid being
prescriptive to LEAS and must refrain from interventions which
might interfere with evaluation. However, six months into the
project MSC staff acknowledged the scale of the problem:

Local authorities . . . are to be asked to provide hard evidence
that they are trying to phase out traditional boy-girl divisions
within their programmes . . . the MSC is to write to all 14
authorities now running schemes to tell them it wants to see an
improvement in the numbers of boys and girls taking up

non-traditional options. It will also expect firm evidence that authorities are developing strategies to overcome sex stereo-typing. (Wilce 1984)

In co-operation with EOC and WNC, a one-day seminar was held in February 1984 in Clwyd LEA for all pilot project co-ordinators. While one participant despaired at the 'repetition of the old circular arguments' the seminar succeeded in bringing equal opportunities nearer to the forefront of local TVEI priorities. At a DES course on equal opportunities held in Birmingham in June 1984, over half the participants were TVEI staff. An increasing number of LEAS have been requesting advice and information packs from the EOC and WNC, both of whom are in a strong position to disseminate examples of good (and bad!) practice. It appears that when the allocation of resources depends on organizations meeting their contractual requirement to provide equal opportunities, there is an impetus for action which has previously been missing.

Practice

The overall proportion of girls to boys in the first year of TVEI was 46%:54%. The proportion of girls was noticeably reduced in the second year in the 14 pilot authorities. The balance within individual authorities varied considerably, with 10/14 LEAS obtaining a greater take-up by boys than girls. In some cases this may have been due to an apparently boy-orientated curriculum. One authority which attracted 183 boys and 120 girls offered fourth-year pupils six subjects in pairs in three option blocks, as follows:

1. Computer studies or manufacturing technology
2. Modular technology or electrical and electronic instrumentation
3. Information technology and industrial studies or information technology and office skills.

This authority hoped to break stereotyping by structuring the curriculum in a way that compelled girls to take non-traditional courses. While girls from the single-sex TVEI schools over-subscribed for these courses, the reverse was true of girls from mixed schools. The course will undoubtedly succeed in putting significant numbers of girls through technological courses but the only real proof of success will be if a high proportion of these girls choose to continue these courses beyond the age of 16.

WIDESPREAD STEREOTYPING: THE IMPORTANCE OF MONITORING

Monitoring course choices by gender in this way has raised the awareness of many heads and teachers for the first time. In one authority, subsequent discussions revealed that girls were excluded from specializing in technology courses because entry was restricted to those (mostly boys) doing maths and physics in the core.

The extent to which the design of TVEI courses promoted or counteracted sex stereotyping was very dependent on each authority's previous experience of equal opportunities strategies. Partly due to the speed with which the first-round projects were launched, not one LEA had counselled TVEI girls on non-traditional subject/career choice prior to making their course options. Many TVEI programmes in their first year had explicitly set 'male' and 'female' options against each other. Two LEAs, whose TVEI courses were based on traditional occupational families, experienced the heaviest stereotyping. Valerie Evans, divisional HMI for the West Midlands, observed: 'In my division I have five TVEI projects. Some are already showing that girls do certain things and boys do other things. The actual statements about the initiative did not support such an idea, but the practice does.' (Wilce 1983) Subsequently, many TVEI staff recognized that individual counselling prior to choice of courses was essential and new counselling approaches were introduced to a number of schools for the second year's intake. Unfortunately the MSC is in no position to ensure that pre-choice counselling becomes part of TVEI programmes as it has no remit to involve pupils outside the scheme (i.e. those under 14 years old). But it is hoped that, as more schools become alerted to the need, we will see more examples of girl friendly careers advice – advice which not only presents girls with information to dispel myths (to point out, for example, that language skills are the best possible basis of success in information technology) but also recognizes that *all* pupils' career patterns should take into account the possibility of domestic and child care responsibilities in adulthood.

ALTERNATIVES TO FREE (STEREOTYPED) CHOICE

The handful of TVEI authorities with previous experience of equal opportunities strategies recognized that 'better counselling' on its own could do little to counteract sex-stereotyped choice. A variety of structural changes and alternatives to 'free' subject choice were therefore considered. A few authorities adopted a 'carousel' system, ensuring that all pupils had a taste of all courses in their first year. But Clywd LEA, recognizing that a nine-week module was unlikely to have a long-term effect on girls' choice of courses, observed: 'Girls are willing to give subjects such as electronics a try for a couple of months but are reluctant to commit themselves for longer. However, unlike the taster courses offered by some authorities, these modules can be used as building blocks towards an examination such as 'O' level'. (Wilce 1984)

A couple of LEAs included non-traditional courses in a core programme to be taken by all fourth-year pupils, e.g., technology at work, world of business and personal and community services. In their fifth year, these students took a total of six modules, having to choose a minimum of one from each of the three compulsory areas. This combined a 'balanced curriculum' with opportunities for specialization; but choices offered within each compulsory area remained stereotyped.

Some LEAs remained firmly convinced that even structural change can do little to counter the influence of parents, employers and the realities of the local employment market. TVEI staff from one authority who were considering compulsory technological courses for girls were concerned about the morality of encouraging girls to consider careers in science and technology when this will 'additionally burden them with the concept of leaving the area' – the employment of technologists in local industry was only 1.3 per cent compared with the national average of 13 per cent. Local employment markets have had a strong bearing on the design of TVEI courses, thereby raising important questions about equal opportunities strategies for girls. Ms Pat White, ILEA's Principal Careers Officer, giving evidence to the WNC's 'Training Opportunities for Women' working party, said that one of the problems in stimulating girls' interest in non-traditional job opportunities was 'that there were few jobs in manufacturing industry in the ILEA area. The absence in some areas of the country of jobs in, for example, the electronics industry and other "new technology" areas made it necessary to hesitate before speaking glibly of openings for girls.' (WNC 1984).

In some areas TVEI staff have felt that local employment traditions inevitably lead to a sex-stereotyped curriculum. A member of one authority said,

> The forestry and landbased skills is a curriculum area where the actual content of the programme and assignments themselves could be externally selective. . . . The local pattern is that girls rarely fell and move trees but they may well plant seeds and saplings . . . the starting point for the student is historically based.

While some authorities state their intention of using employers' involvement on local TVEI steering groups to challenge their traditional assumptions, in practice it is likely that girls on work experience placements will be strongly influenced by exposure to traditional stereotyped attitudes. Although there would certainly be much to be gained from introducing girls to workplaces where women are 'exceptionally successful', such places are not easy to find. In view of this, perhaps carefully structured residential experience has greater potential for 'girl friendly' experiential learning.

COURSE LOCATION, COURSE NAMES

Apart from direct work experience, the location of vocational course components has been shown to have considerable influence on girls. In some LEAs most TVEI courses are school-based. Single-sex schools in particular have seized opportunities provided by TVEI to purchase equipment not previously available to pupils: 'Stevenage Girls School, for example, has used TVEI money to equip two spare rooms for technology and engineering design and craft, and electrical and electronic instrumentation courses. This equipment can now be used by all girls in the school.' (Venning 1983) A striking example from a boys' school was the introduction of a catering course where the boys used the new facilities in the girls' school for their practical work. There are other examples of attempts to attract boys into traditionally female areas, often re-naming options to broaden their appeal. For one authority this strategy raised an important question: by moving the emphasis on business studies away from keyboarding 'to provide managerial-entrepreneurial dimensions, are we not fostering the notion of sex stereotyping?'

A number of projects have recognized the impact of option names on pupil choice. Some have tried to move away from traditional school subject and vocational names to general descriptions such as manufacturing administration and service – the latter including courses like repair and maintenance. Very few course names have emerged that are of equal appeal to girls and boys except where they are new areas, e.g., visual communications, which don't already bear gender tags. Unfortunately many courses located in FE colleges have not undergone the same sort of review as new courses being set up in schools. Girls have therefore been fed into stereotyped courses often taught by instructors from traditional industrial backgrounds: 'The TVEI steering group emphasises the importance of getting the right part-time or full-time instructors, where appropriate, from industry.' (Jackson 1983) Although the LEA may have put on in-service equal opportunities training for members of the immediate TVEI teacher team, others responsible for the TVEI programme – FE lecturers and careers officers – often have no knowledge of, or commitment to, basic equal opportunities issues.

GENERATING AWARENESS OF STEREOTYPING

It was for these sorts of reasons that bodies like the NUT were so concerned that there should be a substantial element of general education for TVEI pupils; this would provide a balance against vocational components and prevent an undue 'narrowing of the curriculum'. A few authorities have built units on sex stereotyping into general education modules – one LEA has included this in communication and personal/social development which forms one of the cross-curricular assignments for the pre-BEC certificates. The work done by pupils has been recorded on film in a documentary-style presentation. Some authorities are inviting TVEI girls who took non-traditional courses in their fourth year to talk about them to the new year's intake.

If LEAS are to meet the MSC's first-named criterion, discussions of the effects of stereotyping need to be held with pupils, parents, teachers and administrators alike. Unfortunately the majority of male dominated project teams and steering groups lack the expertise necessary to achieve this. Many have sought advice from organizations like the WNC/EOC, asking their personnel to assist them in setting up in-service courses within the authority. The few LEAS who have held in-service courses during the first year of the project have mainly aimed at 'raising awareness'. In only two or three authorities have discussions moved beyond monitoring and examining curriculum structures to consideration of the hidden curriculum, although Devon, for example, has produced a resource handbook and guidelines for its staff on producing non-sexist resources and screening published materials. In fact the small pupil/teacher ratios in TVEI provide an excellent opportunity to challenge the traditional hidden curriculum and develop new ways of working with girls in mixed groups. The widespread introduction of pupil profiling provides an ideal opportunity to monitor girls' progress closely, although care has to be taken that personal qualities often valued in profiles – initiative, independence – are not traditionally male qualities on which girls will be downgraded or will downgrade themselves. Small group sizes should also ensure that support can be given to girls entering non-traditional areas or girls from ethnic minority groups who may sometimes be having to deal with sets of new cultural experiences. Undoubtedly TVEI has the potential to generate both awareness and girl friendly curriculum developments in the mainstream curriculum, as has been shown by the introduction of integrated science to some Leicestershire schools. But such potential will only be realized if those responsible for implementing TVEI have both the commitment and the expertise to challenge traditional practices.

Conclusions

There are those who feel so pessimistic about the effects of the new vocationalism on girls that they are tempted to ignore it . . . and hope it will go away. There are those who enthuse uncritically about the new opportunities it offers, seeing TVEI as an excellent opportunity to increase the involvement of girls in traditionally male education and training areas. Both views, while understandable, are too simple, leaving the contradictions for girls unresolved. It is undoubtedly true that the new vocationalism, with its emphasis on technical education, not only has the capacity to draw more girls into traditionally male dominated subjects but also to reduce the status of subjects in which they have traditionally succeeded. There is a clear danger that the new vocationalism will reinforce the position of the majority of girls in an unequal and sexually divided labour market.

There is also a more pragmatic view which recognizes the large sums of money already committed to TVEI programmes in over half the country's LEAS and is determined to ensure that the girls participating gain equal access to the resources available. This view recognizes that, without a clear identification of girl friendly strategies by all involved in implementing programmes, girls are likely to have traditional sex-stereotyped vocational experiences reinforced in schools, FE colleges and workplaces. Faced with a need for rapid innovation in a multitude of areas, it is unlikely that the predominantly male TVEI teams will make equal opportunities a priority and identify positive action strategies for themselves. In this context it is essential that the new vocationalism is not left to its own sex-stereotyped devices, and that those who have identified girl friendly strategies disseminate and promote them vigorously.

The MSC will probably have difficulty in evaluating equal opportunities strategies adopted by LEAS involved in TVEI. Will it look beyond mere numbers to the quality of girls' experience? Will it focus on girls who have taken non-traditional courses or those who move into non-traditional jobs? Or will it examine the success of courses which equally appeal to both sexes and therefore challenge the traditional division of labour? Both the Low Attainers Project and TVEI aim to act as catalysts, to generate curricular changes that will persist beyond the short life of the projects. How possible will it be for LEAS to sustain radical changes in the formal and hidden curriculum once resource levels and pupil/teacher ratios have returned to 'normal'? Perhaps the aim of equal opportunities strategies should be to establish practices most likely to become established features of LEA provision beyond the lifetime of the project – equal opportunities in-service programmes, for example

In the short term ways must be found of ensuring that girls feel that extra funds and new projects are designated as much for them as for the boys. This means resolving a number of dilemmas – should girls choose areas they feel at home in or should they be strongly encouraged to 'take on' new, traditionally male courses? Should boys be encouraged to enter traditionally female areas or should this space be preserved for the girls? Such dilemmas are heightened in projects which have been set up with a distinctive male ethos.

In highlighting sex stereotyping, TVEI has obliged LEAS to address themselves to these sorts of questions; this may prove to be the biggest long-term – if indirect – benefit of the new vocationalism to girls. There has been an abundance of experimentation in new vocational projects from which much has been learnt by LEA staff previously unaware of sex differentiation. Such staff need assistance in moving beyond awareness to positive action. It is here that those with experience of girl friendly strategies have the opportunity to identify examples of good practice, and it is here that LEAS must meet their responsibility towards girls in their schools. The new vocationalism has provided many with opportunities for change; how many of those who have seized such opportunities, have done so with the education of girls at the forefront of their minds?

Notes

1. Aims of Technical and Vocational Education Initiative
   (1) *In conjunction with* LEAS to explore and test ways of organizing and managing the education of 14–18 year-old young people across the ability range so that:
       (i) more of them are attracted to seek the qualifications/skills which will be of direct value to them at work and more of them achieve these qualifications and skills;
       (ii) they are better equipped to enter the world of employment which will await them;

(iii) they acquire a more direct appreciation of the practical application of the qualifications for which they are working;

(iv) they become accustomed to using their skills and knowledge to
solve the real world problems they will meet at work;

(v) more emphasis is placed on developing initiative, motivation
and enterprise as well as problem solving skills and other aspects
of personal development;

(vi) the construction of the bridge from education to work is begun
earlier by giving these young people the opportunity to have
direct contact and training/planned work experience with a
number of local employers in the relevant specialisms;

(vii) there is close collaboration between local education authorities
and industry/commerce/public services, etc. so that the curriculum has industry's confidence.

(2) To undertake (1) in such a way that:

(i) the detailed aims can be achieved quickly and cost effectively;

(ii) the educational lessons learned can be readily applied in other
localities and to other groups among the 14–18 year-olds;

(iii) the educational structures/schemes established to further the
aims of the initiatives should be consistent with progressive
developments in skill and vocational training outside the school
environment, existing vocational education for under-16 year-
old people and higher education;

(iv) emphasis is placed on careful monitoring and evaluation;

(v) individual projects are managed at local level;

(vi) the overall conduct, assessment and development of the initiative can be assessed and monitored by the MSC and the TVEI
unit it has established for this purpose.

References

DES (1984) *Special Project: A Report on Equal Opportunities*, Coventry
LEA.

Jackson, M. (1983) 'More LEAS may join the technical revolution',
Times Education Supplement, 4 Feb.

MSC (1984) *TVEI: Annual Review 1984*, MSC, Sheffield.

Millman, V. (1984) *Teaching Technology to Girls*, Coventry LEA.

NUT (1983) *TVEI – Extension of pilot scheme*, NUT Circular 392/83,
London.

O'Connor, M. (1982) 'Preparing for the real world outside', *Guardian* 23
Nov.

Venning, P. (1983) 'From MSC dream to curriculum reality', *Times
Educational Supplement*, 14 Oct.

Venning, P. (1984) 'And now for something completely different', *Times Educational Supplement*, 27 Jan.

Wilce, H. (1983) 'TVEI may foster sex differences', *Times Educational Supplement*, 25 Nov.

Wilce, H. (1984) 'Professor speaks out for sex equality', *Times Educational Supplement*, 30 March.

WNC (Womens National Commission) (1984) *Interim Report of ad hoc Working Group on Training Opportunities for Women*, WNC, London.

Part Two

Interventions to make schooling more girl friendly

Editors' introduction

The concerns which generated the analyses of unfriendly school-ing have inevitably encouraged the growth of measures designed to combat sexism and promote a more girl friendly environment. The range of approaches described in this section reveal the scale of the task. National and regional initiatives, introduced as a consequence of legislation and policy commitment, create a climate in which change can occur, partly by proscribing certain behaviours, partly by legitimizing the initiatives of educational pioneers.

Most of the interventions detailed here are forms of affirmative action: moving beyond notional equality of opportunity into challenging existing schooling structures and pedagogical practice. It is significant that all the writers interpret the prob-lem largely as one of teacher attitudes and behaviour; thus most of the interventions have been concerned with working with teachers in a variety of guises and with varying degrees of success.

It has been argued that the relatively recent drive to encourage increased numbers of girls into science and technology reinforces the status and worth of male dominated areas of the curriculum and undermines areas in which girls and women have traditionally excelled. Undoubtedly, it has been educationally expedient to focus on these subjects. The emphasis has forged an interesting alliance of industrialists, economists, politicians and feminists.

Tessa Blackstone points out when girls study science and technology they achieve; the problem is female abstention rather than female performance. Most educationalists now perceive this withdrawal as a major female disability: girls are disadvantaged not only in career terms but also in exercising day-to-day autonomy, for science and technology exert a powerful control on our daily lives.

The first chapter describes a range of affirmative action strategies in science and technology and rejects as spurious the notion of access as a means of educational equity. More radical change is recommended: change in the curriculum content of the subject in order to awaken and hold girls' interests. Judith Whyte points out that girls are not intrinsically uninterested in science, just bored by the science they meet in schools. She stresses the powerful influence teachers have in mediating the curriculum to their female pupils and the need to encourage teachers' abilities to reflect on their teaching styles and attitudes in order to bring about change in the classroom and the school. She also notes that those teachers most likely to be opposed to equal opportunities stem from the science and mathematical areas. The refusal by many teachers in the GIST Project (Girls Into Science and Technology) to acknowledge the project as a force for change may be disappointing, though not surprising: educational research makes clear that whatever the extent of resources and political pressure the attitude of teachers is critical in determining whether fundamental change will occur.

This is echoed in the following chapter where Helene Witcher describes her collaborative research with Scottish teachers. In a sympathetic description of her reasons for constructing a feminist model of research, she faces the problem of working with an uninterested teacher who refuses to recognise sex-stereotyped behaviour in her primary class and finds it difficult to accept the need for change. This attitude subverts the non-sexist materials provided in the course of the research. The tension involved in reconciling the importance of countering sexism yet acknowledging the centrality of the teacher's role and individual perceptions is echoed in the next two chapters, which describe larger programmes of INSET with teachers in two London LEAS.

The ILEA was the first education authority to make an explicit policy commitment to the promotion of equality of opportunity for girls; Brent the first to appoint an adviser to encourage work of this kind. Set against a background of political commitment Hazel Taylor describes the comprehensive programme of INSET she instituted in Brent, in which the key characteristics are a fine targeting of participants and the formation of support networks of teacher groups. The importance of working with and through the teaching force is an important element in her strategy. Carol Adams's chapter details the attitudinal difference between male and female secondary teachers on a four-day ILEA course set up to analyse sexist processes in schools; her work has profound implications for the way in which authorities structure INSET work with teachers. Both descriptions of training strategies are in fact expressions of LEA interventions. Jenny Headlam Wells takes us through the processes which brought about Humberside's policy commitment against sex discrimination and the attempts by teachers' unions, politicians and the media to subvert it through hostility and derision. Her chapter also addresses the difficulties of translating policy into practice and recognizes that working within the system, although pragmatic, can be a means of achieving more radical change – though it can also be a mechanism for diluting progress; a cul-de-sac where rhetoric substitutes for action. Andrew Cant's reflective chapter discusses the tension between defining policy and effecting change. With hindsight he advocates a differing approach where the issue might have been more successful had it been perceived less as LEA-controlled. Yet ambivalent, he acknowledges the importance of policy as a means of getting the issue onto the educational agenda.

All the chapters in this section have been concerned to define an alternative view of education. There seem to be divers ways in which this might be achieved. The interventions stress that teachers are both a major obstacle to change and yet the means by which change might be achieved.

This suggests that programmes of action will need to embrace a range of practical strategies which acknowledge this teacher diversity and work from the experience and commitment of the individual teacher. In this way schools may be encouraged to reflect on practice and evaluate critically the processes through which learning takes place. In the long term this may generate radical change which could realize a pedagogic revolution. A small step for woman, a giant leap for man?

Five   Judith Whyte

Girl friendly science and the girl friendly school

Approximately three times as many boys as girls take 'O' level physics and approximately four times as many take CSE physics. Over 90 per cent of entries in all technical subjects are from boys. This means that schoolgirls are ineligible for a wide range of courses in further and higher education and for entry to occupations requiring a scientific or technical base. Female exclusion from science and technology, even if it is apparently by girls' own choice, also means that as citizens their ability to understand and control their environment is limited. Nevertheless, most schools consider they are already providing equal opportunities by neutral treatment of the two sexes (Bloomfield 1984). In effect, ignoring the effects of gender in this way merely reinforces stereotyping because it does nothing to challenge the definition of certain aspects of the curriculum as masculine or feminine.

Girls Into Science and Technology (GIST) was the first major schools-based project addressing problems of sex stereotyping at school, and was an example of 'action research' in education; the project simultaneously took action to improve girls' achievement in science and technology and investigated the reasons for their under-achievement. The project team collaborated with teachers in eight co-educational comprehensive schools in the Greater Manchester area to devise and implement intervention strategies designed to improve girls' attitudes to the physical sciences and technical subjects. Two other schools were involved as controls where attitude testing but no interventions took place.

The actual choice of schools was determined by certain practical considerations and occurred by a process of elimination rather than selection. Since we intended to visit each school at least once a fortnight it was important they should be quite close together and not too numerous. We had also decided to limit ourselves to co-educational comprehensives because this is the type of school in which the majority of British children are educated, and because we felt that in a fairly small project such as GIST we would not be able to deal adequately with the complicating factor of different school types. For the research design it was obviously desirable to have as large a sample of children as feasible and also to establish control schools for purposes of comparison.

One of our ultimate goals was that teachers in the project schools should begin researching in their own classrooms to investigate further the under-achievement of girls in male dominated school subjects.

The action-research plan was as follows:

1. We tested children's spatial ability and their science knowledge on entry to secondary school, and explored their attitudes to science and sex roles. The results were then fed back to schools.
2. We worked with teachers to increase their awareness of the impact of gender on educational achievement and outcomes, and to view it as a pedagogical issue.
3. A programme of visits to schools by women working in science and technology was mounted.
4. On the basis of (2) and (3) above, teachers and schools were invited to mount their own interventions; these included development of more 'girl friendly' curriculum materials, single sex clubs and classes, observation to increase awareness of sex differences in classroom interaction.
5. Children's attitudes to science and to sex roles were again measured for comparison with the initial survey, and their subject options monitored and compared with previous year-groups in each school.

The approach was collaborative: teachers were invited to work with the team as equal partners in the attempts both to investigate and find solutions to the GIST problem. However, very few of the teachers even recognized the issue as one of professional concern at the start of the project, and most of the first two years was spent in establishing the educational importance of the issue and working towards the development of feasible intervention strategies.

The project and its outcomes have been fully described elsewhere (Smail *et al.*, 1982; Kelly, Whyte and Smail 1984; Whyte in press). GIST had more success in altering children's attitudes than their subject choices, suggesting that it is easier to change attitudes and beliefs than actual behaviour. Pupils in action schools became markedly less stereotyped than pupils in control schools. They also had slightly more positive attitudes towards science and scientists and were less likely to define them as exclusively masculine. Despite some evidence of change in teachers' attitudes *and* behaviour, they themselves were reluctant to admit that the project had influenced them. According to an evaluation report this may reflect an unwillingness to admit that in the past schools have been sex biased (Payne, Cuff and Hustler 1984).

The GIST hypothesis was that female under-achievement in science and technology is at least partly socially constructed by the school, an hypothesis based on research evidence as well as critical feminist analysis (see, for example, Kelly 1981). During the project there was a shift away from locating the issue as one of girls' motivation towards attempts to change the nature of school science. One of the main gains from the GIST project has been the clarification of what is meant by a 'girl friendly' science, that is a science which will appeal equally to the interests and concerns of girls as well as boys. This chapter reflects on this concept, and also on the variable success of action schools in meeting the project goals and the implications this may have for a model of the girl friendly school.

Making science more girl friendly

Several interventions were designed to make science more girl friendly. Schools and teachers tried curriculum development to build on girls' science interests, changing patterns of classroom interaction, single sex groups and classes. The largest scale intervention was the VISTA programme, which consisted of women scientists and technologists visiting schools to talk to children about an aspect of their jobs already being covered in the school science syllabus. VISTA made science more girl friendly in two ways: both boys and girls were offered an attractive image of a competent woman scientist, and the talks concentrated on social and industrial applications of science, an element too often missing from science at school. One school was so impressed by the children's positive reactions that they completely revamped the science work in the first two years to include more social and human applications of science.

The survey of children's attitudes helped here: research such as Ormerod's (1971; Ormerod and Duckworth 1975) had shown that girls were interested in the social implications of science, but did not tell teachers what the desirable teaching approach might be in practice. Would science in the home be a starter? A question from our survey asked children whether they would like to know more about how a vacuum cleaner works; hardly anyone did, and girls were even less curious than boys. This told us that any simplistic assumptions about featuring 'female' domestic interests in science would probably meet with failure. The rest of the questionnaire about science curiosity showed that all the children were enthusiastic about learning science, and that girls were keen to know more about nature, the environment and medical science. Over 50 per cent, and in some cases over 60 per cent said they would like to learn about the human heart, germs and illnesses, how our muscles work, what food is good for you, life in the sea, what makes a rainbow appear and how a record is made. It was helpful that these topics also interested boys. At present the science curriculum is structured around physical science interests, on which boys are keener (how motor cars work, atoms and molecules); we were able to recommend that teaching build on the overlapping interests of the two sexes, because girls as well as boys want to know more about human biology and spectacular features of the environment (animals in the jungle, volcanoes and earthquakes, acids and chemicals). The less immediately attractive parts of science could be approached through these interests, for instance teaching 'forces' by beginning with the action of muscles in the human arm, and 'light' via the dissection of a bull's eye. When women scientists employ such approaches, and describe their own work, as happened during the VISTA programme, girls are receiving double encouragement. These examples indicate some of the features of girl friendly science: it builds on girls' interests, not just boys'; it explicitly encourages girls to see themselves as potential scientists, and it includes some of the social and human implications and applications of science.

Other GIST interventions

All the GIST schools were mixed comprehensives, and at first teachers were most unwilling to separate boys and girls at all, on the grounds that it ran counter to their co-educational comprehensive philosophy. Then certain teachers were particularly struck by the evidence of large differences in the interests and experience children brought with them to school. Girls had far less 'tinkering' experience than boys and the connection with their lesser interest in topics like 'how electricity is produced' seemed obvious. Several special science or craft clubs were organized in the lunch hour for girls only and in two schools teachers planned single-sex teaching. As we shall see, it was in these two schools that the largest measurable changes of attitude and option choice occurred.

For a more girl friendly science, it seems vital that teachers should come to see that when all the masculine packaging, evident in textbooks and resources as well as teachers' and boys' behaviour in the classroom, is removed, girls can be very enthusiastic about science.

Members of the team spent many hours observing in science labs and craft workshops. The GIST teachers managed to interact for equal amounts of time with girls and boys, but only with effort. We were looking for inequalities in teacher-pupil interaction, but also for some more clues as to what it is about science that makes girls lose interest. We found that boys acted in a way which made science seem more masculine than it really is; the teachers also helped to create the impression that science is a very macho business. In the very first lesson, teachers often pointed out the dangers of equipment and chemicals in the lab, delighting the boys who in later lessons displayed a great deal of bravado, for instance using a magnet to have a tug-of-war, trying to give each other electric shocks with a 6-volt battery; for the girls, the element of danger was more discouraging. Teachers and boys seemed to be unthinkingly collaborating to construct science as an area of masculine endeavour, excluding girls, who quickly took the hint (Kelly 1984). Just as the Croydon project found boys taking over the computers (see Ward, 1984 in list of unpublished conference papers), so that girls gave up and went away, GIST boys were again and again seen to hog scarce resources, particularly in craft lessons, so that girls would, overall, gain less practical experience than boys. (For a full account see Whyte 1984 and Kelly 1984.)

In the latter article, Alison Kelly sees at least four distinct senses in which it can be argued that science is masculine. First, the pupils, teachers and practitioners of science are overwhelmingly male in terms of numbers; second, school science is packaged and presented to appeal to boys, not girls; third, classroom behaviours and interaction operate to reconstruct science as a male activity, and finally it has been suggested that 'scientific' thinking embodies an intrinsically masculine world view.

The GIST interventions described above relate to three of these: VISTA women, albeit briefly and temporarily, redressed the numerical balance by offering female role models of practising scientists; VISTA and the curriculum development which followed involved a limited 'repackaging' of science to remove its exclusively masculine appeal, and the single-sex classes and classroom observation showed how science comes to be defined as 'masculine' in the mixed school.

The fourth point, the idea that science is intrinsically masculine, can be sustained only by clinging to an irredeemably narrow conception of science and scientific thinking. The industrial and social impact of science on health, on people, on the environment, a focus on the beauty and complexity of the natural world, are notable omissions from the school science syllabus. Girls are not uninterested in science, they are bored by the limited version of it they meet in school.

One of the purposes of an extended period of single-sex science teaching might be to let teachers see how girls approach scientific matters, and to discover, what may well be the case, that girls are just as capable of 'scientific thinking' as boys. Margaret Spear, in a different study from the one reported in this volume, found that for identical work boys were marked higher than girls for supposed understanding of principles, aptitude for science and 'O' level suitability (Spear 1984).

Perhaps a vital skill for the girl friendly science teacher is to study girls' real abilities and interests in science when some of the masculine packaging and the inhibiting presence of male peers are removed.

Outcomes

Children enjoyed the VISTA visits according to the questionnaire returns in the third year; they liked meeting scientists and learning about a range of jobs. Girls were slightly more positive than boys.

Overall, the attitudes of children in the action schools where all the interventions took place became noticeably more liberal, especially on sex role and occupational stereotypes and the 'masculinity' of science. In general, attitudes to science itself became more negative. This is a universal phenomenon (Gardner 1984). Children begin secondary school with high expectations of science, but become disillusioned and uninterested, especially in physics. However, the decline in science interest was less marked in GIST action than in control schools, indicating a possible causal effect of the VISTA visits and other interventions, and on boys as much as girls.

It appears that if girls' interests are catered for, if teachers become aware of the need for careful classroom management to ensure girls' participation, if the social and human implications of science and technology are stressed, girls will respond positively. There will continue to be problems if science teachers are personally doubtful about girls' ability to do science well; even if their doubts are not voiced (and anecdotal evidence suggests they sometimes are), girls are unlikely to respond unless teachers show they believe that girls have something to offer science as well as the reverse.

The significant difference between action and control schools concerning attitudes was not matched by an action/control differ-ence in option choices. In most schools the percentage of girls choosing physics in the GIST cohort increased in comparison with previous years (see Table 5.1). However, the increase in control schools was as large as in the action schools!

The girl friendly school

Unfortunately the pattern of option choice and attitude differ-ences is not perfectly matched within each school. That is to say, certain action schools were successful in changing attitudes, while others were successful in shifting option choices. Only one school was successful on both counts. The implication is that pupil attitude change is not sufficient on its own to ensure that pupils will actually make non-traditional option choices. Presumably the major mediating factors are the teachers, and the school, concerned.

Teacher attitudes

We did not see at the start of the project how we could on the one hand form a collaborative relationship with teachers, and on the other regard them as subjects of research who would complete attitude questionnaires we had devised. The team took copious field notes of responses to workshops and conferences, visits to schools and conversations with teachers. From these notes we became well aware that most of the teachers had rather conserva-tive views about sex roles in general. A questionnaire designed to highlight this might itself have become a source of unwanted antagonism. By the time it became obvious that some measure of teacher response was highly desirable, it was too late to carry out a before-and-after study, and as initiators of the project we could not convincingly claim to evaluate any supposed changes in a non-partisan way, or so we believed.

We therefore turned to some independent sources willing to carry out an evaluation for the small amount of money we had to pay for it. Three male sociologists from the School of Education at Manchester Polytechnic agreed to evaluate teachers' perceptions

Table 5.1 The percentage of girls and boys in the year group at GIST schools taking physics in fourth year, 1980 to 1983

Source Kelly *et al.* 1984

of the project, but actual interviews with the teachers were delayed by several months while the two teams thrashed out how much money could be spent, how the interviews would be conducted, how validity and objectivity could be ensured and how teachers' confidentiality could be protected. The report was finally published in January 1984 (Payne *et al.* 1984).

The most interesting aspect of the teachers' response is their unwillingness to admit to any change of attitude or practice as a result of GIST. Yet both the field notes and the evaluation report provide clear evidence that the staff had become much more aware of, and informed about, girls' under-achievement in science and technology and the possible actions which schools could take. Many mentioned the practical steps they had already devised: altering curriculum materials, deliberately avoiding the use of stereotyped language, studying patterns of classroom interaction and thinking of ways to increase girls' participation. The evaluators noted the grudgingness of teachers to admit to changes in their own beliefs or practices and ascribed it to an unwillingness to accept the implied criticism that previous practice had, even unintentionally, discouraged girls.

A national survey of teachers' attitudes to equal opportunities found that men were more likely to be opposed to promoting equal opportunities than women, but that differences in subject taught were more important than the sex of the teacher in determining his or her attitude. Teachers of maths, physical sciences and crafts were the least in favour of greater equality (Pratt, Bloomfield and Seale 1984). Spear also found in a study of teachers' attitudes to girls and technology that the most sex-differentiated replies came from science teachers (Spear in this volume). On both counts, of sex and subjects taught, the GIST teachers were the least promising group which could have been chosen to promote sex equality.

Alison Kelly worked with some of her students to carry out a minor evaluation of changes in GIST teachers' attitudes in comparison with a national sample (Kelly *et al.* 1984). Women again proved to be more emphatic about sex equality than men, and London teachers were more feminist than others. GIST teachers were slightly less traditional and more in favour of equality of the sexes than other teachers. Teachers in GIST schools were also slightly more likely to agree with statements suggesting that girls 'lose out' in classroom interactions and receive less encouragement in science than boys. This is likely to be an effect of the classroom observation work carried out with GIST teachers (for a full account see Whyte 1984). However, the GIST teachers of physical science were less convinced than their colleagues elsewhere of the importance of finding ways to encourage girls in their subject. It may be that their experience of GIST has given them a better idea of the amount of work and energy involved in trying to change things (Kelly *et al.* 1984).

School atmosphere

Whatever may be the attitude of any individual teacher, if s/he does not receive adequate support from the school in implementing change, s/he is likely to give up, or decide that the innovation is not worth the extra time and energy required.

The GIST project was not limited to changing individual teachers' attitudes, but went beyond that to the attempt to alter school norms. The extent to which GIST was successful in particular schools appears to have been less dependent on the team's efforts than on the existing school ethos and whether it was consistent with responding to the demand for genuine equality of opportunity. In other words, the project probably did not change schools, but change may have been most likely to occur in schools which were open to the innovation and to the ideas of equality presented by the project.

Closer study of between-school differences (see Kelly *et al.* 1984; Whyte in press) shows that attitude change was most marked in three action schools. In one, Moss Green, there had also been an increase in the percentage of girls opting for chemistry, physics and technical crafts. In the other two, Edgehill and Meadowvale, there had been an increase in at least two of these.

These schools appeared to have several things in common: first, each could be characterized as an 'innovative' school in some sense. Moss Green was a custom-built community school, with a commitment to multicultural education and a staff who were used to implementing innovations such as open-plan classrooms, and, more recently, an alternative curriculum for fourth and fifth years.

At Edgehill, the science department was divided into biological and environmental sciences, instead of the traditional biology, physics and chemistry; the head teacher was a conscious advocate of innovation in comprehensive schooling; in the third school, Meadowvale, the science department had decided to redraft its entire first and second year science curriculum, in part because of the children's response to the VISTA visits organized by GIST.

The least successful schools were those which implemented the minimum programme asked for by GIST: administration of questionnaires to children, allowing women visitors into the school and piloting, more or less reluctantly, teaching materials devised by the team. The successful schools, in contrast, took up more GIST suggestions more enthusiastically, or even developed their own ideas for interventions. For example at Edgehill, a GIST pack for discussion of sex roles – *Gender in Our Lives* – was used in the personal and social education lessons, with teachers talking honestly and openly about their personal experience; as it happened they found themselves in the middle of a discussion about fathers being present at childbirth, and the children were obviously fascinated by this new view of their teachers as emotional beings.

At Meadowvale, the head of biology, who was also in charge of personal and social education, used 'active tutorial work' methods to explore children's perceptions of the girls and science problem. The girls were highly indignant about the different treatment they felt they received from most of the science teachers.

At both Edgehill and Meadowvale, the head teachers invited GIST to address the whole staff, at Edgehill in the context of a half day in-service session on equal opportunities.

At Moss Green, a special trip to a local college of building was arranged for third-year girls only, and the school also began an experiment in single-sex setting in third-year science classes, first explaining to the children why they were doing so.

Willingness to talk directly to pupils about the aims of GIST was another feature of the more successful schools. Despite requests from the team to discuss the issue with children, few teachers revealed the purpose of the project to their classes. Some teachers told the evaluators that they did not feel justified in talking to pupils about the girls and science problem, and gave the impression that they felt to do so would be tantamount to propaganda.

At Moss Green, GIST was called in to address the second-year class before they made craft mini-options, to stress how important it was for girls to consider getting a grounding in technology. Far greater numbers of girls opted for technical subjects than had ever done so before. The school also ran single-sex clubs.

In comparison, there was no visible explicit discussion of sex roles at either of the two least successful schools. The GIST workpack *Gender in Our Lives* was used at another school, but a senior member of management had effectively insisted they use it, and some teachers did so with considerable reservations, afterwards reporting almost complete failure to alter children's prejudices.

We had looked for some impact from the presence of women in senior positions in school, but the highest percentage of women at Scale 4 or above in any school was 35 per cent. In the more successful schools, women held relatively more senior posts in the science department or in the school. In the two least successful schools it is notable that the proportion of senior women was lowest, in one case despite the fact that the head teacher was a woman.

In summary, the most successful schools appeared to have the following characteristics:

- teachers who planned and implemented their own interventions;
- teachers who were prepared to discuss the GIST problem with children, rather than simply accepting VISTA and other interventions and hoping that an implicit message would get through;
- staff, especially at a senior level, who had a positive commitment to the aims of the project;
- a progressive ethos which fitted comfortably with the equal-opportunity aims of GIST;
- a relatively higher proportion of women staff at senior levels.

Some of these factors correspond closely to those identified by Lippitt as possible inhibitors or facilitators of change:

- personal attitudes;
- the climate of the school;

— the innovative practice which is being advocated; and
— the physical/temporal arrangements made to encourage change
(Lippitt 1974)

The third element, the innovative practice advocated, became refined during rather than before the project. The use of questionnaires fed back to teachers revealed the base of interest and enthusiasm for science too often missed by schools concerned to promote a curriculum informally based on male interests. Observation in labs and workshops highlighted the depressing effect on girls' performance of the boys' claim to science as their subject. We are much clearer now than at the beginning about how to approach science in a more girl friendly way (see Smail 1983, 1984), and the clarity is in part due to the way we have worked with teachers.

The conditions for a girl friendly school may be more difficult to bring about, for it would seem that teachers must be openly and visibly concerned about equality before pupils will change their choices; schools with traditional norms, limited or formal communication channels, and with few women in senior positions will be much slower to adapt to changed female expectations.

Conclusion

The major impetus behind the GIST programme was the women's movement of the 1960s and 1970s, reflected in the equality legislation of 1975. This brought an upward adjustment in the expectations of women's capabilities, and something of a shift in social values and attitudes about the possibilities for women's work and lifestyles. Zaltman *et al.* (1977) identify as a source of educational innovation the exploitation of a felt discrepancy between an existing situation and what might be accomplished. The GIST project can be seen as a piece of curriculum change originating from the newly recognized performance gap between what schools now do, and what they *could* do for girls.

GIST was not a conventional research project. It was a deliberate intention that by using an action research mode, we would be able to offer policy implications which would ultimately be of benefit to girls. The results of the interventions are not as clear-cut or dramatic as some of those who supported us may have hoped. The ten schools did provide a substantial research sample of nearly 2000 children, but more dramatic changes might have been possible if we had worked instead in only one or two schools. However, then the sample size might have been too small to show up significant attitude change.

Teachers were always busy, and many schools put GIST on a rather lower priority than dealing with the impact of unemployment, school reorganization, discipline or curricular problems. It was often difficult to get schools to provide even basic information such as the breakdown of subject choice by sex, and members of the team frequently had to extract the information themselves from school data. Oddly enough, the control schools, where no interventions took place, were more co-operative and efficient in returning questionnaires than action schools. Similarly, the impact of GIST may have been as great in schools which had no contact with the project at all, because of the changing climate of opinion in which girls' under-achievement in science and technology came to be seen as a serious educational issue.

Acknowledgement

The GIST Project was funded by the EOC/SSRC Joint Panel on Women and Underachievement with additional support from the Department of Industry Education Unit, the Schools Council and Shell UK Ltd. I am grateful to these sponsors and to my colleagues on the project, Alison Kelly, Barbara Smail and John Catton. However, they do not necessarily share the views expressed in this chapter.

My thanks also to Sandra Burslem and Sue Thorne who kindly lent me their word-processor.

References

Bloomfield, J. (1984) 'Option scheme management for equal opportunity', paper presented at Girl Friendly Schooling conference, Manchester Polytechnic 11–13 Sept.

Gardner, P. L. (1984) Summary and cross evaluation of national reports', presented at IPN/UNESCO International Symposium on Interests in Science and Technology Education, Kiel, W. Germany, April 2–6.

Kelly, A. (1981) *The Missing Half: Girls and Science Education*, Manchester University Press.

Kelly, A. (1984) 'The construction of masculine science' submitted to *British Journal of Sociology of Education*, August.

Kelly, A., Whyte, J., and Smail, B. (1984) *Girls Into Science and Technology: Final Report*, GIST, Department of Sociology, University of Manchester.

Lippitt, R. O. (1974) 'Identifying, Documenting, Evaluating and Sharing Innovative Classroom Practices, *Final Report to the Office of Education*, HEW, cited in Zaltman, which see.

Ormerod, M. B. (1971) 'The Social Implications Factor in Attitudes to Science', *British Journal of Educational Psychology* 41(3), 335–8.

Ormerod, M. B. and Duckworth, D. (1975) *Pupils' Attitudes to Science: A Review of Research*, NFER, Slough.

Payne, G., Cuff, E., and Hustler, D. (1984) 'GIST or PIST: teacher perceptions of the project "Girls Into Science and Technology"', mimeo, Manchester Polytechnic.

Pratt, J., Bloomfield, J. and Seale, C. (1984) *Option Choice: A Question of Equal Opportunity*, NFER–Nelson, Windsor.

Smail, B. (1983) 'Getting Science Right for Girls', paper presented to the second International Conference on Girls and Science and Technology, Oslo, Norway.

Smail, B. (1984) *Girl Friendly Science: Avoiding Sex Bias in the Curriculum*, Longman for the Schools Council, London.

Smail, B., Whyte, J. and Kelly, A. (1982) 'Girls Into Science and Technology: the first two years', *School Science Review*, 63, 620–30; *South Australian Science Teachers Association Journal* (1981), 813, 3–10; EOC Research Bulletin (1982), 6, Spring.

Spear, M. (1984) 'Sex bias in science teachers' ratings of work and pupil characteristics', *European Journal of Science Education* 6(4), 369–77.

Whyte, J. (1984) 'Observing sex stereotypes and interactions in the school lab and workshop' *Educational Review* 36 (1).

Whyte, J. (in press) *Girls in Science and Technology* (working title) Routledge & Kegan Paul, London.

Zaltman, G., Florio, D. H. and Sikorski, L. A. (1977) *Dynamic Educational Change: models, strategies, tactics and management*, Free Press, New York and Collier-Macmillan, London.

Personal and professional: a feminist approach

Many teachers, particularly in primary schools, are unaware of the school's role in reinforcing sex role stereotypes, and reluctant to admit the part their own attitudes and behaviour can play in the process. This poses problems for the feminist researcher who wants to promote anti-sexist practice in school while preserving the autonomy of the teacher in her classroom.

The research described in this chapter was concerned with looking at practical strategies which a nursery or infant teacher in Scotland could adopt to counter the effects of sexism and sex stereotyping in the classroom. This concern to develop practical strategies was tempered with reservations regarding the directness of the research approach.

Despite the increased interest in the issues of equal opportunities in many local education authorities in England where advisers and advisory teachers in equal opportunities, conferences, regional policy statements and the development of curriculum materials are proliferating, my experience throughout Scotland indicated that the issues here are largely unacknowledged and are not generally regarded as falling within the professional concern of educators.

It was likely, therefore, that the teachers taking part in the project, as well as being unfamiliar with the issues involved, would hold personal and professional reservations about appropriate strategies to adopt within the project. Thus the research design was devised to accommodate differing perspectives of teachers and was committed to an approach which would base the strategy in each classroom on the individual response and perspective of the classroom teacher. I was convinced that the understanding, interest and commitment of the individual teacher was a pre-requisite for the success of the practical aspect of the project. To have sought to impose anti-sexist strategies, to confine myself within the role of a detached, objective and essentially transient university research student, would have been counter productive.

Introducing new ideas to infant classrooms, or any classroom, is not just a matter of giving the teacher a handbook or set of apparatus and telling her to get on with it. Ideas have to be talked through, rationales explained, but, above all, practical help which takes account of the workload teachers already bear seems essential. Collaboration with the teachers was therefore an essential element of the project.

Where does feminism come in? It was important in this project in two respects. First, the issue of sexism in schools is without doubt a feminist issue. Although studies of sex differences in achievement, aspiration or capability in education have been largely carried out by psychologists over the years, these studies have been mostly descriptive: this is how things *are*, they say. Although such studies may trace the reasons for such differences back to differences in the socialization patterns of the sexes, they are less likely to engage in discussion of positive strategies for overcoming such differences since they are seen not as a problem but rather as a statement of fact.

For sex differences in educational achievement, aspiration or capability to become a feminist issue, they have to be regarded as sexist: that is, containing implicitly or explicitly an imbalance in the power relationships contained within them. For a feminist does not just note that girls are less likely to play with Lego than boys. She notes that

(1) this is likely to be due to the different socialization patterns of boys and girls, and she may discuss how these patterns could be challenged or changed;
(2) this differentiation of experience bears a relationship to girls' avoidance of mechanical and construction tasks in general

and such an avoidance leads directly to powerlessness and dependence;

(3) that lack of three-dimensional experience is significant in terms of vocational aspiration and can eliminate girls from career paths currently awarded status and power in society – science and engineering; and most importantly, she notes

(4) that there are positive ways in which she can intervene to challenge this state of affairs, which a non-feminist researcher would not regard as a problem.

The second way in which feminism was important in the project was in the approach. Although collaborative research is an approach which has been used outwith feminist research as in Lawrence Stenhouse's work (Stenhouse 1975), all feminist researchers would probably support the importance of including the perspective of the researched as well as the researcher, and of awarding status within the research to those perspectives (Oakley 1981). In this way, a feminist approach seeks to alter the power relationship usually maintained in the more traditional types of sociological or educational research.

Traditionally this has entailed a rigid hierarchy headed by the project director (male), filtered down through research fellows (male) and research assistants (part-time women) and, finally, the researched. Often women have been completely excluded from the body of the researched. In compiling statistics about employment, mobility or income, men are often researched as a category from which national predictions and generalizations are made. When women are researched, it is often as a separate group, definable by their stereotyped habits of going shopping or bearing and looking after children.

In terms of methodology Ann Oakley (Oakley 1981) describes the traditional relationship between the interviewer and the respondent as one where the interviewer has complete control, dictates the form and content of the interview and regards the respondent essentially as an object, as part of 'objective' research which can legitimately join the body of academic 'reality'. Of course, the interviewer has at his or her disposal many subtle techniques for eliciting the desired responses, always in an ultimately detailed and objective fashion.

Oakley describes traditional methodology as one which main-

tains a hierarchical relationship between interviewer and respondent, which prohibits respondents from answering back or asking
questions, and which upholds objectivity, detachment and a
regard for 'science' as an important cultural activity taking priority
over people's more individualized concerns. In contrast to the
traditional model, she asserts that 'in most cases, the goal of
finding out about people through interviewing is best achieved
when the relationship of interviewer and interviewee is non-
hierarchical, and when the interviewer is prepared to invest his or
her own personal identity in the relationship.' (Oakley 1981, p.
38) However, although the relationship between a feminist researcher and those she is researching is one where the power
relations have deliberately been minimized, and where an inter-
dependence and a co-operative approach may have been developed, it would be wrong to believe that this leads to a
relationship of complete equality.

The researcher still retains control whether she wants to or not,
particularly if she is writing and presenting the 'findings' or results
of her research. However much she has attempted to accommodate the perspectives and viewpoints of her subjects within her
writing, she will still be presenting them within her own interpretation. She will undoubtedly be involved in the process of
selecting what goes in and what is left out of a report. She is in
danger of engaging in what I regard as a kind of voyeurism, where
she seeks the trust and warmth of an interactive research relationship but then withdraws to academic heights to impart
those parts of the relationship which she deems worthy of
reporting. This is one of the essential dilemmas of a feminist
approach to research which I would like to return to later in this
chapter.

Thus the project pursued two interests, or commitments, at the
same time. It was committed to looking for practical strategies for
Scottish infant teachers to adopt for tackling sexism in their
classrooms, and it was also committed to an approach which took
the teachers' responses to the issues of sexism as a central element.
Of course, it was taking a risk. What if all the teachers were totally
opposed to any kind of anti-sexist strategy and regarded the subject
as a non-starter? If that happened, I was prepared for the project to
be a useful, but far less interesting, piece of research recording

aspects of sex stereotyping in the classroom purely from my own perspective.

The school was selected for reasons of convenience rather than any other, and the three teachers who took part in the project – a nursery teacher, a Primary 1 and a Primary 3 teacher – were given to me by the assistant head as willing volunteers. The project lasted throughout the autumn term of 1983.

The initial stage was primarily for familiarization. I gave each of the teachers background details of what I wanted to do and why. I included some of the schools literature from the Equal Opportunities Commission to lend some legitimacy to the project and to give them the opportunity to become informed of the issues. At the same time, I didn't want to swamp them with literature. I stressed the importance of their responses for the project – how I didn't want them to be polite – that if they thought I was misinterpreting the activities in their classrooms they should say so. And I also tried to get group discussions going so they could support each other.

In order to gain familiarity with the three classrooms I spent about three weeks observing in each one. I avoided a pre-determined observation schedule; I did not want to define the parameters of the situation prematurely, but hoped to gradually build up a picture of the daily activities and interaction patterns in terms of how I saw processes of sex stereotyping. I kept notebooks, used a small tape recorder of my own to talk to groups of children and recorded the teachers with a radio microphone. And I tried to be helpful. I was anxious to present myself for what I was: a primary teacher interested in a specific aspect of classroom life, who wanted the opportunity to learn more. I asked the questions which interested me at the time, and seemed appropriate; I basically trusted myself. By trying to keep very full records and by listening every evening to the recordings it was possible to follow things up, to come back with more questions or to note the implications of something which might have been said or done and look at it again. Two of the teachers undoubtedly became my friends. The third teacher, a young woman in her second year of teaching and still 'on probation', was much more reserved, and I was never able to reassure her fully that I was not a threat.

After the initial familiarization and observation period I wrote a full report for each teacher about what I had recorded in each classroom. I described the classroom briefly in general terms and went on to present my opinion about the sexist or sex-stereotyped patterns of organization or behaviour. Once again the reports invited criticism. They were not academic documents written in sociological jargon likely to impress, silence or confuse the teachers. They were rather mundane descriptions of familiar scenes seen through different eyes. What did they think, I wanted to know. Did they agree with me? Did they see sex stereotyping as an issue? Did they feel they had a role to play in relation to sex stereotyping? If they did, I wanted to help them formulate some strategies for tackling some of the areas of sex stereotyping which I had identified or others which they were personally interested in.

It was the autumn holiday when I left the reports with them and they had a week to mull them over. When school resumed, I conducted individual interviews with the teachers which I taped, to record their detailed responses. In fact, the interviews were conversations. I avoided using a 'schedule' of predetermined questions. I wanted to know whether they felt interested or inclined to talk through the issue of sex stereotyping in the context of practical and immediate examples. After the individual conversations we had a group meeting and exchanged ideas as each teacher had agreed to let the others have copies of her report.

Although sharing certain perspectives – like remarking on the strong influences of the home, the media and the external environment in the sex stereotyping of children – the three teachers presented three very different responses. Accordingly, the subsequent action which was taken in each classroom was substantially different in nature. It would have been indefensible, in feminist terms, to invite their criticisms and responses but then to proceed with a predetermined strategy regardless of the variation in their perspectives.

The Primary 3 teacher was already in favour of positive action and intervention strategies to counter sexism. In fact, her classroom was already non-sexist to the extent that when six children were dramatizing a story with five characters in it and she suggested that one of them should be the director, a boy remarked, 'The director should be a girl. Girls aren't usually directors.' In that classroom we embarked on two weeks of work, which we planned together, designed to 'open up' the topic of sex stereotyping with the pupils. We talked about roles and aspirations, about the embarrassment of being first to do something new; we role played and we encouraged the children to view existing classroom materials critically. Together we extended our understanding of what being anti-sexist in the classroom is all about.

Primary 1 was different. I was never fully convinced that the teacher knew what I was talking about. She politely put down the bulk of my observations to 'chance' or as wrong interpretations. As far as I was concerned one of the most interesting and important elements of sex stereotyping in education was omnipresent in her classroom – boys and control. It seemed undeniable to me that already some of the boys were becoming typed as 'bad boys' and that their behaviour demanded undue amounts of her attention. However, rather than meticulously recording her subsequent interactions systematically over a period of time to try to 'prove' to her that this was the case (and probably still not gain her agreement) I opted for something less close to home.

In the action research project called 'Sex Stereotyping and the Early Years of Schooling' conducted at the University of East Anglia (May and Rudduck 1983), Nick May and Jean Rudduck suggested initially tackling sex-sterotyping issues in locations outside the actual classroom, like the playground, corridors or the lunch hall. In this way, they hoped the teachers would regard any criticism or policy changes as less personal. Encouraged by this approach I suggested to the Primary 1 teacher that we look again at the gym lessons where I had already recorded apparent evidence of sex stereotyping in that the girls appeared to be consistently 'failing' in a certain game. Although not entirely satisfactory, I believe that this attempt to accommodate the teacher's viewpoint was correct. I did not override her response to my report but sought a compromise solution which would still contain both our perspectives.

The nursery was different again. The nursery teacher was obviously very interested in the project and keen to discuss the ideas it threw up. However, she had great reservations about the issue of intervention. Her whole training and experience had been based on the philosophy of 'free play' and the thought of hauling the boys out of the big climbing blocks to try something else and encouraging the girls there instead, caused her considerable concern.

She did not deny that a pattern of sex-stereotyped activities existed in the nursery but was inclined to see the nursery in terms of the year. What might be the pattern this week may change next week was her point of view, and accordingly she preferred not to intervene over sex-stereotyped play patterns but rather wait for the pupils to 'naturally' move from one play area to another 'when they were ready'. In this class, part of my action was to embark on using a systematic observation schedule to record precisely which children were using which activities over a period of two weeks.

This action was selected partly at the request of the teacher because she was interested in the general distribution of the children. Nevertheless, I felt that she might be susceptible to added evidence that the children were not 'naturally' moving on, and that she might therefore begin to entertain the idea of intervention. So once again, the action taken in the classroom was something of a compromise, but was still worthwhile for both of us.

After three weeks of co-operative work I submitted detailed reports to each teacher and invited their comments, this time in a final group discussion. Apart from the details of the findings in each classroom, it was clear that the teachers had felt the project worthwhile in the way that it had encouraged their participation and accommodated their perspectives.

As for the findings, some were inconclusive and most of them posed more questions than they answered in terms of practical classroom strategy. However, the approach had not defined neat parameters from the beginning, and I had expected to open up a Pandora's box. Probably if I had come away with a clear set of 'answers' it would have indicated that the project had radically changed direction and fallen into a more traditional mould.

The three very different responses of the teachers and the differing strategies adopted in their classrooms indicate clearly that anyone concerned with the introduction of equal opportunities policies and intervention strategies in schools should be prepared to work in a variety of ways at a variety of levels.

It is important to allocate time for and acknowledge the importance of talking through the issues involved. Until teacher-training programmes include comprehensive and detailed components on equal opportunities, and local authorities become committed to making informed in-service provision, most teachers are likely to be unaware of the professional implications of the issues and will rely on their personal and perhaps ill-informed beliefs about 'women's lib' and the nature of equality.

The overriding implication of the research is the importance of raising the awareness of teachers and others in education to the issues of sex stereotyping and of placing these issues clearly in an educational context. Indeed, many of them may have doubts about whether the devising of strategies to counter sex stereotyping falls within their professional remit.

The overwhelming message from the work in Primary 1 and Primary 3 relates to the importance of the level of awareness of the class teacher regarding the subtlety of the sex-stereotyping process. The experience in Primary 1 showed a teacher who was provided with explicitly non sex-stereotyped material but who was unable to use it effectively because of her lack of awareness of the issues involved. In contrast, the Primary 3 teacher expressed her heightened awareness of the issues by using the old, sex-stereotyped classroom materials to stimulate the critical faculties of her pupils and to raise their awareness of the taken-for-granted nature of sex stereotyping.

I believe this contrast is important because much of the concern of those active in countering sex stereotyping in schools has been with the removal and replacement of the sexist materials and resources which are to be found in most schools. Their work has usually been undermined by opponents, or 'realists', who point out the overall lack of funds in education to make any such substantial changes. In the current economic climate, teachers have to put up with what resources they already have, and pleas for non-sexist resources seem likely to fall on deaf ears.

It would be useful to pay attention to what can be done with existing resources, and this research suggests some possibilities for the imaginative and aware teacher. By the same token, the experience in Primary 1 indicated that even with a glossy 'package' of non-sexist materials, the impact can be totally diminished if used by a teacher who has not accommodated the implications of sex stereotyping into her teaching approach.

Because of the awareness and commitment of the teacher, Primary 3 provided a testing ground for the idea of explicitly introducing discussion and analysis of sex roles and sex stereotyping into the curriculum. Despite our reservations about the brief and sometimes ill-prepared nature of the work undertaken, the outcome of classroom work showed clearly that such an explicit introduction was not inappropriate.

Indeed, if we acknowledge the significance of the affective development of pupils and the importance of the influences upon them as they construct their self-images for their future expectations and aspirations, then it is on this essentially socializing aspect of their development that we should be focusing our attention. Just as it seems, from the experience of Primary 1 and Primary 3, to be more important to have an aware teacher rather than non-sexist materials, so it is important to have aware pupils. We are likely to be most effective in countering the effects of sex stereotyping on pupils if we seek from the earliest stage in their educational careers to inform them that what seems to be taken for granted need not necessarily be the case.

Teachers have to be relieved of their unease concerning their role *vis-à-vis* positive intervention. They have to be reassured that it is appropriate for sound educational reasons to intervene to ensure that all children experience the whole range of educational resources within the classroom and within the school as a whole, pertaining to both the hidden and the formal curriculum. The limiting effect of gender-typed self-images on the educational aspirations and expectations of boys and girls should be made quite clear. In Scotland, Alison Kelly's work (Kelly 1978), and that of Ryrie (Ryrie, Furst and Lauder 1979), have shown unequivocally that subject choice and occupational aspiration are significantly affected by what boys and girls think is appropriate and expected of their sex.

I was left with the task of 'writing up' and a return to the problem of the illusory nature of the 'equality' of the researcher and the researched within a feminist approach. As far as my relationship with two of the teachers was concerned there was little problem. We got on well and I am as convinced as one ever can be that we understood each other's perspective. I had no qualms about describing how they felt, and felt assured that they would have contradicted me if they had thought I had got a wrong understanding.

However, in the case of the third teacher the situation was quite different. I could not truthfully report her perspective nor even my interpretation of it. I could only say that I felt she was overly apprehensive about the project and that I never became close enough to her to know the reasons why. I could say I felt she had no understanding whatsoever of the issues of sexism and that she actively reinforced sexist practices in her classroom, but this would fail to include her viewpoint.

Inasmuch as I am maintaining my attempts to share the project, it is inevitable that all the teachers will see the final draft. Two of them will feel positive and encouraged. What do I write about the third? This seems to be a crucial dilemma. I am torn between the personal – that is, presenting the sexist teacher in as positive a way as possible out of respect for her feelings and my anxiety not to exert status or power by taking the liberty of defining her for academic delectation – and the professional, where I am dedicated to tackling as truthfully and as positively as possible all the aspects of the teachers' responses which seem important for planning intervention strategies in schools. The Primary 1 teacher's response is very important because, I suspect, it is shared by many other teachers who would react with suspicion and wariness to someone coming into school to talk about sexism in the classroom, in their classroom. Her response should be pulled apart and analysed for every scrap of useful detail and I have the task of doing it in the least hurtful way.

This is why I have reservations about the apparent 'equality' inherent in discussion about the feminist approach to research. It is possible to break down the hierarchies, the interview and observation schedules and to conduct research within an atmosphere of intimacy, trust and personal commitment. But the researcher must never suffer the illusion that total equality can be achieved. She must acknowledge the power relationship in which she finally determines what is recorded and what is not, and in which she must assume ultimate responsibility.

Nevertheless, it is difficult to come to terms with conducting such research in any other way, particularly within a methodology committed to 'objectivity'. A feminist approach, combining the

personal with the professional and genuinely attempting to in-
corporate the perspectives of the researched and award them some
status and 'right of reply', may be more messy and subjective, but it
is one which, personally and professionally, I believe to be more
honest and, in the long term, effective.

References

Kelly, A. (1978) 'Sex differences in science enrolments: Reasons and
    remedies', *Collaborative Research Newsletters 3 and 4*, Centre for
    Educational Sociology, University of Edinburgh.
May, N. and Rudduck, J. (1983) *Sex Stereotyping and the Early Years of
    Schooling*, Centre for Applied Research in Education, University of
    East Anglia, Norwich.
Oakley, A. (1981) 'Interviewing Women: A Contradiction in Terms',
    in Roberts, H. (ed.) *Doing Feminist Research*, Routledge & Kegan
    Paul, London.
Ryrie, A. C., Furst, A., and Lauder, M. (1979) *Choices and Chances*,
    Hodder & Stoughton: SCRE.
Stenhouse, L. (1975) *An Introduction to Curriculum Research and De-
    velopment*, Heinemann, London.
Witcher, H. (1984) 'Responses to gender typification in the primary
    classroom', unpublished M.Ed. thesis, University of Stirling.

Seven   Hazel Taylor

INSET for equal opportunities in the London Borough of Brent

One of the strengths of much anti-sexist work in education is its growth from small groups of committed teachers. Their insights have been firmly based on classroom experience and everyday involvement in the detail of school life as it is experienced by girl and boy pupils, by women and men teachers. The coming together of teachers united in a desire to tackle the issues fosters a solidarity and a sense of mutual support which is powerful in the strength it provides. Yet for the work begun by such teachers to be fully effective, it must be transmitted to others and become part of the culture of the school, while remaining faithful to the visions and commitments which inspired it. How that is done, and indeed, whether it can be done, is the challenge for those responsible for in-service training.

In 1982, the London Borough of Brent appointed an adviser for equal opportunities in its Education Department, with a responsibility for translating the authority's public commitment to equal opportunities into action in its schools. In-service training has been a major means of attempting that formidable task. It is quite clear that if all pupils are to benefit from the anti-sexist insights and practice of a few teachers, then ways have to be found of extending it to many more. Equally, it is clear that simply requiring teachers to change their approach, or requiring them to discuss important policy issues when they are unprepared, or expecting them somehow suddenly to know how to behave differently in the classroom when it has taken those involved in the work many years of discussion, self-examination and trial and error to develop new approaches, is foolish and unrealistic. It is more than that: it is fatal. For the best way of ensuring that anti-sexist initiatives fail is to foist them on teachers (and others involved in education) without preparation or time to reach an understanding of the issues, and then be helpless in the face of things going wrong. The responsibility of in-service training therefore is to provide teachers with sufficient understanding and knowledge to make professional sense of the demands for change being made on them, and sufficient support to enable them to step beyond understanding into action in their schools. This is not easy, for schools as organizations are constructed to resist change, and teachers as individuals are often full of inconsistencies between their educational philosophy and their practice. As Jean Rudduck has remarked,

> There is usually a tough undergrowth of cultural norms that characterises individual classrooms and schools, and this has to be pushed back if innovation is to put down roots. The coherence of an existing set of norms is not easy to displace, and it would be unrealistic to expect that new ideas alone, however exciting they may seem during the course where they are communicated, will be sufficient to carry the would-be innovator through into radically new modes of action. (Rudduck 1981)

Part of in-service training (INSET), therefore, must be the provision of a continuing follow-up programme, and one of the functions of the trainer must be to foster the growth of supportive networks so that much of the follow-up work is taken on by the course participants themselves.

Faced with the task of implementing an unfamiliar policy in a meaningful way across an entire authority, it seemed important to define target groups for different sorts of INSET. It was important to make sure of reaching the most influential teachers, to reach as many different teachers as possible, and to create a web of links between the various groups. In this way, while each group might have its particular needs met in an individual manner, each was aware of and could use the support of the others, and could have a sense that it was not alone but part of a very large body of people working towards a common goal. The in-service work in Brent therefore has fallen into four main categories, not mutually exclusive but each with a clearly defined focus. In this chapter I will describe the main activities within each group and conclude by attempting an interim evaluation of the effectiveness of this type of work as a means of furthering anti-sexist education for *all* our pupils.

One discrete group needing special provision is head teachers and those responsible for managing change in schools. However much one might support a bottom-up model of change, little can be achieved without the active support of those with the power to make key decisions. Head teachers are also crucial figures in that they have a central part to play in leading their staff in new directions and in determining a school's aim and objectives. Ultimately, within a school the responsibility for seeing that school policy is implemented, even by those who may not agree with that policy, rests with the head teacher. In-service work with head teachers or deputies must recognize their management function and offer them support in carrying this out in relation to equal opportunities.

The second category, of equal importance with the first, is that of those committed teachers who have already done a great deal of work and whose common ground is the shared commitment to change. Brought together, they become a very powerful group and it is they who will lead in the development and monitoring of good practice in their schools, who will offer support to each other and to newcomers, who will be called upon to become trainers themselves. They, crucially, must also themselves be acknowledged and sustained.

A third category consists of a large number of groups of teachers brought together by a special responsibility or a common interest. Such groups may consist of teachers of the same subject, with the same post of responsibility, or the same amount of classroom experience. Whatever it is, that connection can act as the focus for in-service work which is relevant to their immediate classroom needs, and also act as a point of contact between the group members. The common ground essentially is not the commitment to anti-sexism, but the shared status or interest of the group.

The individual school is the focus of shared concern for the fourth category of work – school-focused in-service is an essential part of an overall in-service strategy for implementing equal opportunities. Democratic change, with full staff participation, is the only sort of change that can be philosophically acceptable to people committed to equality, and is also the only sort of change likely to be lastingly effective in transforming the culture of the school from one based on male norms to one that is girl friendly. In Brent, a programme has therefore been constructed to meet these four different sorts of needs, and enough has been done to make it possible to offer a description of the work.

Head teachers' courses

For the first target group, head teachers, different approaches were adopted for secondary and primary schools. Within secondary schools in Brent, there were individual teachers who were strongly committed to equal opportunities and who were willing and able to work with senior management to create a girl friendly school. One of the functions of a course for secondary heads, therefore, was to convince them of the value of working with, validating, and giving status to the teachers already engaged in change. A three-day course was planned with a group of four deputy heads. The design provided for an introductory pair exercise through which participants could share their initial perspectives on equal opportunities; a general informative talk, necessary to ensure a minimum of common knowledge about the main issues as they relate to secondary school curricula and organization; choices of specialist workshops, sharing of experience from other schools; and a number of highly participatory activities focusing on central school tasks: writing third-year option booklets and school brochures, deciding on priorities for action within the school, and how to manage it. A bookstall and appropriate handouts were provided.

The Director of Education spoke at one session, making clear the seriousness of the authority's commitment to its equal opportunities initiatives, and representatives of all secondary schools attended – though three schools were not represented at all sessions. The course was far more effective with those who attended all of it than with those few who dropped in and out. The final plenary session was devoted to future planning. Of the many outcomes of the course, several of particular importance can be identified. It radically changed some participants and developed in them a degree of strong commitment which has not wavered since. These people have played a crucial part in substantial changes which have taken place in their schools, and all of them are women deputy heads with curriculum responsibilities. It secured from other participants an acknowledgement of the professional and educational importance of the issue of equal opportunities, even if they were not immediately prepared to prioritize it above other issues seen to be currently important. It fostered a lasting personal relationship between the adviser, who was the course tutor, and the members, so that the adviser subsequently had a link with a senior manager in every secondary school which went beyond the usual professional relationship between teacher and adviser. It led to the setting up in nearly every secondary school in the authority of equal opportunities working parties with an official brief to consider their own schools and report back to the head teacher, through the usual channels for the school, on changes that were needed. It led to a series of regular termly meetings of the same group of people, to discuss their progress and extend their knowledge.

Planning for primary head teachers' needs had immediately to acknowledge that there were many more of them, and that primary teachers tend to see the issues of equal opportunities as of far more relevance to their secondary colleagues than to themselves. A group of five primary heads and the adviser put together a course which was run four times, and was attended by the vast majority of head teachers in the borough; of the few non-attenders most were in church schools. The format was to provide a first day similar to the secondary one; introductory pair discussion of issues, talks providing commonly shared information, and workshops focusing on the very early years. All participants were given an observation schedule and asked to observe a nursery or reception class before the next session. The second and third days each dealt with a major curriculum area – language one day, maths the next – in the mornings after discussion of the observation task. Afternoons were spent on sharing of good practice in local schools and determining priorities for one's own school and realistic steps towards achieving them. The response to these courses was more varied than to the secondary one. At one course, heads who remained untouched by the content dominated discussion in a negative way until changes were made to avoid this. At another, the heads were very enthusiastic and requested further meetings. It is not possible now for a primary head teacher in Brent to trivialize equal opportunities to the level of discussion in the popular press without either being challenged by a colleague, or revealing herself in a way that someone concerned with their professional reputation would not wish to do. The courses demonstrated the serious level of debate required, demonstrated how much there is to know, and also demonstrated that the authority values the good practice of the people who came to share this with colleagues. These things have a powerful effect on the climate of opinion. The courses also deprived people of excuses and of charges of undue speed or pressure from the authority when they were subsequently asked to develop school policies, and part of the follow-up has taken the form of half-day meetings in the following two terms specifically to deal with the management of developing policy in a primary school. Follow-up has also taken the form of visits to schools, provision of resources, and help with developing materials.

In-depth courses for the committed

Running a course for teachers who are committed to anti-sexist education and very keen to be together is an enormously rewarding experience. The course, called 'Gender and Learning', runs for fifteen half-day sessions, and supply cover is available for the teachers who attend. It aims to provide a forum for discussion at a serious level, to extend knowledge (particularly in providing a much wider context for individual classroom work), and to give teachers the opportunity to do some detailed action-research in their own schools. It is clear from working with people who have already taken great strides in their own classroom that there is still a huge gap in the dissemination of information about education for gender equality and that most is gleaned, even by the keen and interested, from the general press. It follows that Dale Spender is almost the only generally familiar name and that teachers are eager to learn of other work that has been done in this field where they themselves are pioneers. It is also the case that popularization of certain issues can lead to attempts at change which are simplistic, perhaps because they do not relate the changed out-come that is desired to what is soundly known about child development or ways of learning. A long course, over a period of time, can allow for reflection and the matching of good educational practice with ideas about gender equality. The 'Gen-der and Learning' course specifically considers gender acquisition theories, classroom interaction, and language and science in the curriculum. One of its purposes is to help teachers become better, more detailed observers of what is really happening in classrooms, and all participants spend an afternoon with a partner observing in a nursery class, using an observation schedule. The field notes form the basis for a session in which observers discuss the action that could be taken to alter some of the events they saw, or to value some things which were going on unremarked. This part of the course is dependent on the goodwill of the teachers and heads who allow course members into their schools, and there are important professional issues to be clear about when conducting observation. It is never easy to be observed, and certainly unfair to be observed and then discussed in your absence by a crowd of strangers who nevertheless are colleagues. It is therefore clearly established that observation is of the children, not the adults, and that play patterns and child–child interaction will provide plenty of information for subsequent discussion. Field notes are always available to the nursery teacher, and a discussion of the session with her should take place (it isn't always possible). There is no question that much can be learnt from observing adult behaviour in the nursery class, but the negotiation for that to take place, the relationship of trust needed between observer and observed, and the assurance the observed must have about the data, do not make it possible for a course session.

The academic input and the observation practice lead to the central focus of the course: the undertaking, by each course member, of a small action-research study, of either her own classroom or something in her school. Every teacher can be their own researcher and find material to reflect upon which will lead to insights and improvements in their own practice; every school can benefit from a close scrutiny of things it may well take for granted. Only close observation can reveal that the cause and effect of teachers' and others' action in schools is frequently quite different from the assumptions commonly made about it. The course members decide on the project topic, discuss it with their head teacher and colleagues (the involvement of colleagues is a vital aspect) and then collect data over a given period of time. They are visited by the course tutor at school to discuss progress, then present a report to the other course members. Two afternoon sessions of course time are allocated for work on projects in school, so that at least some of the work involved in collecting, analysing and writing up observations is done in school time. The range of projects undertaken so far has been very varied, and has led to a great deal of valuable follow-up work in schools. The dissemination of project findings to the whole staff is an important next step, linked with regular recall meetings of the course group and, in some cases, the setting up of smaller support groups. A booklet summarizing the projects from the first course has been published, and the second is in preparation. These will also be valuable aids to the dissemination of ideas about gender equality. There has been much investigation of children's own perceptions about gender in the classroom, and of sex roles; there have been studies of classroom interaction patterns and of the detailed relationship between what pupils know of women and the material the curriculum presents to them. While some of the findings clearly replicate others that are generally available, others do not, and their central value is that they show what is happening in one school, at one time, in such a way that their significance is unavoidable.

Courses for common interest groups

There is a wide scope for INSET activities in the third category, that of special interest groups. They essentially need planning and tutoring jointly with the people responsible for training in relation to whatever the special interest is: teacher-tutors in the case of probationers, subject advisers or teachers' centre subject panel officers in the case of subject teachers, and this in itself can be valuable as the joint planning activity increases the awareness of the subject specialist. Follow-up work can be essentially the responsibility of that person. The equal opportunities specialist has less control over these activities and some compromises are needed. There is considerable doubt about the value, for example, of a one-off day conference for teachers in a specific subject area where it is known there will be little effective follow-up work: the day can do little more than generate some interest and awaken an appetite for more, and the negative effects of subsequent disappointment or belief that a day is all that is needed to have 'done' equal opportunities can well outweigh the positive effects. Ways may be found of providing indirect follow-up, but this is time-consuming and basically unsatisfactory. The patchy nature of subject specialists' commitment to equal opportunities is one of the major reasons why an adviser with specific responsibility for equal opportunities is essential in LEAS.

In Brent the equal opportunities panel, a teacher group attached to the teachers' centre and with access to teachers' centre INSET money, has been increasingly making links with other special interest groups and has held meetings on history, social studies, computing and modern languages in addition to its other activities. The meetings on computing in particular attracted a large number of primary teachers who had not previously been involved in equal opportunities activities, but who have now set up a group to preview software and develop and monitor good practice with girls in primary schools. A day conference on craft, design and technology (CDT) has been held, jointly run by the equal opportunities and CDT advisers. All primary and secondary probationers attend induction sessions on equal opportunities and the quality of their awareness is extremely encouraging, even though they report very little input indeed from their initial training. The most effective special interest activities have been those which were initially designed as long-term. One focus for such activities has been the preparation of classroom materials. Several groups of English teachers have worked together to produce booklets to accompany class readers featuring strong girl characters, and/or sensitive boys. Several groups of primary teachers have worked on developing photographic resources, resulting in a pack of photographs and a teachers' book on non-traditional jobs and books and jigsaw puzzles based on photographs of girls and boys in non-stereotyped activities – including one set of books and puzzles based on photos of the children in an infant school building their own raised brick garden. The photos of girls wearing shalwar kamiz, in total concentration as they spread cement to lay bricks, are superb.

At a Saturday conference, a workshop for primary teachers on jigsaw making shared that skill with many who could then use their own photos. Experience shows that a group of teachers working together on materials production, with some support from an adviser and access to advice about technical skills and printing facilities, will take about a year of meeting together to produce an end-product that can be trialled in school. In Brent, the Curriculum Development Support Unit has been set up to provide such support for development that is anti-racist and anti-sexist, and four teachers have been seconded to support the anti-sexist work. A lot of their work is also in-service training, but is beyond our scope here. Their role in supporting teacher-directed materials production by groups set up by the adviser is crucial in enabling teachers actually to retain control over materials while having them produced to a high standard.

Another productive use of special interest groups has been the running of a four-session course on sex stereotyping in children's books. This course has been repeated six times so that a high proportion of primary schools have been represented. Teachers with responsibility for book buying, or a particular interest in children's books, have come in pairs on the course and at the end of the course have been able to spend a small sum of money in conjunction with their head teachers on non-sexist books for the school. The books are then introduced to the whole staff when they arrive and this, together with the staffroom conversation that arises when two people attend a course together, leads to a wider awareness among teachers in general. Discussion of books in a detailed way can be a very useful first step in raising awareness, as it is a safe area which does not touch on the personal behaviour of individual teachers. However, it cannot be done in a short time because once again the superficiality of a brief discussion can actually reinforce rather than break down prejudices. It takes both time for assimilation of new ideas and plenty of cumulative evidence of the messages in sexist books, and time to examine good examples of non-sexist books, to convince teachers of the need for them. Once convinced, it is an area where awareness expands very rapidly. The course is supported by the Schools Library Service, which keeps a good range of books available for schools to select and keeps updating a booklist which all schools receive regularly.

School-based INSET

The final category of INSET that has been incorporated into the Brent strategy is school-based, school-focused work. This has taken two forms. First, there is the fairly superficial work that takes place when perhaps one or two staff meetings are set aside for equal opportunities and issues are aired without anyone really having to come to terms with the reality of what is happening in their own classrooms. It is very easy for such meetings to turn into the ritual expression of the excuses which enable teachers to avoid accepting responsibility or any power over the children in their care during the time they are there. If this happens, and teachers leave all the more satisfied that the problem lies with society, or parents, or the media, or the phases of the moon, then no good has been done at all. The fact that an outsider comes in to a staff where there are complicated patterns of power relationships and hidden currents of feeling makes short-term work well nigh impossible in an area such as equal opportunities where personal attitudes are intricately enmeshed with professional views. It is not, in my view, possible for participants in equal opportunities INSET to divorce the personal from the professional, and the trainer has to be aware of this dimension. The degree to which a school is a thinking, open-minded school varies, largely according to the lead provided by the head teacher, who can squash enthusiasm by young teachers or work to marginalize the rigidity of the total traditionalist. A lot of negotiation is needed to persuade some heads that a one-off staff meeting is not satisfactory and that a series is needed. But where there are good relationships among staff and a head who is concerned to develop work in a school, a series of workshops can be very fruitful. It can be difficult to hold these after school and involve everyone, because of child-care demands; lunch-time sessions can be unsatisfactory because there are clubs or preparation to deal with, and the nursery staff have different timing of their sessions. However, lunch-time sessions have worked where participants have really wanted them to. Then, everyone is talking about commonly familiar materials for reading, mathematics, topic work and commonly familiar arrangements for assembly, for display, for PE and games. The speed with which change can be effected during and after a shared and honest appraisal of school practices is considerable. It will, however, only take place like that in schools with an established tradition of self-analysis and professional development. The schools where this is not the norm are much slower to work with.

While many schools in Brent have attempted this sort of school-based work, four primary schools have become involved in another, more highly focused and longer-lasting kind: action-research involving several staff over an entire school year. These schools have obtained a small amount of additional capitation and the shared use of an extra teacher, to enable staff to be released to do regular observation and recording. Each school is focusing on a different topic: classroom interaction in one, developing early skills and positive attitudes in girls towards technology in another, developing confidence and strong self-image in girl mathematicians in a third, and working with parents from many different cultural groups in the fourth. The work commenced in September 1984; schools were invited to bid for involvement in the projects, and one of the main aims is to provide very clear evidence of the development of good practice for dissemination to other schools. The professional value to the teachers taking part is very considerable, and they of course become potential trainers of others. The projects will be written up in full after they have run their course.

In-service training is notoriously difficult to evaluate; deep-seated change in schools is notoriously difficult to achieve. How, then, after two years can the work being done in Brent be assessed? It is too early to consider any long-term effects, but it is possible to make some claims. First, the in-service provision reaches a wide range of teachers across the service, so that there are chances that many will fall into more than one category for training. Second, it is precisely prepared for specific groups, so should have maximum relevance. Third, courses are part of an overall programme of authority activity, including follow-up work of various sorts, so that it is not easy to regard the course in isolation. Fourth, the provision of supply cover for the long course, the use of teachers within the authority as workshop leaders, and the existence of an adviser with a designated responsibility for equal opportunities training, give status to the issue and demonstrate the authority's commitment through resource provision and public recognition. There is clearly a large-scale tackling of the issue, across the entire educational age-range, rather than a small-scale picking-off of a few targets. However, if the aim is radically to change the focus of education so that it becomes girl friendly, then clearly not only is large-scale work needed, but also it must continue over a long period of time. It could be claimed that in Brent, after two years, there are groups of deeply-involved people in every secondary school, though the schools vary in their approaches to change. At least one teacher from almost every primary school has been on some sort of course, and is on a contact list or in a network of support. Movement of teachers within the authority is beginning to provide valuable cross-fertilization.

The different strands of in-service provision are also producing identifiable change, especially in primary schools, which have been the main target. The in-service work in this area has tied in with an action programme which requires, among other things, all primary schools to produce a policy statement and school action programme for implementation over a specified period. The fact that heads and many of their staff have been on courses contributes importantly to the quality of policy and implementation. The level of discussion, the climate of opinion and the types of change in classroom practice can be directly attributed to the INSET initiatives. At the same time, courses both establish a base line for equal opportunities and take work forward. The action-research projects, in particular, are providing essential evidence that is simply not available elsewhere. So our teachers are becoming front-line innovators while remaining in the mainstream within the authority. Questions will be routinely asked at interviews about gender awareness; books are routinely examined for stereo-typing; curriculum materials are routinely developed which have gender equality as an underlying value. However, it is salutary to remember that at the last secondary probationers sessions, teachers reported that nothing was going on in their schools, or that the curriculum was far more traditional than it actually is: there are still many teachers who are not necessarily hostile or uninterested, but have not been reached. The continual need is for more effective dissemination, for meticulous organization of networks to involve the maximum number of teachers, for very careful quality control to ensure that rapid growth does not dilute the messages. We've made a good start: come back in five years' time.

Reference

Rudduck, J. (1981) *Making the Most of the Short In-Service Course*, Methuen, London.

Eight   Carol Adams

Teacher attitudes towards issues of sex equality

Introduction

With the recent growth in awareness and activity among teachers and the growing response from LEAs to issues of sex equality, in-service training must be considered one of the key areas for promoting change. It can provide an opportunity for committed teachers to collaborate and to disseminate their work, and it can enable the unconvinced to reconsider their attitudes. A fundamental question is, what are the most appropriate and effective kinds of in-service training, given the wide range of teacher awareness and attitudes? What do teachers of various persuasions want and find most useful, and how do we assess these needs? How do we monitor the appropriateness and effectiveness of the kinds of courses provided?

In an attempt to answer some of these questions, an in-service course on equal opportunities/anti-sexist education for 40 history and social sciences teachers was monitored in terms of teacher attitudes and responses. Although all the 30 women and 10 men participants attended voluntarily, a range of opinions and perspectives was anticipated. Differences were investigated based on age, seniority, subject background, and school – mixed or single-sex, county or voluntary – as well as gender. Somewhat surprisingly, the only significant difference to emerge was between women and men, or more specifically between most of the men and all the women (for further details see Adams 1984).

To date, most in-service training in sex equality has been open for both women and men to work together and there has been a tendency to minimize or ignore differences – at least publicly. There are obvious dangers in appearing to be divisive, or to be encouraging possible antagonism between male and female colleagues. However, the investigation reported in this chapter suggests that the different perspectives of many women and men teachers need to be more closely identified if we want all teachers to become aware of sexism in education and committed to its eradication. Understanding in this area is closely dependent on personal experience which in turn influences professional attitudes and practice.

The study

The first area of enquiry was the teachers' own perceptions of what was being done in their schools. Most women's attitudes were fairly negative and critical, while the majority of men felt positive about what was being done. Women said that their schools either had no policy or public commitment to sex equality, or that where there was one, there was an enormous contradiction between stated policy and reality. Many women had encountered resistance from other staff, especially men in senior positions. Many were anxious to see action rather than policies and statements, and many were highly self-critical, feeling that the measures they were taking by raising issues and preparing materials were insufficient. They were concerned about the lack of participation by girls in mixed classes, and by what they felt was a lack of success in using anti-sexist materials with boys.

The greater optimism expressed by most men was based on using new materials in the classroom and holding discussions on gender bias in language, measures which they felt were combating sexism. One man, however, expressed quite a different view: that in his boys' school, the very idea of sexism being an important issue got 'a response of derision and hilarity'.

These responses suggest a difference not only in teachers'

perceptions but also in their own degree of anti-sexist involve-ment in their schools. Many of those experiencing hostility and questioning their own effectiveness were women who had for some time been active on working parties and had been producing non-sexist materials, while this was not the case to such a large extent among the men. Clearly, greater commitment and activity may produce stronger resistance.

All participants came to the course expecting to learn and exchange experiences about a range of issues, including the curriculum, resources, teaching strategies, whole-school policies, and to consider attitudes – their own, their students' and their colleagues'. Additionally, many women emphasized the need for time out of school to reflect, clarify and refine their own ideas: as one put it, 'time to think and become sorted out and to act as a messianic figure for the school'. They also sought support from other women and 'sisterhood' was frequently mentioned. To women, these factors appeared more important than curricular issues and they wanted to share and exchange teaching approaches in order to increase their competence in anti-sexist education. Women tended not to make a distinction between the personal and the professional; to quote one woman 'the person that I am is the teacher that I am'.

Most men came to the course with the expectation of obtaining information relating to the curriculum and the authority's view. They did not, on the whole, share the women's expectations, except for a minority of men who explicitly wanted to tackle their own sexism, as well as developing ways of challenging it in others. The majority of men approached the course in a professional and rather less personal way than the women, and tended to make a distinction between the two.

Women and men reacted quite differently to the experience of working in separate groups in order to explore issues of personal awareness. Most women enjoyed the opportunity of talking in pairs as part of a women-only group about their experiences as women. Although some were quite critical about the exact aims of this kind of exercise, they appreciated the opportunity to talk and listen without interruption.

The men's experience (as reported by a male observer), was quite different. Members of the group spoke in monologues only, with no exchange of views and in a detached manner, relating only to professional concerns rather than involving personal feelings. Most men had great reservations about the appropriateness both of working as an all-male group and of considering sexism as a personal issue. The majority found the all-male situation difficult and uncomfortable. However, a minority of men felt that single-sex group work was essential to enable men to 'counter the emotional dependency of men on women'.

This raises the important issue of whether and how single-sex groups should be organized on in-service courses. How does one most effectively facilitate personal consideration of the issues of sex equality for both men and women? If men tend not to respond positively to the opportunity of working together, what are the implications for INSET? What should women's response be to the expectation that they should always include men? If single-sex groups on mixed-sex courses appear to be divisive, should separate courses be held?

Teachers' attitudes towards role play as a method of dealing with gender issues in the classroom varied in a number of aspects. Women teachers participated in role-play exercises more readily than men, some of whom appeared to feel uncomfortable and detached. However, when the role play led to discussion in small groups, this was, in the majority of cases, dominated by the men, although they were a minority (talking time was accurately recorded by an independent observer). They also asked the majority of the questions in general discussion. In commenting on the role-play exercises, the women were, on the whole, self-critical and felt the need for more extensive experience before attempting similar exercises with children. The men, on the other hand, felt more positively that they had gained the necessary skills and techniques to use role play on returning to school. Thus the men seemed to have exercised and experienced greater confidence than the women in terms of both group dynamics and developing teaching techniques. They seem to have been unaffected by any apparent discomfort experienced in a possibly risky role-play situation. The women, however, though apparently feeling less confident, seemed to have enjoyed the informality and light-heartedness of working together through role play.

In approaching the subject curriculum, considered a high

priority by both women and men, there were gender-based differences in teachers' responses. Most men expressed a desire for information and resources to be provided and did not necessarily express a wish to produce materials themselves. Most women emphasized the value of working in collaboration during the course to change the curriculum. Many expressed enthusiasm and excitement at the discovery of new historical and sociological evidence, while several men reported that they found the task of rewriting history 'too overwhelming'. Women prioritized involvement and working with others as the key to curricular change, whereas most of the men were critical of the course sessions.

In considering their role in whole-school policies, most men and women had different priorities. Women teachers from all-boys' schools were primarily concerned about the difficulties and sense of isolation they personally experienced, particularly in feeling undermined by a male school ethos when trying to adopt a caring approach with boys. The men prioritized changing aspects of the school's official curriculum. In considering girls' schools, women teachers focused on the enormous amount of conditioning to be overcome in terms of the culture of femininity both inside and outside the school. The resistance to change of many staff, both female and male, was a further important factor. The predominant male view of girls' schools was that resistance would not be as great as suggested by women on the course. During a discussion led by a feminist teacher on single-sex group work for girls and boys in mixed schools, considerable interest was shown by most women. Many were very concerned about the negative experience of girls in mixed schools, and were considering the validity and practicality of some single-sex group work. Many women were particularly impressed by the speaker who had put these ideas into practice. Some men were less enthusiastic about this session, and one explained that he found it hostile because of the emphasis on feminism which, he felt, would increase male resistance. Clearly a feminist perspective, including suggesting that girls need to be separated from boys at times, may present problems for men teachers in defining their role in anti-sexist teaching. It was strongly recommended by the speaker that the role for men teachers should be in doing anti-sexist work with boys, but this was not really taken up.

The greatest divergence in feeling between women and men teachers emerged when the LEA's role and policy was discussed. Many women teachers became very angry, feeling that they were not being listened to, backed up, or effectively supported at grass-roots level. They expressed resentment towards central policies which were, they felt, in contradiction to their own experiences in school, particularly in terms of their own jobs. While not all the women expressed equal anger, there seemed to be general support for the feelings of those who spoke out. The men did not disagree, and in fact many shared the women's views, but they did not share their passionate anger. Men stayed out of the discussion and appeared to be excluded, on the periphery.

Finally, in considering how they would implement equal opportunities/anti-sexist practice on returning to school, the different perspectives of women and men which had developed during the four-day course emerged in some of the discussion groups. Although men had dominated the group talking-time throughout the course, it was the women's views that came through most strongly at this point. They emphasized the problem of official working parties which often aimed at meeting LEA requirements with the minimum amount of effort, but were not essentially concerned with change. Boys' schools were identified as being resistant to all kinds of change – not just sex equality. A major concern was the domination of boys in mixed classrooms and the need to build girls' self-confidence. Strategies for new classroom structures and learning situations to enable girls to be free from boys' domination were discussed. The need to win over all staff, especially senior staff – 'the hierarchy' – was a major focus, and it was felt that although not all men would be won over, the support of a strong committed minority would be enough to 'drag along the uncommitted majority'. In terms of both pupils and staff, sexual harassment was also discussed.

Women dominated these discussions, but their views were shared and endorsed by a minority of men. In contrast, one man expressed concern that the course had been female dominated and that 'offensive and destructive' images of women were being presented along with an 'exaggerated' view of sexism. Thus the women's strength, which became more apparent as the course progressed, had created antagonism for some, though not all, men.

All but two participants, one man and one woman, made favourable comments on the course overall. The aspects of the course most appreciated by women were:

1. a chance to think and develop new ideas to take back to school;
2. the opportunity to exchange and share experiences;
3. the variety of sessions and materials;
4. the informality and accessibility of the organizers.

Comments referred to the pleasure of working co-operatively with like-minded people and the effect this had in reviving energy and commitment. Personal involvement and honest self-assessment were frequently expressed concerning the desire to challenge sexism most effectively.

Men were far more critical of the course, asserting that parts of it were, for them, 'quite inappropriate', 'time-wasting', 'difficult', and 'irrelevant'. There was criticism of particular speakers and sessions and of the 'overburdening of teachers' with more work in preparing materials. Some men were critical that more theoretical sessions had not been provided to examine concepts such as feminism and equality. None of the criticisms made by men were voiced by any women, and none of the aspects of participation and practicality so highly praised by the women were mentioned by the men. One man highlighted the problem expressed by some men in his comment: 'There seemed to be no real examples or solutions for the males on the course – how we could help the problems and solve them as males. More attention should have been given to how male teachers can help in solving the problem.'

This man has pointed to the most significant finding of the evaluation. The majority of men reacted to the course quite differently from women. By its very nature, the course was geared primarily to women, since it is they who have taken the lead and done most of the work in anti-sexist education. At the same time, it was open to men but not geared to their needs in the same way. For some men this was a problem in terms both of working in schools and of providing in-service education, and we have to confront this issue.

A summary of the findings

Throughout the course, differences became apparent between women and a majority of men, which can be summarized as follows:

1. Differing perceptions of the situation in their schools, and differing views of their own reasons for attending the course. Women tended to be more critical of what had already been achieved than were men. They also felt that professional involvement meant personal involvement, whereas men tended to concentrate on the professional and to distance themselves personally.
2. Differing reactions to parts of the course. Women valued participation, working co-operatively, practically. Men tended to want to be provided with information and wanted theoretical background.
3. Men were, on the whole, far more critical and less enthusiastic than women. There was a tendency to blame the course itself when they were dissatisfied. Women tended to regard themselves as responsible for what was happening, and to derive much greater enjoyment from what they were doing.
4. While apparently tending to drop out, and evidently sensing hostility at times, men tended to dominate discussions. In the process, they nevertheless believed that women were dominant.
5. There were two different types of reactions from men, some of whom felt very personally committed and showed sensitivity and awareness, while others seemed to become defensive. Such a division did not appear to arise among women.
6. Although experiencing a sense of exclusion, unclear of their role and wanting role clarification, most men rejected the opportunity of working together to define their own role. It seemed that they wanted to be with the women and wanted the women to provide a role for them.

These findings leave us with some important questions to consider in relation to men and equal opportunities. The experience of the course offers some implications for future action.

Proposals for action

The role of men in anti-sexist education needs to be clarified by women teachers, but men must involve themselves in the work. We need to make much clearer what the different issues are for women and men – that they are not opposite sides of a coin, but unequal aspects of a power structure. Perhaps more dialogue is necessary between the sexes on the educational aspects of sex equality.

It is easy to talk about the need for men's commitment and involvement, but hard for many men to achieve because they have not experienced sexism in the way that women have and are less likely to have a feminist perspective. There is a danger of lip-service responses from men who may think they understand the issues but have not really thought them through. Is there a role here for separate courses for men only, run by men? Do women have anything to gain by joining with men on all INSET, or should they work separately at times? Tackling sexism in depth may be difficult and uncomfortable for many men. Should this be a worry, or is it a sign that something positive is happening and therefore to be welcomed?

There is no reason to suppose that most men teachers will change unless women take the initiative. Women must also be aware and wary of what this could mean. There is the danger that equal opportunities could simply be used by some men to their own advantage – for example, by their insisting that they share control of what happens in education, that measures taken are not too radical, that no-one is too disturbed.

Feminists have raised and discussed 'the problem of men'. In terms of education there are particular reasons why the contribution of men teachers must be seriously considered:

1. many girls are taught by male teachers both in mixed and girls' schools;
2. men play a crucial role in the education of boys;
3. the relationship between women and men teachers in schools is central to the issue of sex equality.

One of the major issues to arise from this study was the question of LEA policy and women teachers' feelings about it. This is germane to the different perspectives of female and male course participants. It was the women who felt angry and unsupported, and it seems unlikely that there would have been such a reaction from the men alone. The sense of conflict between women teachers and the LEA was rooted in a male power structure most resented by women. At the moment, teachers are suffering from lack of job prospects, fewer resources and low morale, and threatened by worse to come. Partly, perhaps, these factors contributed to the animosity that arose. Yet again, women do, and believe that they do, suffer more than men in the current situation because they are, overall, in lower status positions.

The role of LEA equal opportunities policy proved to be a contentious issue. It seemed that the more committed the women teachers, the less relevant they believed policy to be. Their real concerns were with action and implementation, requiring funding, time, information, and personal support. Possibly it is in those schools where there is less commitment that an outside requirement to act is seen as most useful.

Issues for further research

The issues raised here suggest that there is a need for further research into the attitudes of women and men teachers towards equal opportunities in a number of contexts. We need to know more about their respective attitudes and levels of activity in schools:

1. To what extent do men in positions of authority in schools frustrate the anti-sexist work of women teachers as suggested in this study?
2. To what extent are some women equally as resistant as men?
3. To what extent is the teacher's gender significant in terms of anti-sexist work in the classroom, as well as in the school?

It has been found, for example, that pupils prefer teachers of their own sex (Stanworth 1983). How widespread and how significant is this suggestion?

A further issue for research is the factors affecting differences between schools in terms of equal opportunities. Since most initiatives so far have been the result of work by teachers in schools, it would be interesting to know more about the reasons for the variation between the practice of different schools.

Since an increasing number of LEAS are considering or already have equal opportunities policies, we need to know more about the effectiveness of such policies and how they relate to teachers' perceptions. The findings of this study suggest a need for caution in assuming that policies are always necessarily welcomed as relevant and helpful at grass-roots level. We have yet to see the nature of their exact purpose and effect.

More research is also needed into in-service training in equal opportunities, particularly on a practical level with classroom teachers. Far more information is needed on the question of personal/professional attitudes to enable in-service trainers to determine the most acceptable and effective approach in various situations.

Just as the debate concerning single-sex and mixed schools in relation to equal opportunities is unresolved, a debate which needs informing is that of mixed or single-sex courses (and sessions within courses) for teachers. More research is required into teachers' attitudes and responses in both types of situation in order to inform future provision. Finally, while drawing attention to the different perspectives of women and men teachers, this study has also highlighted the striking difference in attitude among men towards sex equality. More research is urgently needed to account for this difference, and to indicate what processes are necessary for men to become genuinely aware of, and committed to, anti-sexism.

This chapter has drawn attention to a major problem in providing anti-sexist education for teachers, which neither has an easy solution nor can be ignored. Ignoring the differences between men and women and the importance of defining suitable roles for men teachers will not advance sex equality in schools, but neither will sexism be effectively challenged if women provide all the answers for their male colleagues.

Acknowledgements

The author would like to acknowledge the help of Sue Warner and her colleagues of the Research and Statistics branch of the ILEA.

References

Adams, C. (1984) 'The significance of gender in teacher attitudes towards sex equality: a case study of an in-service course', unpublished M.A. dissertation, University of London.
Stanworth, M. (1983) *Gender and Schooling: A Study of Sexual Divisions in the Classroom*, Hutchinson, London.

'Humberside goes neuter': an example of LEA intervention for equal opportunities

'Humberside goes neuter' was one newspaper's headline response to the publication in January 1984 of Humberside Education Committee's booklet on *Equal Opportunities and Sex Discrimination*. This chapter describes the background to the publication of the booklet and the responses it received. It also examines some of the issues which have arisen from this example of LEA intervention and draws some general conclusions about implementing an equal opportunities policy.

The background

The most important factor leading to the production of the booklet in Humberside was the commitment of the Labour county councillors who came to power in May 1981 to oppose race and sex discrimination. This commitment was strongly endorsed by the newly-elected chair and vice-chair of the Education Committee. Support from the teachers' unions was also important. The National Union of Teachers (NUT) and National Association of Teachers in Further and Higher Education (NATFHE), in particular, have played an important part in promoting the cause of equal opportunities, both nationally and locally. Both unions had by that time published documents which addressed the issue of sexism and its implications (NATFHE 1980; NUT 1980). Also, the

NUT in Humberside set up an equal opportunities working party in 1981. Following the lead given by the chair and vice-chair of Education, the issue of equal opportunities was given prominence in meetings of the County Consultative Committee for Teachers, where representatives of the teachers' unions meet members of the county council as their employer. In November 1981 the committee resolved 'that the Director of Education be requested to reiterate council policy on equal opportunities and sex discrimination to all county educational establishments'. The NATFHE representative, who was at this time editing a book on sexism and schooling (Whyld 1983), continued to press the issue both within this committee and within the Humberside Teachers' Joint Consultative Committee, where teachers' union representatives meet together with officers. There was little immediate progress. However, in May 1982, as a result of this pressure, the Teachers' Joint Consultative Committee set up its own working party on sex discrimination, with a brief to 'establish current practices, seek information from the LEA and report back to it'. A month later, in June 1982, the LEA requested the Teachers' Committee to nominate six of its members to sit on a county working party on equal opportunities and sex discrimination.

The vice-chair of the Education Committee, Councillor Veronica Wilson, was largely responsible for placing equal opportunities centrally on the educational agenda in Humberside. She set up the working party on equal opportunities and sex discrimination with herself in the chair. The chair of the Education Committee became the vice-chair of the working party. This was a clear sign to education officers, teachers' unions and elected members that the ruling party was taking the issue seriously. Other members of the working party included five Labour and two Conservative councillors, six teachers' union representatives, four representatives of the Director of Education and two co-opted members. The chair of the working party had specifically asked for the nomination of committed members who supported the principles of equal opportunities. By this time the Humberside 'Women in Education' group had been formed and the working party contained five of its members.

Humberside 'Women in Education'

The Humberside 'Women in Education' group began in 1981 when a few women teachers met informally to talk about ways of trying to improve the opportunities and academic performance of girls in schools. One of the members had been doing observational research in a senior high school and had been struck by the lack of awareness and interest among girls concerning their subject choices, their qualifications and employment prospects. Early meetings of the group gave an opportunity for women teachers, parents, governors and researchers to exchange views informally and gave rise to a series of talks aimed at developing a general awareness of sexism in schools.

It was eventually decided to hold a conference to publicize the issues within the county and to encourage national and local initiatives to be more widely recognized. The conference was held in October 1982 at Humberside College of Higher Education where three of the group members teach. The proposal had been approved by the college's Professional Centre for Teacher Education, and the conference, which had the uncompromising title of 'Sexist Processes in Schools: Why Girls Under-achieve', was resourced by the college. The decision to support the conference was clearly influenced by the recent establishment of the county working party. This was the first conference of its kind in the area and it attracted a large audience of local teachers, governors and several members of the working party. The 'Women in Education' group was able to use its personal contacts to attract young teachers and interested governors. Some of the teachers who came reported that they had not seen the conference publicity in their schools: it appeared that not all school circulars and notices for staff reach staffroom noticeboards, but in some cases are 'filed' by head teachers.

The conference was opened by the chair of the working party who made it clear that the Education Committee fully endorsed such an initiative. One of the speakers was Kate Myers, then with the Schools Council, whose description of the development of anti-sexist policies in schools within the Inner London Education Authority (ILEA) came as a welcome revelation to Humberside teachers. Young teachers in particular had two main questions:

'How can I introduce these ideas into my school?' and 'How can I get hold of the resources that will help me to do this?'

Members of Humberside 'Women in Education' found that the conference clarified their aims. The group produced a conference report which included a comprehensive set of recommendations addressed to the LEA and the County Council and contained suggestions for positive action against discrimination in schools. It recommended that the LEA should publish an equal opportunities policy statement and that schools and colleges should develop their own equal opportunities policy, dealing with, for example, issues of organization and management, the curriculum, teaching methods and materials, pupil performance and careers guidance. It also recommended that the LEA should provide in-service training in equal opportunities, initially for head teachers and then for other staff, and should also encourage the development of strategies for achieving equal opportunities in schools. Additionally, the report recommended that the LEA should commission research into sex stereotyping and other discriminatory practices in its educational institutions. The final recommendation was that the County Council should appoint an equal opportunities officer. The report was sent to all members of the working party as a suggested agenda for action.

The framing of a policy

Shortly afterwards the county working party prepared a policy statement on equal opportunities and sex discrimination and this was sent to all schools in March 1983. The statement begins by affirming that:

> Humberside Education Committee believes that girls and boys, men and women, are inherently equal but acknowledges that within the educational system there are many ways in which differential treatment occurs causing one sex to be treated less favourably than the other.

The policy statement commits the LEA, among other things, 'to the elimination of school practices which discriminate between boys and girls and to sustained development of non-sexist practices'. The school circular (3/83) which contained the policy statement also announced the forthcoming booklet and invited contributions and responses from individuals or groups. There were no formal responses from schools at this stage and many teachers reported later that they had not seen or heard of Circular 3/83.

The booklet was written and compiled by five members of the working party. In addition to offering guidance it presents a series of checklists of questions under headings such as 'Class and School Organization', 'Teacher-Pupil Interaction' and 'Teaching Materials'. The booklets were sent out to schools in January 1984. The chair of the working party insisted that a copy should be sent out to every Humberside teacher – about 8000 in all. It was considered from previous experience that unless this were done most teachers would not see or have the chance to read the booklet. Copies were also sent to members of the governing bodies of all schools and colleges and the working party asked them for feedback in two stages. It requested an initial response from both school staff and governors, and a further response in a year's time on ways in which the equal opportunities policy had been implemented. The printing cost was a modest £1540.

Responses to the guidelines booklet

Once the guidelines booklet had been sent out to teachers it attracted an enormous amount of publicity from both the local and regional media. For several weeks the Humberside local press carried headlines such as: 'Equality booklet "sinister"', 'Insult to intelligence of teachers', 'County guide to sexism futile – claim'. Opposition to the booklet was publicly voiced by two main sources, a Conservative member of the working party, and a representative of one of the teachers' unions. The teachers' unions had already decided, through the Teachers' Joint Consultative Committee, that they would make individual responses to the booklet as they were unable collectively to approve it. While the NAS/UWT (National Association of Schoolmasters/Union of Women Teachers) was unable to support the booklet, it did not publicly criticize it. A representative of AMMA (Assistant Masters and Mistresses Association), however, issued a press release which encapsulated many of the prejudices which were later to appear in the early responses from schools. Its opening sentence was widely quoted by the press, 'Although there are amusing overtones to the recently released Humberside LEA booklet *Equal Opportunities and Sex Discrimination* it has its sinister implications as well.'

The press release demonstrated the way in which a teachers' union's national commitment to the principles of equal opportunity can be undermined in practice at a local level. It acknowledged that 'some of the document can be classed as common sense and therefore helpful'. However, it continued, 'unfortunately it has been allowed to be a vehicle for many of the sillier ideas dear to the more paranoiac fringe of the feminist movement'. The writer continued

> In practice, our colleagues, by and large, show a great concern for children as individuals and it seems a pity that money has been spent, at a time of financial constraint, to try and suggest otherwise, and urge a set of practices which would take valuable time and achieve little.

The final paragraph of the press release, under the guise of a 'professional' concern for equality, signalled a refusal to recognize the need for change.

> To attempt to legislate for social attitudes can be counter-productive and the AMMA, whilst reaffirming its belief in equality of opportunity for all, will resist any attempts by politicians to lay down how we go about our professional job of teaching and caring for the children in our charge. Despite opposition from many quarters, many of us still hope to educate 'ladies' and 'gentlemen' rather than 'persons'.

I have quoted at length from this press release in order to emphasize the distance that may exist between an LEA's official policy on equal opportunities and sex discrimination and what happens in schools. What happens may be resistance or indifference, as was seen in some of the governors' responses tabled at the next meeting of the working party in February 1984. A primary school reported as follows: 'The governors, having studied the booklet, *Equal Opportunities and Sex Discrimination*, wish it to be known that they believe the booklet unnecessary, not serving a useful purpose and also being a misapplication of precious financial resources.' Some responses from primary schools indicated that the 'ladies' on the staff were as affronted by the booklet as the 'gentlemen'. One governing body of a group of primary and middle schools reported that it would be interested to have 'views on the attitude of the authority to the encouragement of femininity and gentility'. Many of the early hostile responses reiterated some of the points made in the AMMA press release: intervention was seen as a threat to teachers' professionalism; the production of the booklet was a waste of time and money; and, as teachers treat all children as individuals, discrimination could not possibly occur. Similar responses to equal opportunities initiatives have been noted in other areas (Pratt, Bloomfield and Seale 1984).

Public opposition to the booklet also came from a Conservative member of the working party who attempted, somewhat para-doxically, both to dismiss it as 'a load of rubbish' and to present it as a 'serious threat' to society. The *Hull Daily Mail* had earlier reported this member as saying in a debate on the activities of the working party, 'Feminism is a danger to marriage and the family and the whole basic value of our society.' The principles of equal opportunity were pronounced acceptable, but feminism most definitely was not. The guidelines booklet, then, was presented by the media as a politically divisive document and its under-tones of 'strident feminism' were seen as a threat to established values.

However, when the working party met again in May 1984 a change of tone was apparent in the second batch of responses it considered. These comments from two senior high schools were far more representative:

The Governors welcomed the document and felt that it would provoke thought. It was pointed out that the recommendations were slowly evolving which seemed the sensible way for im-plementation to take place.

The Governors welcomed the report and felt that the Education Committee should be congratulated on their initiative. They felt that a feature of the report was that it was making staff think about this important matter.

It seemed to many members of the working party that once the publicity had died down and teachers and governors had taken time to consider the booklet, their responses became more sympathetic and positive. At times they went beyond the expectations of the working party, as in this response from a junior high school:

> If the Authority wishes to make a significant impact on the promotion of equal opportunities between the sexes and the elimination of sex discrimination it must expand the in-service training opportunities in this area; provide additional resources to enable schools to purchase, for example, non-sexist materials; examine its own policies and practices and determine whether sufficient encouragement is given to women to apply for promoted posts; consider issuing to governing bodies guidelines for interviews in order to prevent female candidates being asked about, for example, their plans to have children and their commitments to looking after children.

Many of these issues were addressed at an INSET conference run by the LEA in March 1984 under the title, 'Towards Equal Opportunity'. Three members of the working party, who had earlier contributed towards Humberside 'Women in Education's conference, worked with a senior adviser to organize the LEA's own conference. The different connotations of the titles of the two conferences are indicative of a question that faces organizers of in-service education in this field: how to present the issues of equal opportunities and sex discrimination in a way that is perceived as neither a threat nor a compromise. There is a need to encourage teachers who are new to the debate, while also offering positive ideas to those teachers who are already committed to implementing non-sexist teaching strategies. The INSET conference was opened by the Director of Education and it was well attended by a considerable number of head teachers and senior staff as well as young teachers. It was considered valuable to have attracted those teachers who have the power to initiate and implement change within their schools. Many of the teachers who attended the conference said they had come as a direct result of the publication of the guidelines booklet.

College-based initiatives

The LEA's equal opportunities policy, while primarily directed towards schools, has also prompted initiatives in two of its colleges. At Humberside College of Higher Education two lecturers, both members of the 'Women in Education' group, submitted a paper on the implications of the LEA's policy for the college. The paper proposed that the areas of student access, curriculum content, staff recruitment and promotion procedures and student services needed to be examined. The paper was presented to a committee of the academic board, after which the Director took the decision to set up a college equal opportunities working party. This move was given further support when NATFHE published its Circular 9/83 recommending that each college should set up an equal opportunities committee as part of its academic board structure. The college working party prepared a report and presented its recommendations to the academic board committee, but there was little progress until the Spring term 1984, when the college governors discussed the authority's guidelines booklet. The governing council gave the equal opportunities policy its full support and shortly afterwards, and not perhaps coincidentally, the college's equal opportunities committee was set up.

In this instance there were three main factors which contributed towards the establishment of a college equal opportunities committee. First, the initial impetus came from a small group of feminist lecturers already identified with Women's Studies teaching, and this seems to be the case in other colleges where an equal opportunities committee or working party has been set up. Second, the Director's attitude was a critical factor in determining whether a grass-roots initiative achieved credibility within the college. Third, it is doubtful whether the idea of an equal opportunities committee would have been supported without the LEA policy. In other words, the local political initiative was crucial, with union representation acting as a supporting but not a determining factor. At Grimsby College of Technology a working party on equal opportunities has been set up in response to the NATFHE circular and the authority's policy statement and it also includes a member of the county working party.

The implications of intervention

The second part of this chapter considers some of the issues raised by this example of LEA intervention and suggests ways in which policy on equal opportunities may be translated into practice. That intervention was necessary in schools was demonstrated, unwittingly, by this response to the working party from a middle school:

> The governors feel that the concept of equal opportunities for all is admirable, but the references to sex discrimination ridiculous to the point of being ludicrous. Governors and staff are confident that the provision of equal opportunities for all is a natural process which will evolve gradually under its own impetus.

Another common response was to assume that discrimination takes place elsewhere – in the home, in 'society', earlier or later in the educational system – and was not, therefore, the responsibility of the school in question. For example the governors of an infant and junior school replied: 'Since the question of equal opportunity does not arise in primary schools, it is felt to be pointless to invite a reaction from the staff and it is, therefore, their intention not to comment on the question of equal opportunities.' A senior high school included in its comments the view that, 'By the age of 13, when students come to us, they are already conditioned by their previous experiences into certain attitudes.'

On the other hand several schools made positive suggestions for counteracting sex discrimination: 'The governors suggested that the Education Committee may wish to consider it appropriate to provide an abbreviated form of the booklet for parents.' 'The governors suggested that the Authority consider sending copies of the booklet to publishers and distributors of educational materials.' The staff of a girls' high school, through its governing body, stressed the important role of the school in counteracting negative social influences on girls:

> Given the often very conservative influence of the home, primary schooling, the press and television (apart from specialist articles and programmes on feminism) with their ingrained

assumptions concerning the traditional roles of the sexes, staff think it especially important that full opportunities should be offered to girls in secondary schools.

Such responses as these, which did not make the newspaper headlines, deserved to be more widely publicized and discussed.

Women in the education system

As we saw earlier, this example of LEA intervention has revealed the distance that may exist between official policy on equal opportunities and practice in schools. This is not surprising when one considers the status of women in education. In Humberside, as elsewhere, women are disadvantaged within the structure of the education system at many levels. At the political level there are far fewer women elected members on the county council – 15 out of a total of 75 at the time of writing. (There are 10 women out of 42 Labour members and 5 women out of 33 Conservatives.) Furthermore, even when elected to membership very few women reach positions of power within their party. On the Education Committee there are only 15 women out of a total of 46 and they include elected members, teachers' union representatives and co-opted members. It is in educational management structures, at County Hall, that women are least represented in positions of authority. In the Schools Branch, for example, there are no women in the management team. In the Advisory Service women are also under-represented. Additionally, women teachers are disadvantaged within their own school management structures in relation to their career and promotion prospects.

Research carried out by two members of the working party in April 1983 showed that Humberside follows the national pattern whereby men teachers predominate in the senior positions in school (DES 1981; Acker 1983). This may be seen in table 9.1. As the table shows, the under-representation of women teachers at senior, and particularly at head teacher, levels is unequivocal. The critical stage in the promotional structure is the move from scale 2 to scale 3 and it is here that the balance alters between men and women.

Table 9.1 Numbers of women and men teachers at various scales in Humberside primary and secondary schools (1983)

Scale	PRIMARY				SECONDARY				TOTAL			
	Men No.	%	Women No.	%	Men No.	%	Women No.	%	Men No.	%	Women No.	%
Head	196	25.76	166	7.23	103	3.47	17	0.89	299	8.02	183	4.36
Deputy	145	19.05	191	8.32	153	5.15	75	3.93	298	7.99	266	6.33
Senior Teacher					99	3.34	7	0.37	99	2.65	7	0.17
Scale 4	4	0.53	2	0.09	464	15.63	80	4.20	468	12.55	82	1.95
Scale 3	181	23.78	340	14.81	824	27.76	310	16.26	1005	26.95	650	15.47
Scale 2	192	25.23	1035	45.10	740	24.93	580	30.43	932	24.99	1615	38.44
Scale 1	43	5.65	561	24.44	585	19.71	837	43.91	628	16.84	1398	33.28
All	761	100	2295	100	2968	100	1906	100	3729	100	4201	100

As a result of these findings the equal opportunities working party sent a recommendation to the Education Committee requesting panels appointing senior staff 'to be conscious of the effect of their decisions on the balance of male/female appointments'. Such an action inevitably prompts the remark from some quarters that 'women don't apply for senior posts'. However, it is necessary to look at the earlier stages of women's careers for one possible explanation. Whereas the responsibility for shortlisting and interviewing candidates for senior posts is shared with, for example, governors, advisers, members and officers, the allocation of scale points within the school is largely at the discretion of the head teacher. Clearly it is vital that teachers are able to progress through the scales in order to be in a position to apply for senior posts at an appropriate age. Many women teachers, however, find themselves unable to progress beyond the critical barrier between scales 2 and 3, as has been recorded in other areas (Clwyd County Council/EOC 1983). The fact that women are so under-represented in educational decision making at the many levels I have described helps to explain the discrepancies that may exist between official LEA policy and the reality of staffroom and classroom cultures. The isolation and hostility that many feminist teachers experience is caused not just by sexist attitudes and prejudices but by very real inequalities in the distribution of power and authority between women and men in schools.

Intervention: a threat to the status quo

While the Humberside guidelines booklet was described by many teachers as a threat to their 'professionalism', one can see how it may also represent a personal threat to many men and women through its challenge to traditional sexual ideologies (MacDonald 1980a, 1980b). An LEA initiative on equal opportunities and sex discrimination presents a double-edged threat to the status quo because of its implications for both girl pupils and women teachers. Such an initiative asks for girl pupils' interests, needs and intellectual progress to be re-appraised and revalued; it also aims to enhance the status of women teachers. Whereas the former may be tolerated, the latter is more likely to meet with resistance. Experience of equal opportunities committee work has shown us that it is the issue of women teachers' and lecturers' career prospects that divides opinion most sharply. Recent studies of teachers' career patterns have revealed and begun to challenge the sexual division of labour within the educational hierarchy and the resulting differential rewards offered to men and women teachers throughout the system (Deem 1978; Buchan 1980; Rendel 1980, 1984; Acker 1983, 1984). The Conservative member who labelled the guidelines booklet 'a disruptive influence' was in one sense right. Such an intervention will, if it is to succeed, cause repercussions throughout school life.

Opponents of the Humberside guidelines booklet, while asserting their belief in the uncontentious principle of equal opportunity, presented feminism and political intervention as twin threats to the established order. In doing so they revealed, perhaps inadvertently, the already political nature of an education system which to a large extent legitimates disadvantage and inequality. When disadvantage for girls is the norm then positive discrimination in their favour, as Stanworth points out, constitutes a politically significant act and is likely to meet with resistance (Stanworth 1981). The booklet's opponents attempted to divide and alienate teachers' sympathies by their crude caricatures of 'strident' and 'militant' feminists. The old weapons of ridicule and contempt were used both publicly and within some schools as a means of ideological control. Reaction of this kind to an interventionist policy is succinctly explained by Roberts, who argues that in Britain there has always been a form of positive discrimination in education, one 'which does not draw howls of protest; it is positive discrimination in favour of men' (Roberts 1984).

Getting policy into practice: what teachers can do

The aim of the Humberside guidelines booklet was to encourage discussion within schools and to raise awareness about sex discrimination with a view to encouraging change. Many responses received from schools, both formally and informally, indicated that no previous LEA document had aroused such interest, whether supportive or antagonistic. The subject of sexism in education appeared on many staff and governors' agendas for the first time. In many cases initial hostility has given way to considered reappraisals and this process continues. There were various factors which contributed towards the introduction of the policy and the booklet. As we saw earlier, the initiative originated in the policy of the controlling political party and was carried through by a committed woman councillor who had the power and authority of the office of the vice-chair of the Education Committee. There was also considerable pressure and support from some of the teachers' unions for such an initiative. When it came to setting up the working party there were several committed women teachers and lecturers who were active in their unions and thereby eligible for membership.

It is very clear that no individual or group is willingly going to relinquish power or privilege in favour of women and girls: it requires a lengthy process of argument and negotiation. The suggestions that follow are based upon the recognition that one's feminism inevitably becomes tempered by pragmatism when working within the educational system. However, as Whyld illustrates in her book, 'working within the system does not mean giving up the fight to change it' (Whyld 1983). It is clear, too, that institutionalized discrimination needs to be opposed through collective action, and teachers need to be aware of the processes of educational decision-making. There is a need for more women to be in positions of authority or influence within educational institutions or through political or union channels. As we have seen, teachers' unions play an important role in policy making through their places on, for example, the Education Committee, the Teachers' Joint Consultative Committee and numerous working parties. Governing bodies can also provide an effective mechanism for getting the issue of sex discrimination onto a school agenda; teachers can be nominated by their political party or as the teacher governor of their own school (EOC 1985). A group of teachers might consider the possibility of setting up an equal opportunities working party or a 'sexism in education' group within their school (Stantonbury Campus Sexism in Education Group 1984).

A local 'Women in Education' group can provide collective support for the teacher who is isolated in an unsympathetic school. It may even be necessary to set up a group. One of its aims would be to establish channels of communication with unions, political parties and the LEA. In Humberside, for example, reports of the 'Women in Education' group's activities, including the conference and a series of talks by local teachers, have been presented to the county working party for discussion. As a result a 'register' has been set up of local teachers who are prepared to speak on aspects of equal opportunities and, specifically, anti-sexist teaching strategies. In July 1984, the chair of the working party set up a sub-group on in-service strategy and several of these speakers will contribute to in-service courses based at Education Centres. The first of these courses, 'Towards equal opportunity – strategies for action', was held at the Hull Education Centre during the Autumn term 1984 and attracted over 50 teachers. This pilot course has given rise to the Humberside Equal Opportunities Curriculum Development Group, which, through the means of further INSET courses, plans to focus in greater detail on the areas of curriculum development, school and classroom organization and the design of teaching materials. The significance of these developments is that equal opportunities education now has a place in the mainstream INSET programme, where it can be seen as being endorsed by the LEA, rather than as a 'fringe' activity provided voluntarily by enthusiasts.

In addition to the direct approach of tackling equal opportunities and sex discrimination as a discrete issue, the working party has recommended that the subject should be placed on the agenda of other specialist groups such as the secondary head teachers and subject heads of department. This process has begun in relation to the authority's 16–19 review working party.

Conclusion

Because intervention of the kind I have described is by its nature 'disruptive' the arguments – often expressed at working party meetings – in favour of compromise have to be taken seriously. The need to maintain a balance between the views of members who want to accelerate the equal opportunities initiatives and the caution urged by LEA officers (who claim that 'if we go too far, too fast, we'll alienate the very teachers we're trying to reach') is a real one. It is important to recognize, however, that bland declarations of support for equal opportunities may often be used as a means of postponing measures of a more practical nature. If sexism in education is to be counteracted, rhetoric must eventually be translated into positive action.

Notes

References in the text not given in the Bibliography are to the published minutes of meetings of governing bodies and the local press in North and South Humberside.

The views expressed in this chapter are those of the author and do not necessarily reflect those of the LEA.

References

Acker, S. (1983) 'Women and teaching: A semi-detached sociology of a semi-profession' in Walker, S. and Barton, L. (eds) *Gender, Class and Education*; Falmer Press, Barcombe.

Acker, S. (1984) 'Women in Higher Education: what is the problem?' in Acker, S. and Warren Piper, D. (eds) *Is Higher Education Fair to Women?* SRHE & NFER-NELSON, Slough.

Buchan, L. (1980) 'It's a good job for a girl (but an awful career for a woman!)' in Spender, D. and Sarah, E. (eds) *Learning to Lose: Sexism and Education*. The Women's Press, London.

Clwyd County Council/EOC (1983) *Equal Opportunities and the Secondary School Curriculum*, EOC, Manchester.

Deem, R. (1978) *Women and Schooling*, Routledge & Kegan Paul, London.

DES (Department of Education and Science) (1981) *Statistics of Teachers in Service in England and Wales*, HMSO, London.

EOC (Equal Opportunities Commission) (1985) *Equal Opportunities and the School Governor*, EOC, Manchester.

Humberside County Council Education Department (1983) *Equal Opportunities and Sex Discrimination*, Humberside County Council, Beverley.

MacDonald, M. (1980a) 'Socio-cultural reproduction and women's education' in Deem, R. (ed.) *Schooling for Women's Work*, Routledge & Kegan Paul, London.

MacDonald, M. (1980b) 'Schooling and the reproduction of class and gender relations' in Barton, L., Meighan, R. and Walker, S. (eds) *Schooling, Ideology and the Curriculum*, Falmer Press, Barcombe.

NATFHE (National Association of Teachers in Further and Higher Education) (1980) *The Education, Training and Employment of Women and Girls*, NATFHE, London.

NUT (National Union of Teachers) (1980) *Promotion and the Woman Teacher*, NUT/EOC, London.

Pratt, J., Bloomfield, J. and Seale, C. (1984) *Option Choice: A Question of Equal Opportunity*, NFER-Nelson, Slough.

Rendel, M. (1980) 'How many women academics 1912–1976?' in Deem, R. (ed.) *Schooling for Women's Work*, Routledge & Kegan Paul, London.

Rendel, M. (1984) 'Women academics in the seventies' in Acker, S. and Warren Piper, D. (eds) *Is Higher Education Fair to Women?*, SRHE and NFER-Nelson, Slough.

Roberts, H. (1984) 'A feminist perspective on affirmative action' in Acker, S. and Warren Piper, D. (eds) *Is Higher Education Fair to Women?*, SRHE and NFER-Nelson, Slough.

Stantonbury Campus Sexism in Education Group (1984). 'The realities of mixed schooling' in Deem, R. (ed.) *Co-education Reconsidered*, Open University Press, Milton Keynes.

Stanworth, M. (1981) *Gender and Schooling: A Study of Sexual Divisions in the Classroom*, Women's Research and Resources Centre, London. (Revised edn (1983) Hutchinson, London.)

Whyld, J. (1983) *Sexism in the Secondary Curriculum*, Harper & Row, London.

Ten   Andrew Cant

Development of LEA policy:
Manchester

Manchester is one of the largest authorities in the country, and has
already adopted wide-ranging policies and strategies for multicultural and anti-racist education. Progress on equal opportunities
for girls and boys seems to have been much slower, and this
chapter describes the early development of an LEA policy on
sexism.

It is now nearly four years since issues of sexism and sex
stereotyping were first raised at LEA level in Manchester. A
number of reports and papers, including 'Guidelines for Good
Practice in Secondary Schools' endorsed by the Education Committee in 1981, testify to the sustained efforts of various working
parties and to the forbearance of teachers in completing questionnaires, but the impact on schools shows little consistency. The
'issues' are on the agenda (notably for a number of secondary
schools) but there is a measure of uncertainty as to how best to
make progress; the issues themselves often lack definition so far as
teachers are concerned, particularly where teachers are yet to be
'tuned in' to the taken-for-granted and institutionalized nature of
sexism within the school.

In reviewing the experience of developing an LEA policy on
sexism, the genesis of that policy and strategies proposed to
encourage its implementation, there are grounds to suggest a
possible re-think with a view to shifting the impetus for change
from the LEA to the schools themselves. With hindsight the

environment for change, that is the context within which both teachers and schools were working, needed clarification. It might well have been more fruitful to work *through* schools (perhaps on a pilot basis initially) rather than have sexism seen as an issue imposed from outside by the LEA. The *process* of identifying sexism within one's own school and devising a school-based policy offers the prospect of a whole-school approach which sets out the implications of anti-sexist strategies for all staff and for the school as an institution. Developments in Manchester highlight the fact that a 'top-down' model of innovation and change is in itself insufficient. While it is crucial for those in the field to feel their efforts are supported and made legitimate by the LEA's statement of policy, the 'top-down' model needs to be complemented by 'bottom-up' developments at school level.

At the time of the LEA's 1980 initiative the whole question of sexism in education was increasingly being raised in the press and research projects were underway in various parts of the country. In Manchester a number of schools were participating in the Girls into Science and Technology (GIST) project. Members of the Education Committee had expressed a committed interest in seeing the issue of sexism raised and a group of officers and teachers who shared that interest came together to devise a local initiative. Two working parties, chaired by a member of the Inspectorate, were established for the primary and secondary sectors respectively. The latter readily defined its brief: the production of a useful and acceptable set of recommendations for 'good practice'; not a finished or definitive document but a source of suggestions for a school or departments wishing to develop their own initiatives. Unfortunately the primary working party found it harder to get off the ground. There was a feeling that guidelines *per se* would have a limited impact (there had been a plethora of guidelines on different aspects of the primary curriculum) and that something in the way of a discussion paper/checklist of suggestions might be more helpful. In large part the problem lay in defining an objective. In the secondary sector issues such as the under-representation of girls in craft and science subjects were readily identified and were obvious targets for intervention. In the primary sector the question of sex stereotyping was perceived as being far more diffuse and it took some time for the working party to work through to the stage where the issue could be broken down into a manageable form. With hindsight the division between primary and secondary working parties proved something of a handicap in itself. There has been little contact between the two groups and therefore little prospect of making appropriate links between primary and secondary education and of examining the interplay between the two.

Initially, the primary working party decided to look in detail at one area where it might be supposed that boys' and girls' learning experiences are constrained by sex-typed expectations; 'free activity' periods in nursery/infant classes. An observation schedule was sent to all schools with nursery and infant age children and staff were invited to record children's choices (a simple head count) on at least six different occasions, preferably at different times of day and on different days of the week, rather than on (say) consecutive Monday mornings. There was a very good response and figures/ observations were recorded for over 100 nursery and infant classes. While the data indicated a number of areas where there is only a marginal difference in boys' and girls' choices, for example painting, there were other areas with more marked differences, and which might have longer-term educational implications. Boys tended to engage in constructional play, including the use of 'boys' toys' such as bricks, cars and trains more frequently than girls (a ratio of between 2 and 3:1). Conversely, boys were consistently under-represented in activities centred around the 'home corner'. The data also illustrated an interesting trend as children passed from the nursery to the infant class, suggesting that as children get older they become more aware of activities 'appropriate' to their sex; boys, for example, were significantly less likely to engage in 'social play' as they moved up to the infant class.

Many staff made observations on the nature of children's play. There was a frequently expressed belief that there were no significant differences in choice of play activities as between boys and girls, but in some schools it appeared that the teachers' perception of play activities was not borne out by their recorded observations. For example, one teacher noted that 'the boys are just as much at home in the Wendy House as the girls are in the brick corner': yet in this school 17 boys and 1 girl had been observed playing with 'bricks, cars and trains'. Another dimension which emerged was the kind of role boys took on in areas of social play: 'When boys do choose to play in the Wendy House they often want to be robbers or dogs!' It was apparent that the completion of the observation schedule had provoked discussion among staff and to that extent achieved the twofold purpose of gathering data and raising awareness of the question of sex stereotyping in the primary and nursery school.

By way of follow-up the primary working party drafted a more comprehensive questionnaire as a means of identifying areas on which future work might focus. Again a very good response from schools and the comments of teachers suggested that the questionnaire had been raised as a matter for discussion in the staffroom; in one school there was a feeling (positive? negative?) that 'sex stereotyping is an issue which polarizes opinion' among staff. Questionnaire data ranged from staffing matters, for example the finding that as children move up the age range the chance that they will be taught by a male teacher increases progressively, with male teachers forming 9 per cent of the total at J1 and 44 per cent at J4, to the choice of reading schemes and aspects of school organization and the hidden curriculum. The working party has now broken down into sub-groups focusing on the following areas:

– an 'in-service pack' for developing a whole-school policy
– science and technology
– physical education and games
– reading schemes and classroom resources
– working with parents

and is working towards a series of papers the form of which is likely to vary according to the subject matter, namely advice and checklists regarding school and curriculum organization; in-service or classroom materials; recommendations to schools and/or the LEA. A likely pattern for the initial use of materials will be through pilot schools receptive to developing an anti-sexist approach. A further development will be on the link-up with secondary schools, a theme ('transition') which is now attracting a lot of interest in other areas.

The secondary working party's guidelines dealt in the main with ways of opening up the curriculum and in particular redressing the imbalance of girls taking craft and physical science. A guiding principle was that if pupils were to have a *realistic* choice of options in years 4 and 5 the first three years needed to be carefully organized. As a realistic choice is only possible on the basis of experience, opportunities to take non-traditional subjects (for example, in the lower school) must be real, sustained opportunities, not token gestures. It is not enough to claim that every individual has freedom of choice when it is not one's alternatives which are controlled but one's motivation to choose anything but prescribed or 'acceptable' alternatives. For example, a survey of secondary schools showed that while most schools offered some form of craft circus or integrated craft course to all pupils during years 1 and 2, over a third of schools reverted to a pattern of single sex 'traditional' craft subjects in year 3, with serious implications for subsequent option choices.

The working party brought together recommendations on curriculum organization, options policy, careers advice and work experience along with proposals to the LEA on matters such as staff appointments and provision of in-service training.

So far as the development of an anti-sexist approach at school-level was concerned the working party recommended 'That responsibility for co-ordinating staff procedures to ensure equality of opportunity between the sexes and for eliminating sex-stereotyping socialization be given to a member of the Senior Management Team'; that is, someone with sufficient authority over heads of department. Schools were asked to identify a 'named person' to take a co-ordinating responsibility, but there was some uncertainty as to their role and the steps they were to take (short and long term). Some schools were reluctant to propose a nominee, in others the head teacher nominated him/herself less as a measure of commitment than as a way of ensuring the matter went no further. In an attempt to define the co-ordinator's role a day conference was held (it also served as a launch for the guidelines). For the co-ordinators the main issues highlighted were:

1. how to raise the question of sex stereotyping in schools: at a staff meeting? at departmental level?
2. how to put sexism across as an issue: a data base of facts at school level could provide useful evidence;

3. the need to establish a central loan collection with both in-service and classroom materials;
4. the need for consistent advice and support from the LEA Inspectorate;
5. the need for a network so that co-ordinators might meet and offer mutual support on a regular basis.

The co-ordinators' network has been established (on a district basis) but each of the district groups (representing about twelve schools) appears somewhat uncertain as to what steps to take next. The lack of definition of the co-ordinator's role has had a carry-over effect on the district group. There has been a tendency to want to start afresh with a new questionnaire, leading perhaps to new guidelines, checklists, etc. There has also been the often time-consuming matter of inducting those who have not been party to earlier discussions. The need for cathartic discussion of the issues and one's own experience of their effect may hinder progress of a more practical nature. In so far as the district groups are now seeking to define short-term objectives the preparation of appropriate in-service training materials is to be a priority. The co-ordinators' network has, however, succeeded in providing support to colleagues who might otherwise feel very isolated within their own institutions. Another way of trying to break down that sense of isolation and to establish sexism as a high-profile issue is through a newsletter to all schools (published termly) giving contact names/addresses, details of courses, developments within the LEA and elsewhere, examples of good practice, etc. There are now a number of initiatives being taken in some Manchester schools to tackle girls' under-representation in craft and science subjects; for example, the girls' school which has established a successful 'link' course with the local Further Education College to give a 'girls only' workshop experience which school facilities would otherwise fail to provide. However, such initiatives are something of a patchwork across the LEA and are dependent for the most part on the enthusiasm and commitment of a particular teacher or department rather than as a response to a whole-school policy on sexism.

With hindsight the experience of the last four years suggests that we neither assessed sufficiently the environment for change within which we were working nor identified/deployed our allies (whether teachers, pupils, parents or governors) to best effect. We could, for example, have made more use of a particularly committed department or sought to have the question of sexism raised via the governors. We might also have forged better links with other parts of the education service, for example with initiatives on 'work with girls' in the Youth Service. The need for co-ordination points now to the need for a full-time post at inspectorate level. At the outset such an appointment seemed in a sense to run contrary to the notion that sexism is something about which we should all be concerned, that to pigeon-hole responsibility could be counter-productive. In the event such a view seems to have been overly optimistic.

Assessing the context within which we were working might also have caused us to query the value of official-looking guidelines. In retrospect it might have been more effective to start with the schools, identifying a co-ordinator and working through her at school level. Many teachers have seen the LEA's concern about sex stereotyping as an imposition on an over-crowded curriculum. Having the initiative taken up from within the school and having schools develop home-grown strategies implies the valuable experience that the *process* of policy formulation entails. School-based approaches seem more likely to encourage a sense of ownership, a recognition that the problem is one for the school to tackle, albeit with the help and support of the LEA.

The development and effectiveness of an LEA policy in Manchester remain problematic. If LEA policy is to be more than a paper exercise it needs translating into practical action in the schools themselves. In reviewing the experience of the past four years it sometimes seems as though one is running up against the same resistance and scepticism first met in forming a working party and drafting an LEA policy and guidelines. The achievement of Manchester's policy has been to get the issues firmly on the agenda. The question of policy implementation remains but increasingly it needs to be seen as a problem that the school needs to define rather than one which can be solved centrally.

Note

The views expressed in this paper are those of the author and are not necessarily those of the Manchester LEA.

Part Three

**Reflections on intervention:
where do we go from here?**

Eleven   Lynda Carr

Legislation and mediation: to what extent has the Sex Discrimination Act changed girls' schooling?

The Equal Opportunities Commission's (EOC) interest in girl friendly schooling derives from its statutory duty to monitor and enforce the Sex Discrimination Act 1975 (SDA), and to make recommendations to the Secretary of State for Home Affairs for amending the legislation as appropriate. It is a matter of concern to the EOC that while sex discrimination affects both girls and boys, the disadvantage to girls is more far-reaching in its implications. Boys may leave school lacking valuable communication and life skills, but these have less relevance in terms of gaining access to post-school education and employment than the lack of scientific, technical and mathematical qualifications which adversely affect the majority of girls. Girl friendly schooling has been actively promoted by the EOC for many years.

In 1978 the EOC undertook its first major task in an educational context, which was to explain the implications of the legislation to schools and to local education authorities, and this was done through the issuing of guidelines entitled *Do You Provide Equal Educational Opportunities?* (EOC 1979). The job was an important and necessary one but it had the unfortunate effect of branding the EOC in the eyes of much of the educational world as an unsympathetic body with extensive legal powers which were not matched by an equivalent educational experience or understanding. It is interesting to observe, therefore, that almost a decade later the EOC finds itself widely accepted as an informed educational resource while its legislative powers under the provisions of sections 22 and 23 of the SDA remain untested.

The legislation, however, has not been ineffective in the main areas of complaint in education, which are: access to educational benefits including selective education and the curriculum, and access to employment including promoted posts. Generally speaking, sections 22 and 23 of the Act are concerned with the curriculum and section 6 with employment. The EOC acts on the basis of authoritative legal opinion and its interpretation of section 22 of the legislation has yet to be challenged by a local education authority. *Every* complaint of sex discrimination which has been made to the EOC concerning educational provision and benefits in schools has been resolved. Furthermore, the LEAS concerned, almost without exception, have demonstrated a willingness to comply with the legislation and to improve the educational facilities for the pupils concerned. The unlawful discrimination is thereby removed on both legislative and educational criteria, but case law is not established.

The lack of case law has been interpreted as a weakness in the legislation, though in practical terms the Sex Discrimination Act does work. The presence of legislation focuses the attention of local education authorities on sex discrimination in schools, and the threat of legal action has been used effectively by the EOC many times.

The weakness in the educational provisions of the Sex Discrimination Act is that it places the onus upon the parent to take his or her complaint to the county court. The EOC is empowered to provide financial and legal assistance but considerations other than finance have proved problematic. County court proceedings would involve the child concerned in the pressures of the judicial process and in cross-examination. A county court case is an adversarial situation; the presence of a complainant and respondent are essential, and with the parents and the school on opposing sides there are evident disadvantages which might ultimately reflect on the child.

The court is not primarily concerned with matters of principle – the side which makes the best case wins – and many feminist educationalists regard the elimination of sex discrimination as a matter of educational principle as well as sound educational practice. Furthermore, the county court will not necessarily be able to provide access to the particular provision to which the child was denied access even if the case is won. The length of time taken in preparing a case and arranging for it to be heard is several months, by which time the damage has been done and another academic year may have passed.

It is arguable, therefore, that the *threat* of legal action has been more effective in reducing sex differentiation in the curriculum than the legal process itself would be, and that the lack of case law is not as significant as has been suggested. Nevertheless, the means are available by which the disincentives to pursue cases under the educational provisions of the Sex Discrimination Act may be removed. The SDA is a piece of reforming legislation and among the statutory duties of the EOC is a requirement to recommend amendments in order to make the legislation more effective. The Commission's first set of proposed amendments were published in 1980 (EOC 1982) but time has not been found by Parliament to debate them. Further amendments are now in mind and it seems likely that the Commission, with the benefit of greater experience, will re-frame all the proposed amendments and will campaign more vigorously for the amending of the legislation within the foreseeable future. As far as the education sections of the Act are concerned, the earlier amendment sought 'to make clear that the requirement that pupils/students of one sex should make a request while pupils/students of the other sex are automatically admitted to a particular course of study, does constitute less favourable treatment within the meaning of section 1 of the SDA'. Such an amendment would go a long way towards resolving the majority of curricular complaints made to the Commission which relate to the allocation of pupils to traditionally sex-segregated craft subjects. A more wide-ranging and potentially more effective amendment, however, would be to give the EOC itself the power to bring a case to a county court on behalf of a parent; the Commission is empowered already to take direct action in the case of discriminatory advertising and such cases are also heard in a county court. The educational provisions of the legislation are most relevant in terms of curricular change but the appointment and promotion of women teachers is also covered by legislation under the employment sections of the SDA. Three cases have been of particular significance: *Gates* v. *Wirral Borough Council*, *Dick* v. *University of Dundee*, *Hay* v. *West Lothian College of Further Education and Lothian Regional Council* (EOC Information Leaflets). Ms Gates claimed that she was discriminated against at interview when questions were asked concerning her relationship with her husband and her intentions about starting a family. The industrial tribunal ruled in Ms Gates' favour: the personal questions put to her were clearly discriminatory, similar questions were not put to the male candidates, and the questions were part of the 'arrangements' made by the respondent LEA.

Mrs Dick claimed sex discrimination when she was made redundant from a part-time post under the terms of a staff review. She submitted that the university would not have dismissed a male part-time employee in a situation where the post from which he was about to be discharged was his only employment. The tribunal found indirect discrimination because the review, as a result of which Mrs Dick was made redundant, affected a greater proportion of the female employees than the male employees because more women work part-time.

Mrs Hay claimed that she was discriminated against when the college at which she had been teaching for eight years failed to shortlist her for interview for a promoted post to senior lecturer in the Business Studies Department. She also claimed indirect discrimination with regard to the requirement that applicants should have a background of managerial experience in industry. The tribunal found discrimination on both counts and she was awarded compensation.

Two of the formal investigations which the EOC has undertaken in the area of education have been concerned with the appointment and promotion of women teachers and have alleged unlawful acts. The formal investigation into the appointment and promotion of women teachers to senior posts at Sidney Stringer School and Community College (EOC 1983) was concluded in 1983 and did not find discrimination, although the Commission was critical of the procedures by which appointments and promotions were made. As a result of the investigation, two publications were produced by the Commission, *Equal Opportunities and the Woman Teacher*, (EOC 1985b) and *Equal Opportunities and the School Governor* (EOC 1985a); both documents make strong recommendations for good practice in making appointments to the teaching profession.

The formal investigation into Ebbw Vale College, Gwent, (EOC 1984) found discrimination against women lecturers in the college's Business Studies Department. Improvements which were made to the college's procedures caused the Commission not to issue a non-discrimination notice. Nevertheless, where discrimination is found in employment a non-discrimination notice may be served by the Commission. Monitoring then takes place and persistent discrimination may result in further legal action with heavy fines and the ultimate threat of imprisonment. The Commission receives too many complaints from women teachers who allege discrimination at interview or in the arrangements made for appointments and promotions for such allegations to be easily dismissed – as often seems to happen in the schools concerned. The Commission's belief was confirmed by the findings of the NUT research *Promotion and the Woman Teacher* (NUT 1980) undertaken in 1980, and the 1984 survey *Women's Careers in Teaching* (ILEA 1984). In terms of taking a case to an industrial tribunal, however, hard supportive evidence, in the form of corroborative statements by members of the interviewing panels, is hard to come by, and the argument of 'better candidate on the day' has been seen to refute claims by women teachers with better qualifications and longer experience than the person appointed.

The Sex Discrimination Act is a very complex piece of legislation and in discussing its relevance in terms of educational change over-simplification is inevitable, but a detailed guide is available from the EOC called simply, *A Guide to the Sex Discrimination Act 1975* (Home Office 1975). There is, however, nothing simple about proving sex discrimination which is often hard to pinpoint and even harder to prove. Furthermore, the kind of discrimination which is 'provable' is only part of the problem; deep-seated prejudice affects attitudes towards women of all ages and its implications for schools are very far-reaching.

In many respects the EOC has been an important influence on girls' education. The legislation and the presence of the EOC have given a legitimacy to matters of grave concern to women and provide a framework for all the other initiatives which take place. The enormous demand for the EOC's educational materials reflects the practical help which it is able to give and it is now EOC policy to relate its promotional work in education very closely to its legislative work.

Schools need to know not only which of their practices are unlawful but also how to implement change and good practice. However, it is the legislative powers and duties of the EOC which differentiate it from other curriculum development bodies and which make the EOC a potentially stronger and more effective force in the girl friendly schooling issue. In terms of girl friendly schooling there is a fine balance to be struck: on the one side is the kind of curricular and organizational change which is brought about by understanding of, and commitment to, the principle of equality between the sexes in the education system, and on the other side is legislation which has the potential to force change whether or not the reasons for doing so are accepted and understood. The satisfactory solution of such an equation may depend upon the length of time allowed to tackle it, but a growing degree of impatience is discernible and a more confident use of the legislation would help to hasten progress.

It was, perhaps, inevitable that a period of time would elapse before a reasonable analysis of the effectiveness of the legislation could be made, but nine years is enough. The legislative power with which the EOC is invested is unique to the UK and as there is evidence to suggest that the presence of legislation has had a positive effect it is time to build on this presence by amending the legislation in order to make it more directly effective.

A great deal of progress has been made during the past decade and the issues surrounding sex differentiation in the curriculum and sex discrimination in education are widely understood. Understanding is essential but it does not necessarily promote change. Strategies for change are needed now and as long as change is dependent upon principle and personal commitment, a coherent national policy for equality of opportunity in education will not emerge. Curricular development is a matter of choice, sex discrimination is a matter of law; the way forward is through legislation and a stronger determination to use it.

Note

The contents of this chapter reflect the personal view of the author; they do not represent the policy of the Equal Opportunities Commission.

References

EOC (1979) *Do You Provide Equal Educational Opportunities?* (revised edn 1982), EOC, Manchester.

EOC (1982) *Proposed Amendments to the Sex Discrimination Act 1975 and the Equal Pay Act 1970* (As amended), EOC, Manchester.

EOC (1982) EOC Information Leaflet: *The Case of Gates* v. *Wirral Borough Council*, December.

EOC (1982) EOC Information Leaflet: *The Case of Dick* v. *University of Dundee*, December.

EOC (1983) *Report of the formal investigation into Sidney Stringer School and Community College*, EOC, Manchester.

EOC (1984) *Report of the formal investigation into Ebbw Vale College*, EOC, Manchester.

EOC (1985) EOC Information Leaflet: *The Case of Hay* v. *Lothian Regional Council*, EOC, Manchester.

EOC (1985a) *Equal Opportunities and the School Governor*, EOC, Manchester.

EOC (1985b) *Equal Opportunities and the Woman Teacher*, EOC, Manchester.

Home Office (1975) *A Guide to the Sex Discrimination Act 1975*, HMSO, London.

ILEA (1984) *Women's Careers in Teaching*, ILEA, London.

NUT (1980) *Promotion and the Woman Teacher*, NUT/EOC, London.

Further Reading

Pratt, J., Bloomfield, J. and Seale, C. (1984) *Option Choice: A Question of Equal Opportunity*, NFER-Nelson, Slough.

EOC (1982) *Towards Equality, A Casebook of Decisions on Sex Discrimination and Equal Pay*, EOC, Manchester.

Twelve   Lesley Kant

A question of judgment

The law in question

One of the fundamental tenets of the constitution of this country
has been the principle of equality before the law but in common
law its parameters have been narrowly defined.

> The limits of Common Law must be remembered because the
> Judges are imprisoned within them but a survey of the decided
> cases suggests that Judges have made their prison more con-
> fining than it need have been; they have grown to love their
> chains. (Lester and Bindman 1972)

The law is rooted in individual rights yet the British Parliament
has never guaranteed basic human rights; some consideration of
these has been enforced both through Britain's membership of the
United Nations, which in its charter affirms fundamental human
rights, and through the Treaty of Rome as members of the
European Economic Community (EEC). Directives of the EEC are
binding but member states can now decide how to put them into
practice and the Sex Discrimination Act of 1975 was the result of
the EEC directive on equal treatment for men and women.

Over the past hundred years common law has tended to suppress
rather than uphold fundamental human rights for it has consistently been invoked in order to justify sexual inequality; the
capacity of the law to be used as an instrument of either oppression

or reform is nicely documented by Dr Rendel, who comments: 'Anti-discrimination legislation . . . provides an exacting test of the effectiveness of law as an instrument of reform because it is law which is concerned with behaviour based on prejudices which are unconscious and irrational.' (Rendel 1976)

Witness the words of Mr Justice Caulfield, only a few weeks prior to the enactment of the Sex Discrimination Bill:

> Even in present times, when there is a movement by women for equality with men, a sensible wife, certainly in a united home, does not generally make the major decisions. A solicitor should not take instruction from the wife when the husband is available. (McMullen 1978)

The Sex Discrimination Act renders sex discrimination unlawful in employment, training and related matters; in education; in the provision of goods, facilities and services, and in the disposal and management of premises. Discrimination can be attacked in two ways – through individuals seeking remedies for discrimination they have suffered, and through an attack on discriminatory practices; responsibility for the latter rests primarily with the Equal Opportunities Commission which was set up with the statutory function of 'working towards the elimination of discrimination'. From 1976 up to and including 1983, approximately 1700 applications were made under the Sex Discrimination Act. Of these roughly a quarter were made by men. Complaints under the Sex Discrimination Act are referred to industrial tribunals and of these a negligible 10 per cent have been successful. Over the years 1976–83 there were approximately forty-five tribunal decisions involving teachers. Of these, about 15 per cent have been successful.

Industrial tribunals

Industrial tribunals are a judicial mechanism through which the bureaucracy and expense of the traditional machinery of judgment can be minimized; it was also anticipated that it would render the law less daunting and more accessible. Most industrial tribunals consist of three individuals; one a nominee of the Confederation of British Industry (CBI), one a nominee from the Trades Union

Congress (TUC) and the chairman who has a specifically legal background. Despite the demystifying intent, it appears that the formula is insufficient to escape the legal strait-jacket: legal reasoning is both inductive and deductive and requires considerable precision in wording. A feature of the English legal system is its inculcation of extreme pedantry. 'When determining whether a woman should be included in the category of person they employed the same format as to decide whether a wooden hut was a building for purposes of planning.' (Sachs and Wilson 1979)

Tribunal decisions or judgments in the cases brought by teachers have reflected the legal system's strict adherence to technical details in preference to the spirit and ethos which engendered the law in question. In the majority of cases judgments have consistently been made by using the available methods of classification without questioning the assumptions about sex that underlie them.

Teachers

School teaching has been traditionally dominated by women and colleges of further education and institutes of higher education by men. In the primary sector women outnumber men by more than 3 to 1. However, the concentration of men in the junior sector and the overwhelming proportion of women in the infant sector may itself offer some clues to this particular statistical pattern. Although the proportion of men in the primary sector represents only 27 per cent of teachers overall, men account for 60 per cent of headships and 43 per cent of deputy headships; positions where responsibility for decision making and influence extends not only to the field of school curriculum but to the employment of subsequent staff.

In secondary schools the sexes are more evenly distributed and women account for almost 45 per cent of the total staffing; despite this only 15 per cent of all headships and 35 per cent of deputy headships are held by women (DES 1980). Although women account for 62 per cent of the second master/mistress posts, which is disproportionately more than at any other senior tier level, this figure declined between the years 1965 and 1974, despite the

Burnham Committee's (positive discrimination) ruling, which provided for the appointment of a person of the opposite sex in third-tier posts in co-educational schools (see *Mrs K. Castle v. Surrey County Council*, the case described on p. 171)[1]. In teaching we see a profession where the representation of women at management and middle management levels is in inverse proportion to their actual numbers. Ironically, despite the fact that female entrants to the profession tend to be better qualified than their male counterparts, the under-representation of women teachers in the upper echelons of the teaching profession is rapidly accelerating. Of the 15 per cent of women secondary heads, only a tiny proportion are in fact heads of co-educational schools. Thus the move from single-sex schooling to co-education has itself contributed to the decline in senior positions for women.

It might have been anticipated that the sex discrimination legislation would remedy the situation and it seems appropriate to examine cases involving teachers as a means of appraising the efficacy of the legislation. The context is particularly fitting: the historical background of female education and women in teaching has witnessed a continuing debate over women's rights and past struggles might have given impetus to present opportunities. Additionally, a major feature of the legislation (section 22) is the commitment of the education profession to the promotion of equality and in recent years a number of schools have scrutinized both the formal and informal processes of education in order to widen the horizons of their female pupils. Yet the legislation has done little to enhance the status of women teachers. A very small proportion of cases brought by teachers has been upheld and the similarity of the circumstances in which the tribunals reached favourable decisions is significant and worth scrutinizing in greater detail.

Equality enforced

In *Blackburn and Craig* v. *Red House School* (1977) the applicants were the female members of the full-time teaching staff of a co-educational boarding school, where they were paid according to the Burnham Scale for teachers. In addition to their salaries they were allowed half remission of school fees in respect of any children educated at the school. The complaint was that all the men on the staff were allowed full remission. It was agreed by all parties that the male members of staff had extra-curricular duties substantially greater than those of the women, although one exception was a Mrs Smart who had assumed considerable extra-curricular duties as time went on. The headmaster, Mr Ryan, recognized this contribution by increasing her benefits to the point where she was granted full remission of fees in respect of her child.

The tribunal ruled that despite the fact that male members of staff undertook considerably more extra-curricular duties than the women, these duties were not specifically defined as they arose out of the interests, skills and function of each member of staff and 'the request made of him by the Headmaster'. That the fee remission did not represent the rate for the job was evidenced by the fact that one male member of staff had no child who could qualify for fee remission and thus undertook duties without this benefit. The position of Mrs Smart was deemed to have no particular bearing on the matter, and the tribunal found for the applicants.

This case reveals similarities with an influential judgment in *E. Coomes (Holdings) Ltd* v. *Shields* (1978) which came before the Court of Appeal. The bookmakers opposed equal pay on the grounds that men were expected to act as bouncers. The ruling that 'the male bookmaker was only required to perform the function of a protector because he was a man' is of particular relevance, although not explicitly noted in the Red House School judgment. Similar expectations by the headmaster had percolated into the thinking and performance of the women teachers. Supervision of preparation was cited by Mr Ryan as one of the many extra-curricular activities engaged in by the male staff and the tribunal was informed that prior to the question before the tribunal none of the female teachers had wished to supervise preparation. 'He (Mr Ryan) says that experience shows that one man can do this supervision and it is appropriate that a man should do it from the point of view of discipline, the variety of work being done and the preponderance of boys.' It is hardly surprising that given Mr Ryan's explicit and implicit assumptions about the roles male and female teachers were expected to fill, no females had previously volunteered. Apart from the use of the adjective 'one' which is set in unspoken opposition to 'two or more women' there is the association of male teachers with the maintenance of discipline and polymathic capabilities as well as the echo of the National Association of School Masters' argument of the 1920s that males should be responsible for schoolboys: 'a male adult who is produced by a man teacher is, in our judgement, bound to be a superior being as compared with one taught by a woman teacher' (Partington 1976).

Such expectations of limited female competence in these areas of education contribute to a socialization process through which gender differences for boys and girls are established. This view was even reinforced by Mrs Craig, who told the tribunal that the differences in remuneration for men and women were due to the fact that men made teaching their career. The tribunal refuted this, stating unequivocally that

> it is today and has been for many years, common practice for married women to pursue a career throughout their normal working lives . . . there is no evidence that either applicant has had any intention other than to make teaching her career . . . it is because she is making a career of her profession that she is entitled to the fee remission.

Married women are commonly viewed as having a superficial work commitment, though their subordinate status and discriminatory attitudes undoubtedly fuel such perceptions.

The issues raised in *Mrs K. Castle* v. *Surrey County Council* (1976) are interesting, both for the past prejudices they reveal and for the success of the application which ended the Burnham opposite sex ruling on third-tier posts in co-educational schools. This Burnham rule was challenged on the technical ground that the provisions of the Burnham Report were financial only. The real case being fought behind this technical argument was, however, a fundamental principle of the Sex Discrimination Act: that all jobs must be open to both sexes unless a case could be established for a genuine occupational qualification. The LEAs were unable to decide whether they were arguing for a preserved quota system or a genuine occupational qualification. Mrs Castle was successful and afterwards appointed to the post in question, and the authorities removed the rule from the Burnham agreement.

This case revealed both confusion and lack of direction over both staffing policies and the thinking which precipitated this Burnham regulation. The main defence of the Burnham ruling was that it would provide an opportunity for the minority sex, men in primary and women in secondary schools, to achieve promotion; another justification was that the education of boys and girls is best served by having senior people of both sexes in schools. The first argument is specious: if there had been a real desire to achieve equality between the sexes then all the senior posts would have been subject to the ruling. The second argument, that pupil welfare is best served by having a senior teacher of the same sex, is arguable. It implies that the pastoral needs of boys and girls are diverse and incompatible and that only the same sex is competent to understand or offer direction; it polarizes rather than reconciles the sexes and is an implicit negation of the principles underlying co-education. Nevertheless, women in senior positions present an important role model to girls and allow boys to perceive that women are capable of occupying positions of leadership and discharging them efficiently. In practice, women in senior positions tend to assume responsibilities for counselling, pastoral care and social activities; men take control of the construction of the timetable, direct studies and curriculum development. Yet it is through the latter route that the avenues for promotion to headship lie (Richardson 1973). Of course these might well be the routes to promotion because they are trodden by men and thus valued accordingly.

In *Mrs Whitehouse* v. *Highlands Regional Council*, Mrs Whitehouse, a former school teacher, applied for an ancillary post which was one of three posts created under the government job creation scheme. At her interview she was informed that her application could not be considered as she was a married woman. The tribunal reported that during the interview her marital status was discovered; she was immediately informed that the Manpower (sic) Committee had decided as a matter of policy to exclude from consideration for such posts married women other than those in 'sole support' or 'breadwinner' categories and that the vacancies were not open to married women. She was subjected to further castigation because she had a husband who should be able to support her and that in a period of high unemployment it was wrong that a husband and wife should both have jobs. She would be doing a married man out of a job. She must have been sent for interview by mistake and the Jobcentre would be told to send no more married women for interviews.

There was no dispute that there had been unlawful discrimination but the tribunal also had to decide the matter of compensation; for this she was awarded £100.

The discriminatory attitudes and practices revealed in this case echo the earlier antagonism towards married women teachers that resulted in disqualifications such as the marriage bar. Opposition to the employment of married women conveniently surfaces at times of grave unemployment; witness Lord Spens' suggestion that married women should give up work. As this case arose out of a scheme set up to combat unemployment it is revealing that the tribunal chairman stated that the policy, while unlawful, was 'comprehensible', giving substance to the claim that 'Judges (using the word in the broadest sense) are content to adopt modes of classification without questioning the assumptions about power, property and sex that underly them' (Sachs and Wilson 1978).

A favourable judgment was also allowed in the case of *Mrs Phyllis Hay* v. *Lothian Regional Council* (1983). Mrs Hay was a senior lecturer 1 in the Business Studies Department of West Lothian College of Further Education. When the council advertised a senior lecturer 2 post in the Business Studies Department at the college, Mrs Hay had considerable difficulty in getting hold of the post particulars and was not called for interview. Following interviews of five candidates, a male colleague was finally appointed to the post.

Mrs Hay's academic qualifications were at least as good as those of the successful candidate and, following considerable equivocation by the college council, the only relevant distinction the industrial tribunal drew between Mrs Hay's experience and that of the successful candidate was in the area of work experience. Furthermore, the successful candidate was not teacher-trained whereas Mrs Hay met all the job description criteria. The tribunal discovered that a *post hoc* justification of the chosen candidate had taken place. In the course of the hearing it was also established that the type of industrial experience which the college preferred was much more likely to be found in men than in women and thus amounted to a form of indirect discrimination.

The pattern of employment in the Business Studies Department in the college reflected the norms that are found elsewhere in employment as well as in schools: women teaching mainly secretarial studies within the Business Studies Department; business studies accorded higher status and taught mainly by men. The college's internal structure reinforced a situation where women would have found it very difficult to gain promotion. Thus the socialization which was perceived in the Red House School case was also evident in the West Lothian College. The tribunal suggested that on the basis of the evidence before them it appeared that any efforts made by women to move from teaching secretarial studies into teaching general business studies had been unsuccessful. They drew the inference that women were not encouraged to move out of the secretarial studies side and that this effectively limited the avenues available to them. An important point that emerged from the tribunal judgment was that discriminatory practices are justified by subsequently agreeing criteria which favour the successful male applicant.

In all four cases judgments were favourable to the teacher applicants. In all cases there was no necessity to dispute the presented facts. The tribunals had a fairly straightforward task of applying the law without having to weigh disparate or contradictory evidence or to draw conclusions where no concrete information had been produced. The cases next considered reveal the difficulties faced by applicants in the substantiation of discriminatory practices, particularly with regard to interview procedures. This discrimination is compounded by judicial bias on the part of industrial tribunals.

Judgments in question

In *Mrs Lake* v. *Essex County Council*, Mrs Lake claimed discrimination on two counts: first, indirect discrimination because as a part-time teacher her security of tenure was more vulnerable than that enjoyed by full-time employees and that selection for redundancy was partly on the grounds of her sex or marital status; the second, direct discrimination in the appointment of a man to fill a vacancy for a history teacher. The case for the indirect discrimination is lucid and persuasive and is reproduced in full at the end of the chapter.[3]

The claim for indirect discrimination was dismissed. The tribunal rejected the argument, though not the statistical evidence, which they held irrelevant, paradoxically on the grounds that the Act explicitly uses 'can' rather than 'do' and therefore, although more women do part-time work, despite the arguments presented below they are held to have the capacity for full-time work. In a later significant judgment, *Price v. The Civil Service Commission* (1977), the Employment Appeal Tribunal upheld a case of indirect discrimination because of the Civil Service Commission's age bar and maintained that 'on a narrow construction it could be said any woman *could* comply with the Civil Service requirements, since no woman is obliged to marry or have children. However, such a construction would be wholly out of sympathy with the spirit and intent of the SDA.'

In the appeal tribunal's view it was necessary to see whether women could comply in practice (knowledge and experience tended to suggest they could not). However, the tribunal's expeditious dismissal of the evidence which demonstrated the extent to which women are unable to make such choices is accompanied by the statement that 'if there is sex discrimination here, it is not by the employer but between husband and wife in the way that family duties are shared'. The assumption that the solution lies merely with the family, and is extraneous to the patterns of distribution of labour and the roles enforced by society, is breathtaking in its arrogance. The judgment is further revealing; 'it would be possible, and does actually happen, that a wife or daughter does full-time work outside the home and a male member of the family looks after the home'. The absurdity of instancing as a justification for dismissal an hypothesis which the legislation was designed to render concrete is a Dickensian syllogism. Redistribution of domestic responsibilities is only possible if the wife has the opportunity to be appointed to a full-time position; as she is not appointed she claims she is discriminated against; her judges inform her that her defence is untenable because she has the choice of working for pay or assuming responsibility for domestic work.

In support of her claim for direct discrimination Mrs Lake also invoked a 1976 circular to head teachers from the Area Education Officer which imposed a duty on a head teacher who was terminating or arranging the termination of a part-time post to give the teacher concerned 'the first opportunity to convert to a full-time permanent appointment where a vacancy exists'. Mrs Lake claimed that this put the head teacher under an obligation to appoint her to the vacant Scale 1 post as she was a Scale 1 teacher of history; in failing to appoint her he was influenced by the fact that she was a woman. The tribunal ruled with an unreasonable interpretation stating it may be required of the head teacher 'to bring to the notice of the redundant teacher the permanent full-time vacancy'. This elliptical reading of such a straightforward direction to allow part-time teachers to become full-time should there be an appropriate vacancy is disturbing; equally puzzling is the tribunal's disregard of Mrs Lake's additional evidence in support of direct discrimination.

Mrs Lake was told informally by the Head of the History Department that he presumed the head teacher would appoint a man. While the head teacher denied this had ever been the case and possibly with justification, the prejudices of the head of department are nevertheless exposed. 'She got the impression that Mr Davis himself wanted a man appointed as he stressed how difficult some of the fifth-year boys could be and mentioned a young lady who had been greatly upset when she had tried to teach fifth-year boys.' Mrs Lake, quite reasonably, assumed he was trying to put her off. Despite the statement of another male witness who confirmed that Mr Davis 'had said more than once in his hearing that the post was unsuitable for a woman', the tribunal chose to disregard this evidence: it held that it was inconsistent, in other words unbelievable, because Mr Davis had successfully suggested the promotion of a woman to deputy head of department. This logic smacks of the 'some of my best friends are . . .' reasoning which implies that if you treat any individual charitably, *ipso facto* this renders you incapable of baser actions to the rest of humanity.

Mr Davis the Head of Department, was on the appointing committee and it would be unusual if the other members did not defer to, or at least allow themselves to be influenced by, his feelings on this matter. It was admitted that Mrs Lake was asked about her family commitments but not about her academic qualifications. It was also suggested that 'lady governors' almost invariably ask 'lady teachers' about their family commitments but this is to put the candidate at ease and has no discriminatory intent. Yet it reveals the opposite: how deep rooted and unconscious is prejudice. The tribunal tacitly accepts that domestic responsibilities are those of women, but makes it clear that in order to achieve in employment terms women must shake off the stereotype perpetuated by such judgments.

This teacher's experience reveals the assumptions made about the roles of males and females and their domestic commitments; it is unlikely that such assumptions fail to influence the selection process. This was further underlined by Mr Greevey's statement that 'the decision was based on qualifications and experience and the impression given at the interview'.[3]

Impressions are transient judgments, relevant perhaps if a candidate's job is bound up with fleeting exchanges (a travelling sales person, for example), but not in a job where stable, long-term relationships are involved and where children's perceptions might be presumed to be the most relevant. Impressions can be no substitute for qualifications and experience.

Criteria employed to select candidates at interview are rarely made explicit and, as demonstrated in the earlier case of Mrs Hay, not even delineated at short-listing stage. The subjectivity of the selection procedure is further illustrated in other tribunal cases where discrimination is alleged as a result of non-appointment. The judgment in *Mrs Walker* v. *Fife Regional Council* stated: 'We accept entirely the evidence as to the manner in which the interviews were carried out, the impression which they formed and the conclusion which they reached . . . The Rector found what he described as "lack of sparkle on the part of Mrs. Walker".' Eileen Byrne voices suspicions shared by many: 'I suspect overt and indirect sex discrimination by both men and women on governing bodies who reproduce unfounded doubts and assumptions' (Byrne 1978).

Guidelines from the Equal Opportunities Commission (EOC 1978) state

> Questions put to the applicant must be relevant to the applicant's suitability. Questions relating to marriage, plans for children are seldom asked of male candidates . . . the requirement not to discriminate against married persons, or against women can best be met by leaving questions relating to marital status and dependants to be followed up with the successful candidates after the appointment has been made.

Such advice was contravened in the evidence submitted in *Mrs Oliver* v. *Farnborough College of Technology*. The applicant claimed she was asked more questions about her family than were the two male candidates. She said that these questions should not have been asked just because she was a woman or else the questions should have been asked of all the applicants. There was some justification for the latter claim as both the appointed candidates were married. The tribunal ruled that because the panel denied concern with the applicant's sex and marital status and because both men appointed were themselves spouses, then discrimination could not exist; thus adducing that any problem created by marriage applied equally to men and women. The usefully ambiguous phrase 'less dedicated' was levied as a reason for non-selection. Whether the fact of being a woman by definition generates the allegation of less dedication might be worth pondering. Criteria for establishing dedication are notoriously difficult to come by. However, the assumption that marriage dilutes a woman's dedication but concentrates a man's is unjust and unreasonable, but highly predictable. Lack of commitment on the part of women teachers has frequently been alleged but it is difficult to see how women can evidence this commitment when society has seen that they will automatically undertake an extra job on marriage; that they will defer to their husband's work thus rendering them immobile, and that these expectations are reinforced by discriminatory assumptions when they do offer themselves for selection. Moreover, when a woman fails to reflect this model more insidious discrimination becomes evident.

In *Miss Gates* v. *Wirral Borough Council*, the applicant had applied for the post of head teacher of an ESN school in Merseyside.

She had previously been deputy head at the school and then moved to Newcastle upon Tyne when she was appointed as head teacher. After marriage Miss Gates continued to use her original name. As her husband's employment was in Merseyside she lived in Tyneside during the week and returned to Merseyside each weekend. Two years after her appointment she decided to apply for the headship of her former school, although it was a job of equal status with the one she already held, because she could then return to live full-time with her husband. Miss Gates was short-listed for the post and interviewed with four other persons including the candidate who was eventually selected.

In terms of qualification and experience Miss Gates was clearly the better applicant. She was a head teacher whereas the selected candidate was a Scale 3 assistant; his experience was in a school for physically handicapped; he had no experience in a school for esn(m) children. Her first degree was a B. Ed. (Hons), his first degree was a B. A. from the Open University. She was currently studying for a Master's degree in Special Education and he was studying for a Diploma in Special Education. She was aged 33 with twelve years' teaching experience, he was aged 34 with five years' teaching experience. In the course of the interview the panel eliminated the three other candidates and selection was reduced to Miss Gates and the successful candidate.

Before Miss Gates was interviewed there was some discussion on her use of Miss as opposed to Mrs. A strong case was presented to the tribunal that the interview was discriminatory and that the interview started off on the basis of different treatment setting a prejudicial tone in some of the panel members' minds through the unnecessary debate on the applicant's use of Miss, Ms or Mrs. Extraordinarily, the tribunal discounted such a claim. They noted: 'If a married professional woman continues to use her maiden name it is a matter related to courtesy rather than prejudice to let the panel know this before the interview starts.' Yet anyone who has been subject to such discussions knows it is an expedient way of making explicit the antagonism to female assertiveness. Ironically, Miss Gates' collected performance in the face of objectionable questioning also seems to have operated against her interests. Both the interviewing panel and the tribunal accept that she performed 'less well' than the successful candidate, yet the tribunal rejected the idea that the attitudes of members of the interviewing panel could have generated a weaker perform-ance than anticipated.

This case is particularly significant because of the double standards employed: commitment would have been highly rated in a man yet was considered suspect in a woman. Rosemary Deem notes that commitment itself could well do with some analysis: 'Balanced delicately between advancement in a career through constant mobility from school to school and remaining in one school but showing strong commitment to the pupils in that establishment' (Deem 1978).

All the above candidates alleged discrimination as a result of the interview procedure. In *Miss Baker* v. *Harper Adams Agricul-tural College*, the applicant claimed discrimination primarily under the section of the Sex Discrimination Act which provides that it is unlawful 'for a person to discriminate in relation to employment in the arrangement he makes for the purposes of who should be offered that employment'; Miss Baker had applied for the job as Head of Animal Husbandry which specified particular qualifi-cations, including teaching experience and research work. In the fuller particulars of the post it was further stated that 'sound practical knowledge' was essential. Nineteen people applied for the job but Miss Baker was not among the five short-listed nor were her references among the eleven taken up. Her claim rested substantially on the fact that the appointee's qualifications and experience in research areas were more limited than her own. However, on considering the evidence of all the documents to which Miss Baker gained access on the first day of the hearing, the tribunal decided that the successful candidate's experience in lecturing and farming was far greater than Miss Baker's and the reason she had not been short-listed for the appointment was that the college had reasonably thought she was a research specialist and author and lacked both practical farming experience and recent academic office 'rather than because she was a woman'.

The criteria for selection appear to have shifted for each candidate short-listed and it is well known that research has demonstrated that curricula vitae attributed to women are judged less favourably than identical or similar cvs attributed to men (Simpson 1969). Miss Baker was caught also in the part-time trap when this part of her experience was judged inferior to that of the appointee. The fact that Mr Alan had in recent years been in full-time remunerated employment in the same field in which he was seeking a more responsible appointment was an important consideration. Part-time teaching is deemed, whatever the actual time equation, of inferior worth compared to full-time. This constitutes indirect discrimination if the ruling established in the *Price* case were to be applied. However, Miss Baker is attacked on two further counts: through her marriage by virtue of the constraints placed on her professional undertakings, and for bringing the case in her own rather than her husband's name. 'The applicant is a married woman who made her application in her maiden name and has been referred to throughout these proceedings as Miss Baker.' Females are still identified in terms of marriage, family and domesticity rather than in terms of personhood and individual identity. In cases where men are the applicants, marital status is completely ignored. The unnecessary allusion to the maiden name itself reveals some ignorance of the law, carrying as it does the assumption that the legal name is the married name. The legal name is that which one chooses to be known by. Miss Baker had every right not to change her name on marriage (Cousins 1978).

Further prejudices are later revealed over the wording of the post particulars which used the male gender throughout. In *Stuart* v. *Strathclyde Regional Council* the tribunal accepted that the use of the female gender was off-putting and agreed that future advertisements should be gender neutral. Here it is recorded that 'it is right . . . that Miss Baker appreciated that in documents the male gender is often deemed to include the female . . . unless the respondents were prepared to use the word "person" which many of us would regard as a grammatical abomination and abuse of the English language'. Miss Baker was penalized for expressing similar strength of feeling in her view on the case. Having frankly told the tribunal that whatever the decision she would always believe she had been a victim of sex discrimination, the tribunal proceeded to refer to her as 'obsessive'. What seems particularly regrettable is the partisan way in which the tribunal interpreted a previous case brought by the applicant: 'The fact that she had apparently obtained some position in South Australia by using a sex discrimination legislation of that state and this might possibly lend support to the contention that she believed that by bringing the proceedings she might get some sort of offer.' The eclecticism of this instancing lends some support to the theory that 'if women do not show initiative in actively seeking promotion they are over-looked because initiative is a desirable quality in senior management. However, women who have agitated for better prospects of promotion, or more equal treatment, are branded, only too often it appears, troublemakers.' (Walters *et al.* 1971)

This appeared to be the tribunal's attitude in *Mrs V. A. Mason v. Coventry City Council.* Mrs Mason's complaint was that she was not appointed sixth form head at Sidney Stringer School, Coventry. In an application which was dismissed, the tribunal itself recorded with some depreciation that 'during her evidence she showed us she was a strong willed lady, competent no doubt, but unless the school was run entirely with her approval she would not hesitate to crusade for a change'. *Pace* Miss Buss and Miss Beale!

In all these cases the tribunals were faced with the problem of establishing issues that were in dispute, and given this context it is virtually impossible for an applicant to be successful. Apart from the central difficulty of the burden of proof which rests with the applicant, these cases in general illustrate a number of problems facing those who claim against discrimination.

Marital status was cited by all applicants as the basis for discrimination and indeed specifically, though irrelevantly, intro-duced into the judgments. Pre-occupation with marital status appears, however, to be no proof of prejudice and unless respon-dents unequivocally admit marriage as a barrier, as was the case with Mrs Whitehouse, it would seem that this section of the Act can have little application, particularly as the employment of married men is accepted as proof of non-discrimination while the subordinate status of women in marriage is implicitly accepted through many of the judgments.

The stereotypes of females and males which are presented as evidence of discrimination are compounded in many tribunal judgments. It is presumed that women are responsible for domestic and familial duties while men's responsibilities lie in earning a living and gaining professional qualifications; that certain tasks are best performed by women and others by men: that any interests outside these areas should be subordinate to domestic duties. It is no coincidence that time and time again applicants were described in terms of their marital status or parenthood when this was irrelevant to the claim in hand. The woman is thus defined first through her husband and secondly through her reproductive facilities. In Miss Baker's case her reclassification according to the tribunal's assumptions of what constitutes an appropriate name was evidence of this attitude. Lord Denning in the Court of Appeal ruling on *Marcia Poynton* v. *University of Sussex*, irrelevantly describes Dr Poynton as 'mother of two children'. It may reasonably be questioned why she should not be described as a university teacher or a researcher in sociology? If judges choose to reclassify women according to the images they prefer them to accommodate, then the case is lost before the hearing.

Paradoxically, the difficulties faced by women in terms of leaving work to raise families, working at home, working part-time because of the pressure of familial and domestic commitments and pursuing full-time employment while undertaking a full-time job at home, are rarely considered in a positive sense; it might be argued that instead of penalizing women for these undertakings, as was accepted by the tribunals who saw less value in part-time work and interrupted careers, women should be positively assessed for the difficulty they have overcome.

In most cases discrimination was alleged as a result of interview and it is in this area that the tribunals appear to have been at their most naive, or suspect. If the assumptions about women's place, performance and commitments are held by a panel of interviewers then however unconscious might be their prejudice it is unlikely that bias does not occur. Yet most of the tribunals have accepted without question the respondents' simple defence that no discrimination had been intended. Intent is no substitute for practice, as the tribunals' ignorance of their own bias amply demonstrates.

Beyond the question

Few teachers have won redress through the Sex Discrimination Act and legal advances have in practice been minimal. Even where the law is applied less pedantically it is clear that the parameters of the sex discrimination legislation are too limited. As with other areas of the law in this country, the Sex Discrimination Act and Equal Pay Act are framed in the individualistic tradition which fails to recognize collective rights, thus ensuring an exhaustive system of independent applications; the fact that the law fails to recognize that industrial relations and groups of workers have collective rights places a considerable onus on an individual teacher who sets out to claim redress.

In addition to the isolation faced by teachers who pursue their redress through the statutes that outlaw discrimination, their task is compounded by the male dominated milieu and the complex legal structure devised by men and barricaded against female participation, in theory until the Sex Disqualification Removal Act of 1919 and for most practical purposes up to the present time. Time and resources as well as the prospect of victimization are also relevant. It has been noted that 'justice delayed is indeed justice denied, more than that an individual organisation and impersonal entity is using staff time. With ordinary luck an individual would give up, go away or die before any concession comes to be made', (Rendel 1976). All these factors militate against women resorting to the law in order to safeguard their rights for this will be in addition to the two or even three jobs which they will have to undertake simultaneously in the course of their normal working lives.

Another problem occurs in the specific provisions of the Sex Discrimination Act. The burden of proof rests with the applicant, although in the earlier government White Paper the burden of proof rested with the respondent once the complainant had established that the respondent had acted to the complainant's detriment (HMSO 1975). The current legislation means that a teacher has to persuade the tribunal that her version is the most probable.

No doubt the burden of truth would be less intractable were applicants to have access to all the documents relevant to their cases. In a number of cases involving teachers there is little doubt that their difficulties were increased by not having access to relevant documentation. In Miss Baker's case she requested a modest selection of the requisite documents, i.e., the College prospectus, a copy of the original application, a copy of each of the publications listed by the applicant appointed. Although these were eventually made available Miss Baker had no further information about any of the other applicants, which was essential in view of her claim. The words of the judgment are revealing: 'It appeared to the tribunal that it would be in the interest of justice to provide the applicant with information with regard to other applicants, although Miss Baker had not requested this information prior to the hearing.' Miss Baker told the tribunal the reason why she had not done so was that she had been advised she would be more likely to be granted her modest request if she did not press for information about the other applicants as well. It appeared to all members of the tribunal that information about the qualifications and experience of the other applicants might be very material to their decision in this case.

In this matter the tribunal was more enlightened but it also underlines the problems raised in the issue of disclosure. Although Miss Baker was later allowed full sighting of the documents, the tribunal stressed the importance of the information to their decision making. The equally important aspect of Miss Baker's capacity to marshal an effective case on the basis of the information is ignored but, given the burden of proof, an applicant must have the opportunity to point to concrete evidence. Miss Baker's pessimism over her chances of obtaining anything but the most limited information is equally perturbing.

In the Court of Appeal ruling in *Nasse* v. *Science Research Council*, it was decided that the industrial tribunal could not order or permit disclosure. The judgment of Lord Denning revealed an intriguing definition of the constituents of fairness:

> In the present case, fairness includes fairness to those who make and receive these reports. It also means fairness to the public services and industries and industrial concerns. They have to cope with the problems of discrimination and should be trusted to deal with them fairly.

This concern with protecting rights of others which override those of the applicant must be construed as a hierarchy of rights which hardly squares with the concept of natural justice: to guarantee impartiality and objectivity in order that the law is applied equitably to all. Lord Denning, in an intemperate outburst, went on to rail about the process of discovery and disclosure in these terms: 'They demand to see documents made in confidence and to compel breaches of good faith which is owed to persons who are not parties to the proceedings at all. You might think we were back in the days of the general warrants.'

The teacher is thus trebly disadvantaged. She has to discharge the burden of proof but is disadvantaged by reason of having no legal right to disclosure of the confidential documents which might reveal that proof. Judges reveal their antipathy to the powers vested through statute in bodies such as the EOC and CRE. This publicly expressed hostility permeates the attitudes and influences the decisions of many who are called to sit in judgment. Lord Denning expressed concern lest disclosure leads reports to be neutral but this would be preferable to the subjective, inaccurate and discriminatory assessments that at present militate against women's success in competition for employment.

The hostility displayed by Lord Denning highlights another aspect of the judicial process which further undermines the female position. The interpretation of statutes becomes the common law but the theoretical impartiality expected of judges is illusory. Griffith (1977) suggests that 'public interest in the preservation of a stable society' leads judges to support conventional established interests. If women are to grasp their full entitlement under statute then the system would be in danger; for the judiciary has resorted to extraordinary lengths to ensure that sexism has been enshrined through a hundred years of legal judgments.

In the field of schooling in education, as opposed to employ-ment in education, only one case of alleged discrimination has been tested in the county courts: *Helen Whitfield* v. *Croydon County Council.* Helen Whitfield was a minor and the case was pursued by her mother and next friend. At her co-educational school she and the other girls were allocated to home economics courses while boys were allocated to craft work which included woodwork, metalwork and design technology. At the age of 14 girls transferred to an all-girls school where there was no provision for girls to take such crafts. It was considered essential for girls to study home economics at middle school so they could take the subject to 'O' level at the next school. The case was brought after

Miss Whitfield's mother asked if Helen could take woodwork. The head teacher eventually responded by offering Helen the option of craft work, including woodwork, instead of home economics.

This offer was rejected on the grounds that by opting in she would be the only girl studying the subject. Miss Whitfield's case that she had been less favourably treated on the grounds of her sex under section 22 of the Sex Discrimination Act was rejected on two counts:

1. The home economics course was more advantageous to the girls and it was not perceived that a craft work course was of any greater value.
2. There was no discrimination since boys were also placed in the same position of opting into home economics.

This notorious judgment has done little to promote the case of equal opportunities in schools or to strengthen the power of the EOC. Nevertheless, in more recent years education and persuasion have been held the most effective and politic means of eliminating sex bias and sex discrimination. If schools are to play a major part in the fight for education equality, the areas of the school curriculum in which inequality is fostered need challenging and changing; not only those aspects of the curriculum in which the most glaring sex differences occur but also those sections of the informal curriculum which have a major influence in socialization. Schools need to analyse not only what is taught but process as well as content. This informal curriculum is not only represented through the values, attitudes and expectancies of teachers: the status of women teachers is central to this representation and women teachers share the subordinate role of women everywhere.

The Sex Discrimination Act and Equal Pay Act provide a legal means of pursuing equality and in the cases analysed a number of women in education have attempted to challenge a system which they believed denied them the same opportunities as their male colleagues. The campaign for educational equality launched by Emily Davies in the nineteenth century is logically extended into the twentieth century and many of the insidious attitudes that were present in 1860 can still be detected today. However, if education is a key to change it is axiomatic that women must be afforded that status in education which will enable their female pupils to appreciate that their horizons can be extended. Education must not continue to provide an image of woman as inferior, muted and subservient; education must prove that goals are obtainable. A number of women in teaching have resorted to the Sex Discrimination Act and by this have revealed that they are not content to accept this subordinate image. However, both the conditions which generated their action as well as the judicial processes reveal that sex discrimination continues apace. If education is to be a successful instrument of change then female teachers are necessary role models from which the society of the future may learn. The Sex Discrimination Act had the potential to bring about change; that potential has not been met and equity in education has proved an ill-matched partnership.

Notes

1. The Burnham Committee consists of Representatives of the Secretary of State, teachers and Local Education Authorities. The Committee keeps under review and formulates salary scales and grading structures with the school.
2. (i) In the teaching profession, as in employment generally, the proportion of part-time posts held by women is far greater, both in relation to total employment and in relation to part-time employment than the proportion held by men.
    (ii) This is so in the teaching profession, even though women teachers also exceed men in numbers in full-time posts.
    (iii) The majority of part-time teachers in the employment of the respondent Authority have a Fixed Term type of contract which is said to be less favourable as regards security of employment than the permanent contracts given to most but not all full-time teachers.
    (iv) The differences between the fixed-term contracts and the permanent contracts were not shown by the respondent to be justifiable, irrespective of the sex of the person to whom they are given.
    (v) By making the terms of part-time employment less attractive than those of full-time, the respondents are indirectly discriminating against women under section 1 of the Act and against married women under section 3 since it is shown statistically that a lower proportion of women do take full-time employment and it is to be inferred that their domestic duties make it difficult

to the point of impossibility for many married women to take full-time employment.

(vi) The applicant could not previously take up full-time employment because of her domestic responsibilities and therefore suffered the detriment that she did not enjoy the security of employment that a permanent contract could have given her.

3. The judge in *Saunders* v. *Richmond upon Thames Borough Council* (1977) held that it was lawful to ask differing questions of males and females as long as the result was not discriminatory! Miss Saunders had applied for a job as a golf professional but had not been appointed; during her interview she was asked sex-specific questions. However, in a later particularly significant judgment, Lord Lowry in *Wallace* v. *South-Eastern Education and Library Board* (1980) said that

> only rarely would direct evidence be available of discrimination on the grounds of sex; one is more often left to infer discrimination from the circumstances. If this could not be done, the object of the legislation would be largely defeated, so long as the authority alleged to be guilty of discrimination made no expressly discriminatory statements and did not attempt to justify actions by evidence.

The implication of this is that discriminatory questions are entitled to be used as evidence of discrimination.

References

Byrne, E. M. (1978) *Women and Education*, Tavistock, London.

Cousins, P. (1978) *What's in a Name*, National Council for Civil Liberties (NCCL), London.

Deem, R. (1978) *Women and Schooling*, Routledge & Kegan Paul, London.

DES (Department of Education and Science) (1980) *Statistics of Education*, HMSO, London.

EOC (1978) *Legal Information Bulletin*, 104, January.

Griffith, J. A. G. (1977) *The Politics of the Judiciary*, Fontana, London.

Home Office (1975) White Paper *Equality for Women*, HMSO, London.

Lester, A. and Bindman, G. (1972) *Race and Law*, Penguin, Harmondsworth.

McMullen, J. (1978) *Your Rights at Work, Workers' Guide to Employment Law*, Pluto Press, London.

Partington, G. (1976) *Women Teachers in the 20th Century*, NFER-Nelson, Slough.

Rendel, M. (1976) 'Law as an Instrument of Oppression or Reform', *The Sociology of Law*, University of Keele, Keele.

Richardson, E. (1973) *The Teacher, The School and the Task of Management*, Heinemann, London.

Sachs, A. and Wilson, J. (1979) *Sexism and the Law*, Free Press, New York.

Simpson, L. A. (1969) 'Attitudes of higher education employment agents towards academic women', *comment* Wayne State University, Michigan, 12, 1, 41–6.

Walters, P., Allen, A. J. and Fogarty, M. (1971) *Women in Top Jobs*, Allen & Unwin, London.

Thirteen   *Hilda Davidson*

Unfriendly myths about women teachers

One of the least friendly aspects of schooling from girls' point of view is the relative lack of women in senior management positions in the school. As Lesley Kant shows (Chapter 12), girls and boys are more likely now than in the past to acquire the idea from school that men are in charge, and women are natural subordinates. Why should there be so few women in leadership positions when teaching is a predominantly female profession? This chapter explores the possible causes in one local authority.

The research presented in this chapter forms part of a larger study established by an LEA in conjunction with the Equal Opportunities Commission to examine the secondary schools within that LEA. While the main thrust of the work was concerned with the curriculum it was recognized that teacher attitudes would be crucial to the success or otherwise of any programme for equal opportunity in schools. Information was obtained from returns made by schools to the LEA, questionnaires to schools and individual teachers and in many cases personal interviews with members of staff.

Each secondary school head teacher completed a staffing form listing each member of staff with qualifications, years of teaching experience, subjects taught and academic and/or pastoral responsibilities. The forms showed that there was not a great deal of difference between males (55 per cent) and females (45 per cent) and that there was little change between 1980 and 1983. The

Table 13.1   Percentage of posts held by female and
male teachers in Project LEA in January 1983

	Female	Male
	%	
Head teacher	—	100.0
Deputy head teacher	34.4	65.6
Senior teacher	9.0	91.0
Scale 4	22.0	78.0
Scale 3	34.2	65.8
Scale 2	47.7	52.3
Scale 1	67.3	32.7
N =	887	1101

difference in numbers was not great enough to warrant the
comment that 'higher levels are male dominated, but then, there
are many more male teachers' (Scale 2 male teacher). The actual
numbers may have shown little difference but there was, however,
considerable difference in the positions held.

When the figures in Table 13.1 are compared with those of
Table 13.2 it can be seen that nationally female teachers hold
more of the senior posts.

In the authority examined in this project the position for

Table 13.2   Percentage of posts held by female and
male teachers in England and Wales in January 1983

	Female	Male
	%	
Head teacher	16	84
Deputy head teacher	37	63
Senior teacher	19	81
Scale 4	22	78
Scale 3	37	63
Scale 2	50	50
Scale 1	63	37
N =	110,308	132,308

Source: DES *Statistics of Education* (1983), HMSO, London.

women at the two most senior levels of head teacher and deputy
head deteriorated during the period of the research 1981–3, with
the result that there were no female head teachers and two
schools did not have a female deputy. Twenty-seven of the 34
schools did not have a female senior teacher and 9 did not have
female teachers at senior teacher or scale 4 level. Only 17.6 per
cent of male teachers were on scale 1 but 45.1 per cent of female
teachers were on the lowest scale. When women were in Head
of Department posts it was usually in the traditional areas of
domestic subjects, girls' physical education, English or languages,
although in some schools there were some interesting anomalies:
two were in the design area and one was in the pastoral field. In
these instances the higher scales were not for extra duties in
other areas.

	Heads of Department	*Scale*	*Male*	*Female*
School 1	Woodwork	4	1	
	Metalwork	3	1	
	Art	3	1	
	Cookery & needlework	2		1
School 2	Boys' craft	4	1	
	Girls' craft	3		1
School 3	Heads of house	4	3	
	Heads of house	3		2

It is not just the position held, however, which needs to be
examined but the 'title' and responsibilities which are allocated to
the post. The 'title' given to female deputy heads was in many
cases that of Senior Mistress even when the job for which they
applied and were appointed was that of Deputy Head. Sixteen
female deputies were called Senior/Second Mistress. Only one
man appointed was called Second Master while eleven appointed
either as Academic Registrar or Senior Master were known as
Deputy Head. To be called Senior Mistress does not give the same
status as Deputy Head.

If it is assumed that a future head is being 'trained' while holding
the position of deputy, then the major tasks managed by a head
teacher will be learned as a deputy. A head must be well versed in
day-to-day management, curriculum development, timetabling,

staffing, examinations, etc. and these are the areas of responsibility quite clearly in the hands of the male deputies in the LEA studied. The responsibilities given to female deputies such as girls' welfare, lost property, school bulletin, charities, minutes of meetings, social functions and refreshments cannot be held to give equal status with their male counterparts or training for a future headship. Female deputies know this, as the following quotes show:

> I feel that because I am a woman deputy my career has been held back because of the unequal allocation of duties among the deputies.

> Throughout my career I have progressed through a solid performance at what are considered in educational terms 'low level tasks'. If I am to progress any further in my career it is vital I achieve self-confidence in other areas that are regarded by educators as 'high level tasks'.

Female senior teachers were clearly aware that their roles were mainly pastoral and that this did not fit them to compete with men for deputy headships or headships.

In the mathematics and science areas men outnumbered women (63 per cent and 74 per cent) and also held the majority of the Heads of Faculty and Department posts. There were two mathematics departments and four science departments which were all male and a further nine mathematics and eleven science departments which had only one female teacher. In English and languages the majority of staff was female (66 per cent in each case) but women did not occupy a corresponding majority of senior posts. In fact in two English departments and six language departments where the entire staff, with one exception in each school, was female, it was the one male teacher who had the head of department post.

One common assumption was that it was married women who reduced the overall promotion figures for female teachers. This was not proved to be the case with the study authority. Of all the female teachers (887) in these secondary schools, 72 per cent were married and they held a slightly higher percentage of the posts above scale 1.

Table 13.3 Percentage of female scale posts held by married women in the study authority in January 1983

Deputy head	84.4
Senior teacher	75.0
Scale 4	72.7
Scale 3	72.8
Scale 2	77.6

Promotion

It is argued by some that women do not want headships. Perhaps some do not. However, if they never get the chance to move up from scale 1 then their promotion to senior positions is blocked forever. When promotion does come the way of female teachers it is rarely in the 'important' fields which offer adequate training and the enthusiasm for higher management levels. During the course of the research programme 199 female teachers and 202 male teachers were asked to give interviews or take part in questionnaire surveys. Of these, 64 per cent of the female teachers and 69 per cent of the male teachers agreed to take part. While these teachers may not be considered to be completely representative it is for the reader to decide whether their comments are pertinent or not.

A number of beliefs were given as the 'reasons' why women do not receive promotion and these were examined to see if facts supported the claim.

'Women do not want promotion and responsibility.'

The research did not reveal that there is a low promotion orientation in women teachers. When asked, most of the teachers had a clear idea of their ultimate goal in teaching with only approximately 5 per cent of men and women who did not know. The percentage hoping to reach the top posts was roughly the same for males and females. The figures shown in Table 13.4 do not appear to support the myth that women teachers are not interested in promotion.

Table 13.4 The ultimate goal for the sampled teachers

Goal	Female	Male
Head teacher	9.4	11.9
Deputy head teacher	17.0	13.4
Head of faculty	5.7	7.5
Head of department	28.3	20.9
Head of year/house	15.1	9.0
Adviser	3.8	7.5
Further education	3.8	3.0
LEA administration	—	1.5
Don't know	5.7	4.5
Present post	11.3	20.9

In fact a higher percentage of women than men would like to achieve the position of head of department and posts in charge of pastoral care while nearly twice as many men as women saw their present position as their final goal. The desire to reach their ultimate goal is, however, tempered for women by their awareness of the reality of the situation.

Impossible to rise from scale 1 to anything above scale 2 regardless of any qualifications one might possess (e.g., industrial experience, six years as a Careers Advisory Officer, Social Studies degree before Certificate of Teaching) which do not appear to be sufficient qualifications for a pastoral/career post. (scale 1 female teacher)

It appears to be [authority] policy to have a male as overall head of PE departments, therefore little chance of furthering my career promotion wise. (scale 2 female teacher)

I feel I have the experience and ability necessary for headship, but since there are very few girls' schools in existence and none in [the authority], I doubt whether I will attain my ultimate goal. I shall however apply for any headships advertised within driving distance of my home. Had I remained in [the authority] I might well have been appointed as head of a girls' school. Ironically I prefer co-education but feel that single-sex schools provide more opportunities for the promotion of women. (female deputy head)

Posts in schools are hierarchically arranged and equated with salary. Certain factors are considered to influence promotion and the sampled teachers were presented with a list of thirty-two factors which might be thought to have such influence, such as length of teaching experience, administrative ability, ability to control children, and were asked to rank them. Items which were thought to be very important were then considered. There appeared to be gender differences in the answers to the following: for male teachers there was a closer relationship between 'Experience in a variety of schools' and 'Willingness to move to other areas' than there was for female teachers. Men also considered 'Personal/social contact with people who can influence' and 'Conformity with views of advisers/inspectors' as important factors. Women's responses indicated that they saw advantages for men who were married. This attitude was summed up by the following quote: 'Being married and a parent are helpful to a man but affect a woman adversely.' (scale 3 female teacher) One (male) head teacher claimed that the concentration of women on the lower pay scales represented the 'fact' that they did not want to have promotion: 'it must be understood that women are quite content to leave school at the end of afternoon school and take home their scale 1 salaries with them'. This statement was made 15 minutes after the end of the afternoon session while standing in the staff car park. As there were only three cars apart from his own and the car park was usually full, it would appear that few men let alone women were staying after the end of the afternoon session on that day.

During the study it seemed from my observation that there was little relationship between the scale posts held and staying on after school and it was as likely that both men and women on scale 1 posts stayed behind for professional activities as those on higher posts (see Table 13.5).

Certainly the percentage of women who became involved with these activities was as good as, if not better than, that of their male colleagues. However, the myth was still present that the women did not contribute to the same extent as the men.

The sole basis of consideration for promotion should be professional ability and not the cost of supporting a home, a wife and children. The argument about dependants is never considered in

Table 13.5   Teachers in the case study schools reported to be taking part in extra curricular activities

	Female			Male		
	total staff	taking part in ECA	%	total staff	taking part in ECA	%
Scale 1	47	10	21	18	4	22
Scale 2	21	5	24	37	7	19
Scale 3	5	4	80	35	12	34
Scale 4	7	3	43	15	2	13
Senior teacher	—	—	—	9	3	33

relation to single women who could be supporting elderly parents, which is arguably more expensive than supporting a wife. Married women reported that during job interviews they were questioned on their role outside the school with the implication that it was detrimental to their work in school. Activities and family commitments undertaken by male teachers outside the school were not questioned nor were they considered to be detrimental to their work within the school.

Women teachers are far more career-minded than they are given credit for. However, as in schools in the project LEA, where there is no open advertisement or genuine competition for internal promotion, then the promotion process seems to favour male aspirants.

> '*Women teachers aren't promoted because they are less well qualified than their male colleagues*'

The teachers taking part in the survey reported their 'teaching history' from the time of training (Table 13.6).

It will be seen that more women than men entered the profession with a certificate but 'being a graduate' was placed quite high in the list of factors which influence promotion by both male and female teachers. The argument that women teachers do not further their qualifications is not true of the sample group (see Table 13.7).

When tabulating present posts held by entry graduates and

Table 13.6 Sampled teachers' initial training

		Female	Male
			%	
Teachers' certificate		52.8	39.7
Degree or equivalent		20.8	20.6
Degree + postgrad. cert.		26.4	36.8
	N =	53	68

Note: Some of the men entered the profession without any degree or teacher training.

non-graduates who have attended a course of further professional training, it becomes clear that for the female non-graduates in the sample, completing the course had not significantly affected their present position. Seventy-seven per cent of them are on scales 1 and 2. Some felt that being a graduate was seen as more important than teaching ability. 'Lack of degree qualifications, age, marriage responsibilities are all factors in the minds of governing body members.' (scale 4 female teacher)

A further claim made by male teachers was that women did not apply for courses of further professional training. The figures for those granted secondment for twelve months to three years are shown in Table 13.8.

It is argued that women could not expect to receive as many secondments because they did not apply in the same numbers as their male counterparts. However, they should at least have received the same percentage of places as men if they had been afforded equal opportunities. This was not the case. Only 20 per cent of women who applied to take master's degrees were

Table 13.7 Sampled teachers who attended a degree or diploma-awarding course of further professional training

		Female	Male
			%	
Graduates		33.3	43.6
Non-graduates		44.8	44.8
	N =	53	68

Table 13.8 Percentage of secondments granted to female and male teachers in the secondary schools of the study authority

	Female	Male
	%	
1981/2	21	79
1982/3	37	63
1983/4	28	72

The courses for which these secondments were granted in these three years were as follows:

	Year	Diplomas	B. Ed.	Master's
Female	1981/2	2	—	2
	1982/3	6	—	5
	1983/4	8	—	2
Male	1981/2	2	—	17
	1982/3	10	1	8
	1983/4	16	—	8

successful whereas 31 per cent of men obtained a place. For those following a diploma course the percentages were 53 per cent of the female applicants but 64 per cent of the male. In conversation, a senior official of the authority expressed the opinion that the reason women were not granted secondment was because they were not of the same calibre as the men and without the qualifications of men. This rather places women in a 'Catch 22' situation. They cannot get promotion because they lack qualifications and do not try to get them, but when they do try to get them they are not allowed the opportunity to gain extra qualifications because they lack them in the first place. Men on the other hand are granted secondment to get higher qualifications because they are already well qualified.

The teachers in the sample were also asked about their attendance of part-time courses and the overall picture presented was one of high attendance. The percentage of women attending was greater than that of men (84 per cent female, 67 per cent male) and their reasons were the same, *viz.* to acquire skills, further their careers and improve their teaching performance. In the course of conversation a number of women on scales 1 and 2 said they felt that courses did not help promotion.

1. A scale 1 female teacher with nine years' experience of teaching mathematics felt she would never get any higher and resented this.
2. A scale 1 female drama teacher responsible for the subject throughout the school, including productions, and with many years' experience, felt strongly about still being on scale 1.
3. A scale 1 female English teacher with many years' experience saw no hope of promotion having been told that at 42 she was too old.
4. A scale 2 female English teacher applied for internal promotion but failed because 'they wanted a man' in the position 'to maintain a balance'.

'Women do not have the same number of years
of experience as men'

A group of secondary deputy head teachers expressed the opinion that women did not receive promotion because they did not have the same number of years of experience as men. But the figures for the sampled staff (Table 13.9) did not show a wide variation.

This same group of deputies was also of the opinion that all teachers needed a good solid grounding of about ten years' experience before climbing the promotion ladder and it is at this time that the women are 'out' having children. The 10-year 'pre-promotion' experience does not seem to apply so rigidly for the men. Some men received high levels of promotion in that time (Table 13.10).

Table 13.9   Years of teaching experience for female and male teachers in the sample group

	0–5 years %	6–10 years %	10+ years %	N
Female	18.8	20.8	60.4	53
Male	22.0	26.5	51.5	68

Table 13.10 Percentage of female and male teachers in the sample group with 10 or less years of experience

	Female	Male
	%	
Head teacher	—	—
Deputy head teacher	—	6.6
Senior teacher	—	6.2
Scale 4	19.5	17.9
Scale 3	32.0	34.5
Scale 2	59.1	67.9
N =	53	68

Men moved more quickly from scale 1. Only 1 per cent of men were on that scale after ten years whereas 9 per cent of women were still on scale 1.

'Women no sooner enter the profession than they leave to have babies'

The average woman can expect to complete her family by the age of 30–35 and then be available for continuous employment for the next thirty years. These days, a woman of over 35 is much less likely than her predecessor of 40–50 years ago to have young children to look after. The picture has changed due to the change in social attitudes and increased economic pressure. The low pay of women cannot be accounted for wholly by the fact that some married women have a break in service to bring up a family. It certainly cannot be used as an excuse for the relatively poor position of single women. The male teachers in the sample felt more strongly than the women that mothers should stay at home – 41 per cent of men against 15 per cent of women. The women felt that 'women have much to offer'; 'society should not be deprived of an educated mind'; 'as long as one parent cares for the children it does not matter which one'. The men felt that 'working women cause juvenile delinquency'; 'it would help unemployment with only one breadwinner (male)'; 'male pride would be hurt if the man stayed home while his wife worked'.

The claim that large numbers of women were away having babies was not really upheld in the secondary sphere. In the project LEA the percentage of full-time women teachers who had taken maternity leave in 1981/2 and 1982/3 was 3 per cent for each year. At the same time 1.5 per cent of men and 1.5 per cent of women were absent for periods from one to twelve months yet this was not held to be a reason against promotion. It is assumed that women teachers are married with small children to attend to and that these responsibilities will take precedence over their jobs. Comments by female teachers indicated that they felt that gender was certainly an influence on their promotion hopes: 'I saw the lack of opportunity when I was told by my headmaster that having left teaching for two years to have a family, I should say "good-bye" to real opportunities.' (scale 2 female teacher) Another respondent said she had recognised that she would not achieve her ambitions for promotion, 'when I realized that being "female" was taken as a sign of weakness'. (female deputy head)

> I have attended interviews where there has been great reluctance to employ married women teachers – with children – and I have also been told this as a married teacher with a family. I see no relevance in my perception of my job when statistics can show – regarding ability and experience – that at present in teaching there isn't any significant improvement in the opportunities for women since the 1975 Act. This authority may officially have repealed the old policy through the work of the EOC (but) it has not changed its philosophy. (scale 2: female teacher).

It appears that women are penalized because they have children, whereas men receive promotion because they have children to support.

'Women are absent from work more than men'

A group of male head teachers expressed the view that it was the women who were always absent from school. They did not have figures to substantiate the claim but all agreed that 'everyone knows it is always the women.'

A survey of absences covering all the teachers employed in the secondary schools of the survey LEA was taken over the whole term September–December 1981. This was the time during which the above statements were made. The reasons for absence and the number of days lost were taken from the returns sent in by the secondary schools and covered only the days on which the schools were open. Overall the figures were low for all teachers. Working on the absences reported by schools it was possible to break down the figures into categories (Table 13.11). Some may be subject to variation by individual schools and it was possible that some absences were not reported or not viewed as absences. These figures showed the expected differences but they were slight and were not statistically significant. There could be a change in the pattern if the proposed EEC legislation on paternity leave is accepted and becomes law.

When a male senior teacher saw the above figures he remarked that it was the married women who were away much more for the family than single women. When it was pointed out that there was little difference for married and single women he said that was because the married women put down that they were ill themselves rather than a child being ill. When asked for figures to support that claim his reply was 'everyone knows that's what they do'. He then added that men never did that!

The other reasons for the absence of teachers from the classroom (Table 13.12) again showed little difference for men and women. These figures could be less reliable if 'courses' and items under 'other', e.g., union duties, magistrate duties, jury service, were not all recorded as absences from school. What these figures

Table 13.11   Percentage of time lost by female and male teachers in the study from September to December 1981 for personal or family reasons

	Female	Male
	%	
Personal illness	3.29	2.68
Family	0.19	0.12
N =	858	1080

Table 13.12   Percentage of time lost by female
and male teachers in the study from September
to December 1981 for courses, visits, etc.

| | | *Female* | *Male* |
		%	
Courses		0.39	0.51
School visits		0.15	0.17
Examinations		0.04	0.05
Other		0.17	0.28
	N =	858	1080

indicate is that although men were absent more than women in
these categories, the male absences were considered acceptable.
The small difference between the sexes was certainly not sufficient
to support the claim that women are always absent, causing extra
work for their colleagues.

'Women only work for pin-money'

The assumption that women teachers are married with small
children and that their domestic responsibilities take precedence
over their school duties does not take into account the fact that
not all women are married or have children. The feeling that
women only work for pin-money because they are not the breadwinners is a blanket assumption. It does not appear to be considered that there could be male single-parent families or single
men with elderly parents.

When the sample teachers were asked for their reasons for
entering the profession (see Table 13.13), slightly more women
than men put that it was their first choice as a career.

It seems to be expected also that a married woman's future
career is secondary to her husband's and that career moves will be
dictated by where her husband goes, as the following statements
show:

'my husband's career has always come first', (female deputy
head);
'problem of working around employment location of husband',
(female deputy head).

206   *Reflections on intervention*

Table 13.13   Reasons given by female and male teachers
in the sample group for entering the teaching profession

	Female	Male
Career	30	41
Academic	18	19
Working conditions	11	21
Interest in children	8	7
Respected position	—	4
To use expertise	—	4
Had ability to teach	—	2
Holidays	—	2
Security of employment	—	2
N =	53	68

Note: the teachers were able to give more than one reason

The women teachers saw their own career as equally important as their husbands'. The claim that women work for pin-money because their husbands are in better jobs is not always correct. Neither is the claim ever reversed to suggest that a male teacher married to a doctor, solicitor, etc., is working for pin-money and is therefore not committed to his job and does not need promotion. The time spent by women on their homes is claimed to be detrimental to their school work, but the time a man spends at the golf club or the leisure centre is not seen in a similar light.

> 'Men are the breadwinners, therefore they should
> have the promotion'

To claim that men must have promotion because they are the breadwinners does not take into account the many different responsibilities of women teachers. Not all are married but most none the less have a home to maintain; a number are widowed or divorced and therefore have responsibilities equal to those of a married man. The attitude of many men that promotion must be viewed in relationship to the breadwinner of the family rules out the fact that it should be the best person for the particular post, with the good of the pupils in mind. As one female teacher said:

'To have a family and a husband who has a job is to have two grave disadvantages in [this authority].'

'Men are better teachers and pupils prefer male teachers'

The sampled teachers were asked whether they considered female teachers were more, less or about as effective as male teachers and administrators. Only 2 per cent of women felt that female teachers were less effective but 18 per cent of men felt this to be so. The reasons generally given were lack of discipline, lack of commitment to the job and frequent absences – but two put it more strongly. 'Males are more positive and dependable.' (male senior teacher); 'Women have to develop skills of control and teaching techniques which men have naturally – few women develop them.' (scale 2 male teacher)

As far as women administrators were concerned, 28 per cent of females considered women more effective because they were more conscientious, more thorough and had a greater awareness of the feelings of colleagues. For men 18 per cent felt that women were less capable than men because they were not dedicated and their 'emotional make-up' made it difficult for them to 'enact their duties'. Strong comments were: 'It grates on me to have a woman in any position of authority over me' (scale 3 male teacher); 'Men do not give women a chance because they resent them in authority and expect little of them' (male deputy head).

The majority of male and female teachers felt that pupils did not mind who taught them so long as they were competent. Male teachers reported that students who preferred male teachers did so because males had better discipline, a greater sense of justice and were more effective as teachers while they object to 'bossy females'. Female teachers reported that students preferred male teachers because they were suspicious of women in authority, particularly in non-traditional areas.

It would appear that the tendency of women to occupy the lower status positions in the secondary schools is 'explained' by a number of assumptions about their motivation, qualifications, experience, career pattern and expectations. Not all female teachers, however, are married with young children: women teachers are as varied in age and marital status as any part of the

community; they include the single, married, widowed and divorced, and single parents, as do male teachers also. To see all
women teachers as conforming to a sex-stereotyped pattern is not
only wrong but dangerous in terms of their professional advancement. The evidence from this research does not support the 'myth'
that women are not interested in promotion. Most of the data
reveals that teachers' attitudes and perceptions of sex roles are
often very traditional and presumably therefore contribute to
maintaining sex-role stereotypes. It is vital that all teachers come
to understand their basic sex-role images and expectations, the
effect these have on schools and pupils and how these images and
expectations are sustained by the school. If schools continue to be
run by people with stereotyped attitudes then one of the most
important consequences is the model presented to children by the
profession. The model now presented is 'the male runs the show'.

Where now?

If there are to be changes then everyone in education must be
prepared to try to understand the complexities of the situation.
Male and female teachers as well as LEAs must examine their own
assumptions about masculinity and femininity. Women must no
longer accept the traditional treatment they have previously
accepted as correct. Eliminating discrimination will not be easy
and schools alone cannot bring about the change – they must be
supported by all members of the LEA and school governors. The
letter of the law is not sufficient and there must be a change of
traditional attitudes. To bring this about each LEA should issue a
policy statement about equal opportunities. They should run
training programmes for LEA staff, teachers, governors and
parents, and establish a working party to study ways of eliminating
stereotyping and discrimination. Each school should also establish
a working party to consider ways of eliminating traditional attitudes towards promotion and ensuring that all internal posts are
open to all men and women. Women have for so long accepted a
lower position in the teacher hierarchy that they will need special
encouragement to apply for secondment to improve their qualifications and apply for senior posts.

Is 'girl friendly schooling' really what girls need?

Introduction

'Girl Friendly Schooling' is not a title that would have been used for a conference or a book on girls and schooling a decade ago. Then, we would have been far more likely to title our concern 'Equal Opportunity for Girls' or 'Girls as a Disadvantaged Group', or perhaps 'Sexism in the Curriculum'. In the mid-1970s our analysis of the problem, the strategies we were concerned with, the stock of experience we had to draw on, were all somewhat different from those at work today. Different too would have been our reference point for analogies and ideas. A decade ago, the technological sphere was not quite so pervasively the touchstone for progressive developments – 'user friendly computers' was a term we would scarcely have heard about, far less played with.

In this chapter, the concept of 'girl friendly' schooling is used as a focus for some evaluation of past developments, present strategies and current dilemmas in the area of girls and schooling. The empirical focus here will largely be the developments and strategies at work in the Australian movement for non-sexist education, but the types of activities and concerns discussed here can be found as well in England and in other western countries which have shared a concern about equal opportunity in relation to girls in the period under discussion. However, the relative emphases of different countries may vary, and are certainly affected by differing political and economic climates as well as by the form in which education systems are organized.

The first section of this chapter will trace the way in which initial concerns about the issue of girls and education were framed in the mid-1970s and will discuss some ways in which strategies have moved from a deficit model to a 'girl focused' or 'girl friendly' one. The second section of the chapter will look in more detail at two popular current equal opportunity activities, the concern with language and classroom dynamics and the campaigns to promote non-traditional careers, in order to discuss two potential traps for those working for non-sexist education. These are an over-concern with 'friendliness' or the immediate experience (which incorporates some naivety about schooling in its social context) and an over-ambition about the manipulations which schooling can immediately accomplish. The interpretations being made in this chapter are based in part on a comparison of analyses and strategies concerned with class and those concerned with gender in education.

The shape of developments 1975–84: from disadvantage to the sexually-inclusive curriculum

When an attempt was first made to demonstrate at a national policy level that there was a problem to do with sexism in schooling, the emphasis, not surprisingly, was placed on the 'hard facts' of inequality.[1] Reports set out to show that girls did not receive an equal share of educational resources: they had less money spent on them, had access to less space and equipment, were debarred from certain studies. In addition the reports had, on the one hand, to demonstrate that different patterns of access and achievement by girls could not simply be written off to innate ability or natural urges, and, on the other, to justify from social statistics the necessity and rightness of preparing girls and boys equally for a range of employment and domestic situations rather than continuing to channel them along traditional and stereotyped paths.

Now although the material in the reports contained a host of possibilities for taking action on behalf of girls in school, the action which generally followed from these was both limited and, to some extent, problematic in its directions. In Australia the response made at government level to the reports (that is, when and if there was finally a response) took two main forms. One was to show commitment to the area by making a token appointment of someone to be responsible for the area. The other main form of response was to make some moves to equalize resources for girls: for example, to make it illegal to deny girls entry to subjects which were offered to boys; to give some financial support to projects and publications which added girls to the illustrations in textbooks; to publicize trade careers to girls as well as to boys.

While the moves outlined above were all very important as a first move in recognizing some injustices in the schooling of girls, they were a limited approach to changing anything about the process of schooling. For one thing, in terms of purely quantitative effect in the financing and organizing of public schooling, the moves were very much a tinkering at the edges. In general, the main lines of both the overt and the hidden curriculum stayed as they were: the range of subjects offered, the forms of assessment and selection, were little touched by the moves here. This marginalization of the concerns was partly the result of the ways in which Equal Opportunity appointees, units and resource centres were set up and funded: junior and short-term appointments, uncertain funding, conditions of dealing with schools which necessitated occasional and one-off contacts, etc. all worked against mainstream change in either the centralized directives or the school-based activity (Yates 1984).

Second, as we should have recognized given the extensive experience with and analysis of issues of class and schooling, the moves here were a weak means of providing 'equality'. Certainly both the enacting of legislation to make sure that girls (or boys) were not actually debarred from taking certain subjects and the moves to check the relative amounts of money spent on them were of benefit to some students. However, the types of sociological analyses which started to develop in the early 1970s in England in recognition of the disappointing results of comprehensivization (for example see Young 1971; Open University 1971; Dale, Esland and MacDonald 1976) and the types of schooling policies developed in the Whitlam period in Australia (especially the Karmel

Report which is extensively discussed in D'Cruz and Sheehan 1978) had already made it clear that a simple policy of equal offerings was a naive approach to social equality. Given the very different out-of-school experiences of girls and boys, to give them at school the same offerings, resources and advice was not likely to affect them equally.

Finally, even where stronger moves to encourage girls were being made here, they smacked of a deficit approach, one which blamed the victim. They tried to persuade girls to do what boys were doing (act assertively, choose mathematics, perform competitively). Such programmes may be of value to some individuals, but the problem is (as the much-discussed Headstart project in America had indicated) that overall such approaches are likely to make only marginal gains. This is because where the criteria of success and the norms of teaching and curriculum are still defined in terms of the already dominant group, that group is likely to remain always one step ahead with the other groups trying to catch up. For example, one case study in Australia of a programme which tried to develop assertiveness in girls and sensitivity in boys was not successful because the boys, who already had the solidarity and competitiveness the girls lacked, were able to use these to ridicule and undermine the attempted programme (Waugh and Foster 1978). The general issue has been extensively discussed in more abstract terms by Bourdieu and Passeron (1977).

Moreover, in many ways it is questionable whether the disadvantage model was appropriate for understanding the experience of girls in school. In contrast with class and race, even in 1975 in Australia it could be argued (and was by some, see Yates 1983) that in terms of overall retention and average success rates girls do not lose out at school. Girls were of course losing out in terms of later job entry (both with unemployment rates and with the status and rewards of jobs entered) and in post-school participation in education, as well as in a whole range of acquisitions which are not so easily quantified by statisticians (beliefs about themselves and the world, modes of action, etc.). To some extent too such outcomes might be related to how school treated girls (for example, in channelling them to make certain subject choices, or in reinforcing personality characteristics and beliefs about male and female attributes which lead to assumptions by both job applicants and employers that jobs involving the exercise of authority or involving what is seen as mechanical or dirty work will be inappropriate for women). But this is clearly not the whole picture. The later patterns may be the result of institutional or structural forms which work against women irrespective of the relevance of their educational experience. Work requirements, for example, may themselves be incompatible with women's domestic burdens, and the competitive profit requirement in a free enterprise system can work against women of child-bearing age. Again, a model of disadvantage implies the possibility of overcoming disadvantage through the acquisition of what was lacked. But as many studies of women and language have suggested, such a path to equality when girls and women are at issue is less clear-cut. The taking on of more self-confident, assertive language forms by women may well be interpreted as a sign of aggression and bitchiness rather than as strong and authoritative behaviour (see, for example, Lakoff 1975; Spender 1980); and the question of what might change the tendency for women's motivations to be interpreted as personal and emotional when men's are seen as rational and externally-oriented is obviously a complex one (see, for example, Grieve 1981).

Nevertheless, whatever the problems with the way in which inequalities were being understood and tackled at this time, the public recognition of inequality was a first step in focusing attention on what happened to girls in school, and in the decade since then work on the area has flourished. In Australia, as a result of very vigorous lobbying by those involved, equal opportunity or women's advisers have now been appointed in each state, and in Victoria the Equal Opportunity Unit has grown from one temporary appointee in 1977 to eleven positions funded by the Education Department in 1984. There are also paid appointments by the teachers' unions; funding of projects on sexism by bodies such as TEAC (Transition Education Advisory Committee) and its successor, the Participation and Equity Programme; many conferences on relevant issues and much academic research focused on the area. This is not the place for a full-scale analysis of the ways in which a developing social movement outside education and changing policies, lobbying and strategies within education are intertwined (and sometimes at odds). But it is important to note that changes in our appreciation of the problem have been influenced in particular by work at three levels: the experience of ongoing school-based projects (and the equal opportunity and TEAC officers who service, advise, digest and collate the various projects); the work of academic researchers in education; and developments in feminist theorizing and public practice (including, for example, the types of issues publicized by Equal Opportunity Boards). Aspects of the problem (and sites for intervention) are now being recognized that were either not recognized or only embryonically recognized in the earlier period.

The first of these areas of current action is that of gender relations in classroom dynamics: the behaviour of teachers and students in mixed and single-sex groups, which includes attention to issues such as quantity of participation, use of space, types of encouragement and discouragement, form of language, conversational politics (similar to the sort of material cited in Spender and Sarah 1980; Stanworth 1983 and Kelly 1981). In Victoria, for example, this is an issue which has been probably the most commonly discussed item at the range of school-based and regional in-service discussions which have been held on sexism; it is mentioned in virtually every publication by the Equal Opportunity Unit (for example, in a discussion of teaching computer studies, or on teaching in primary schools) and is the subject of some recent videos and kits produced by that unit. In terms both of practical projects in schools and of the work of researchers in education, there is now a sensitivity to *gender* issues in interpersonal dynamics and a knowledge of a range of substantive findings about these which are largely the product of work of the past decade.

A second area of concern now, which was not mentioned in the mid-1970s, is sexual harassment. The issue was made prominent with a lead editorial and article in *Ms Muffet*, the publication of the Victorian teachers' union's counter-sexism project, in August 1981, and was reported as one of the most popular workshop areas at the Conference on Sexism as an Industrial Issue held by the teachers' unions in Melbourne in October of that year. The issue was one clearly felt strongly by teachers whose consciousness had been raised in relation to issues of sexism, and who experienced personally reactions by their colleagues in the staffroom and the union. Attention here was developed also by moves in the wider community, when the tribunal which met to consider claims of discrimination in employment began to give attention to such pressures. Finally, the issue in some cases at least was being raised by students themselves once they were given conditions that enabled them to speak freely on issues that concerned them. One report from a project involving six schools in an inner-Melbourne suburb reported that: 'Sexual harassment can be seen as the key to unlocking the whole debate on the inequality of education for girls.' (BRUSEC 1982, p. 21) This report also acknowledged that to take such a position represents a considerable development in the thinking about equal opportunity and the problems to be confronted if schooling is to be friendly to girls: 'as our thinking about Equal Opportunity develops, and we become more aware of the power relationships underlying sexism, e.g. sexual harassment as a powerful force operating against women, the more challenging and controversial the Project's ideas and programmes become to the status quo'. (BRUSEC 1982, p. 12)

A third area of current development can be seen in some attempts to re-think the shape of the overall curriculum of a school in the interests of working towards a culture that does justice to and is in women's interests. The moves here are at an early stage and have taken a variety of forms. The term 'sexually-inclusive curriculum' for example, was first used by Jean Blackburn (Blackburn 1982) when trying to talk about an approach which would avoid the imbalance on the one hand of the conventional curriculum which in so many ways made women invisible, and on the other hand, that of the focus of much of the work of non-sexist education, which had treated issues such as raising girls' self-esteem as an isolated problem and had given too little attention to the development of a worthwhile curriculum content for all students. (Many people who have taken up Blackburn's orientation now use the term 'gender-inclusive curriculum', or simply 'inclusive curriculum'.) A rather different approach has been that of writers and workers who talk about 'feminist curriculum' (for example, Dugdale 1983; Spender 1981; and see Weiner in list of unpublished conference papers). Again these writers are concerned with ways in which earlier approaches took piecemeal actions and also with the way in which they were in danger of incorporation, leaving the concern with girls as a marginal and welfare-oriented concern. They argue that those concerned with 'feminist curriculum' should explicitly acknowledge the political nature of their enterprise: that the 'problem' with girls and schooling involves a major critique of existing educational institutions, and that feminists should be concerned not with equal access to what is, but with offering a quite different experience in education (including teaching about how women have been oppressed), and that political battles in working towards this are inevitable.

In terms of practical work towards a more gender-inclusive curriculum in schools, one school-based project in Victoria (Gardner *et al.* 1984; also Fowler 1983) has operated by taking a number of subjects in turn, deconstructing the traditional offerings (both as content and as activity) and working on reconstructions which have as their base both feminist concerns and some respect for worthwhile knowledge. The project has included working on some more tactile and communal dimensions to the year 7 mathematics course, and re-working the history of Australian squatters (early land-settlers). The latter exercise included the usual attention to 'writing women in' by giving attention to the experience of women in colonial life. It also included some games and physical activities as attempts to work out how a culturally, geographically and historically specific concept like squatting could have any meaning for migrant adolescent schoolgirls. A practical strategy of a different type has been the development of a Women's Studies Association by interested teachers. This Association has worked to make Women's Studies one of the prestigious year 12 subjects but also to help women's studies penetrate other subjects.

What the developments and strategies outlined above might be taken as signifying is the following: first, and most superficially, there has been quantitative growth in the concern with the issue of sexism and schooling. In terms of funding, personnel working in the area, and schools and teachers who have been directly confronted by some aspect of work in the area, there has been a slow but exponential growth since 1975. Second, the problem is now seen in far greater complexity: on one side there is attention both to the micro-level of interpersonal relations and language of

students and teachers and, on the other, there is greater recognition of the way in which the problem is embedded in social
relations generally (the work on sexual harassment) and of the
extensive scale of curriculum change that would be needed to
begin to counter this. Third, the understandings and strategies
outlined above have developed, at least in part, by a *focus on girls
and women* as a means of understanding the problem. This is
seen both in feminist theoretical work which filters into the
educational sphere and in the way a number of school projects in
Australia are now beginning to be organized.

In other words, I have been suggesting in this section that a
concept of 'girl friendly schooling' has some significance in label-
ling where the concern with sexism and schooling or the 'problem
of girls' and education has moved: from an initial recognition of a
problem (one whose hidden allegiance to the status quo was not
always recognized) to a recognition both of the complexity of
issues in the area and of the need to focus centrally on girls and
women in resolving them. The foregoing analysis, however, is
merely trying to point to some ways of thinking about strategies
over the past decade. It is not a report on how far concerns about
sexism have now penetrated education and policy generally (an
analysis of which would have a far more pessimistic flavour) nor of
what are the quantitively-measured dominant themes among
teachers. The next section of this chapter will discuss more
extensively two strategies that are currently dominant among
concerned teachers in Australia.

'Girl friendliness' and two current directions

What is a 'user friendly computer'? It might depend on whom
you ask. In the words of the marketing agency, for example,
the 'user friendly computer' is likely to be portrayed as an apt
description for 'your technological friend who is here to help
you'. Not only is the computer programmed in your own language,
so that you will actually be able to use this wonder of modern
high technology, but it is designed to make you feel good by
occasionally giving little pats on the back, or even cartoons for
light relief as you go along. The responses of actual users might

range from those who are made to feel good by using the equipment (they enjoy it, they feel clever, they are able to do things with it) to perhaps the occasional dissenter who has never quite mastered it[2] and is increasingly irritated by its patronizing response. For social theorists who try to work out some broader perspectives on social change, the 'user friendly computer' might represent something else again: a device which is successful in encouraging more and more people and institutions to organize their lives and their society in computer-appropriate forms while making this form of domination appear to be a freely-chosen benefit. So with schooling perhaps we might need to ask, 'What do we mean by girl friendly?', 'What are we trying to draw girls into?' and 'Why do we want to do this?'

'Girl friendly' schooling, like user friendly computers, might be interpreted in many ways. In the first section of this chapter, the term was used as meaning something like 'girl-focused and in their interests', taking it as a positive approach to the problem of sexism in comparison with the apparently even-handed but possibly limited concept of equal opportunity. However, this section of the chapter looks at some problems we might face both in using the term and in the directions at work in current strategies.

The problems with the concept of 'girl friendliness' to be discussed here are these. First, as the computer analogy suggested, an assessment of what is happening can take place at various levels. The obvious interpretation of 'friendliness' is how the experience *feels* to girls. Less obviously, there is a more extended sense of 'friendly', that is, what the institution of schooling does which is *actually* of benefit to girls. Of course what the experience feels like may be an important part of whether it is of benefit but, I want to argue, the relation between these two aspects of the process is by no means unproblematical. Moreover, it may be that the very use of the term will encourage an emphasis on the first of these definitions (the immediate experience), in my argument the more limited one. We may thus be led to ignore some of the issues that sociologists and practitioners in the past two decades have been working through with regard to class and schooling – although I will also argue that the case of girls is not quite parallel to that of class, and there is a somewhat greater rationale for focusing on the immediate experience in the case of girls.

(As it happens, the issues I will raise here regarding an over-emphasis on the immediate experience are not at all the dominant emphasis in the various contributions to this volume. My interpretations were based on emphases at work in Australia. With regard to the chapters in this volume, perhaps the opposite point should be put: given the theme of 'girl friendly schooling', has there been sufficient attention through this volume to the experiences and lives of the girls at school?)

The second type of problem I want to discuss here (by looking at the alternative careers campaign) is not one of strategies which over-emphasize the immediate, since the non-traditional careers campaigns, like GIST and like many of the chapters of this volume, are concerned with producing real changed social outcomes. The problems I will raise here are that if we do want to work towards 'girl friendliness' in this more substantial way, in some important regards we scarcely know where to begin.

'Classroom dynamics' and what school feels like to girls

The extent to which attention to language and classroom dynamics has caught the imagination of teachers and other appointees concerned with intervention in Australia is very striking. Many projects use checklists to monitor what girls and boys and teachers do in school and in class, and it is a subject widely discussed at conferences and in staffrooms, as well as in the many newsletters and publications which circulate among teachers.

The first point to be made about this is that if we are concerned with change in schools, then the question of why a strategy is popular and widely practised deserves analysis as well as the more usual research on the nature of the problem. In the case of language and classroom dynamics, an initial interpretation might suggest that popularity is related to the fact that the associated practices offer something that is immediately do-able (though 'doing' in this case might be simply noticing, monitoring, and discussing them). This is in contrast to the point reached by this period with regard to the concern with and analysis of class biases in schooling – among radical teachers and theorists in the late 1970s, both in England and Australia, there was a loss of confidence and a lack of direction as to what might be done with working-class students.[3] Moreover, the attention to monitoring interpersonal dynamics could be a source of enthusiasm both for those in the mainstream of liberal approaches to education and for those most solidly involved in feminism. For the former, this could be an exercise in empirically checking the facts of what went on in school: a quantifiable way to begin to discuss equality and fairness. For the latter, one of the key contributions of feminism to analysing the oppression, alienation or disadvantaging of girls and women was the theme that 'the personal is political' (see Stanley and Wise 1983). So not only did attention to interpersonal dynamics reveal new things about what was going on in the classroom, but there was a rationale about why this was important and about why change in this regard might really be seen as getting somewhere.

Nevertheless, there are some potential traps in an over-attention to classroom dynamics and to making school 'a nice place to be'. For a start, although the details of such studies are often ambiguous, it does seem that for some time more girls than boys have completed secondary school in Victoria, and often girls are more positive and enthusiastic about their experience of school than are boys. Girls may have inferiority experiences reinforced by school, particularly in certain subjects, but we should not exaggerate the extent to which the problem has simply been one of girls feeling uncomfortable in that environment.

Some similar points may be made about the extent to which the issue is to give girls power within the school environment. If we again take the experience of the Victorian radical education movement of the late 1960s and early 1970s, we can see that in various ways (for example, in community schools, in negotiated curricula) there were attempts to prepare students to be powerful and active by allowing them, in fact directing them, to take considerable control of their lives at school and to transform school structures accordingly. Gradually through the 1970s some disillusionment with these approaches in their original form was seen. The people and institutions involved, without renouncing their ideals or their concern with the lives of the students, are now increasingly giving attention to what types of knowledge are 'enabling' in the wider society, and devising ways to make sure that students gain these.[4]

As noted earlier, with gender even more than with class, a

concern with the phenomenological meaning of interactions is important. However, attention should not be given to the process or form of the teaching-learning situation in a way which detaches this from the content of the exchange and from the wider structures in which the school is embedded. To some extent the focus on gender dynamics is valuable in beginning to make such connections. It provides a means for moving from the micro to the macro, for giving students some insight into gender relationships, and this is an important and legitimate subject for their education. On the other hand, the school is not the society and the forms of the former do not automatically produce the same forms in the latter (Bernstein 1971; Yates 1983; and see note 4). The compliance of students with a different balance of power between boys and girls may be achieved because of the framework of the teacher's authority and power, with only limited gains in the long term. Moreover, because of the immediacy of the rewards when concentrating on the immediate experience, there has in Victoria been relatively less attention to thinking about some of the deeper effects of arrangements of subject-teaching.

That the issues that I am discussing here have raised themselves as a practical and not just theoretical dilemma can also be seen in the split between those whose concern is with interpersonal relationships and who, as a result, resist any moves to impose central compulsions on what school and teachers do, as well as any formal assessment of this, and those whose concern is more with the outside structural arrangements that shape women's fate, and who wish to support forms of compulsion which will ensure certain types of common learning for girls and boys and/or will prevent girls taking 'short-sighted' options which will circumscribe their later chances.

Non-traditional careers and the problem of what is a 'friendly'
act in an age of unemployment and rapid social transformations

Since the concern with equal opportunity for girls has been recognized with government funding in Australia, a considerable part of this funding (possibly a disproportionate part) has been channelled into promotions to persuade girls to take on non-traditional jobs, in particular manual trades requiring apprenticeships. Photographic kits, booklets, videos, registers of speakers, in-services for careers teachers, 'try-a-trade' days for female students, have all been mounted. As well there has been a host of research on the attitudes of girls and their parents to their future careers (for example, Saha 1982). All, to date, to very little effect (see, for example, Foster 1984): girls may try out and enjoy trade activities at school, but the job patterns of girls and boys have remained very traditional (other than, that is, for the steadily mounting unemployment).

The strategies and the dilemmas I am discussing here bear some similarities to strategies in England such as the GIST project. However, there are some differences of emphasis. The campaigns in Australia on which my discussion is based have been concerned with direct careers advice, especially to girls who will leave school before year 12, and have focused a good deal on apprenticeship-level jobs. GIST was especially concerned with influencing subject-choice in schools and also had a rather greater emphasis on the higher-level careers and the requirements of university science courses. Much of the work in Australia has been carried out by government-funded equal opportunity workers, who are usually ex-teachers rather than women coming from academic fields, in association with school projects. As a result there has been reasonable access to facilities for producing materials and for holding meetings, but there has been less attention to an academic justification and monitoring of procedures such as GIST attempted. It may be of interest that in the period under discussion, where there were government guidelines for evaluation of the Australian projects,[5] they usually required demonstrations of wide participation in the on-going project and dissemination of news about it rather than a product-evaluation of results.

In the case of the non-traditional careers strategies, there are, again, two sorts of questions to be raised. For researchers and theorists an important question is why have such campaigns been popular, to what concerns of teachers, parents and policy-makers do they speak? For teachers and workers in the field of equal opportunity in schools, the questions are why have these campaigns had so little success in producing measurable change, and can and should they be revamped to be made more effective?

In their social location, the origins of the alternative careers campaigns were twofold. First, they stemmed out of the equal opportunities arguments most favoured in the early period. Although at any time those working in the field of equal opportunity encompass a variety of political positions, in the mid-1970s there was quite a commonality of approach. This emphasized a criticism of claims of differences between girls and boys, an acceptance that different outcomes were due to social stereotyping, and a working towards change in which sex differences would not be a major part of the social fabric: in particular, that there should not be stereotyping of role and of paid work by gender. (In the period since then however, feminist theorizing has begun to give more attention to focusing on what has been specific to women, especially their involvement with child rearing and family, so that feminist models of change are not always cast in an androgynous mould. See, for example, Eisenstein 1984; Elshtain 1981; O'Brien 1981). As well, there was a wide attention in the late 1970s to the range of jobs which girls entered and the contribution of schooling to this because it was becoming very apparent that, due to technological change, the relatively small range of traditional female jobs was being eroded at a rapid rate (*Girls, School and Society* 1975; Sweet 1980a, 1980b; Byrne 1978; Deem 1980).

In terms of problems with these campaigns and accounting for their apparent lack of success, we might return to the concept of 'girl friendliness'. To some extent, the approaches here might be accused of not being 'friendly' to the girls at whom they were directed in the sense of either the immediate experience or in the wider sense. In the immediate sense, the problem is that the videos and kits can take the form of fairly crude propaganda, propaganda which does not take account of or connect with the current realities of the students. It is schooling trying to preach to its students about what is best for them. Such approaches often fail to take account of why boyfriends and their views, and the prospect of marriage and babies, *are* so much more powerful an immediate reality; nor do they always see the class division between students and the glossy figures portrayed (cf. McRobbie and McCabe 1981). In one video showing girls in non-traditional careers, all appear to be thoroughly middle class, at least two of them announce that they took up a trade after trying and rejecting tertiary education, and none of them are seen to do it as an alternative to the factory, the shop or the office, not to mention the dole (and a similar pattern is revealed in the projects and cases reported by Foster 1984). As well initially, though less so today, the campaigns did not adequately take account of the competition and the isolation faced by girls seeking apprenticeships.

The strategies here seem to have taken little account of the work that has been done on the culture of girls, especially working-class girls, and of schoolgirl 'resistance' (such as McRobbie and McCabe 1981; Thomas 1980). Yet the fault here is not simply on one side. Sociological studies which produce further understandings of what life is like for girls at school often circulate in a different world (or discourse, to use the current jargon) to those concerned with doing something to produce change through education.[6]

In the wider sense of 'girl friendly', the idea of acting for girls, it now seems that one could also raise questions not just about the form of the teaching involved but regarding the directions involved in the campaigns. First of all, it is clear, given total job vacancies and registered unemployed and given the predictions of most economists and politicians, that high unemployment, and especially youth unemployment, will continue even if we were to rearrange somewhat the availability of jobs (for a good discussion of some campaigns and the possibilities see Earley 1981). So what do the campaigns do for the potential unemployed? Might there not be a danger of a new form of 'blaming the victim' for her failure to take the jobs portrayed? Questions have also been raised about whether the campaigns are not doing more to persuade boys to enter non-traditional jobs such as kindergarten teaching rather than expanding the possibilities for girls (BRUSEC 1982).

Second, given that part of the impetus of these initiatives was to reduce the relative extent of girls' and women's unemployment, has there been concentration on the right types of jobs? The area of manual skilled trades is one where employment is decreasing due to automation. Similarly, the associated campaign to ensure that girls continue with mathematics was based on the premise that 'All the indications are that the career areas in which there will be growth in the 1980s and 1990s are mining, finance and related business services, and those with a technological orientation, requiring such secondary subjects as double unit mathematics, physics and chemistry.' (Jones, Reading and Thurgood 1981) But are the indications in this regard so clear? It might be that although new types of jobs are opening in these technical areas, the total job growth will not be high, due to the effects of computerization. The potential for real growth may be in the area of personal services.[7]

Third, questions have been raised about whether the alternative jobs campaigns might have the effect of devaluing traditional female areas of employment, such as office work, and/or 'inadvertently increasing the prestige of the technological over human and environmental values' (BRUSEC 1982).

Although these questions raise some negative issues concerning 'non-traditional' jobs campaigns this is not all that is to be said about them. They did have the effect of combating some very sexist elements of traditional careers counselling and resources (see Allen 1978). As well, when used sensitively by teachers, they may work very well to inform students about the range of jobs that exists in society and about areas of developing unemployment, and to open up some discussions about the nature of work and gender relations in it. Finally, some of the practical activities associated with the campaigns (the learning of additional manual skills, greater help with mathematics) may be of value in themselves, no matter what paid job (or lack of it) the students eventually acquire.

Here I am suggesting that although there are some problems with the way the non-traditional careers strategies have operated, there is equally a problem in accepting that they be evaluated only in terms of quantifiable immediate change in who does what. Schooling *is* a limited venue for producing social change, but it does help to form the consciousness of the next generation, so the *educational* aspects of the attention to non-traditional careers should not be dismissed.

Nevertheless, I wished to draw attention to some problems with the types of interventions both because they have attracted so much support and because they are symptomatic of the difficulties in our present era of trying to develop schooling which offers the best basis for development in the future of the students in it. In so far as schooling is seen as a preparation for productive life, teachers are faced with trying to have some answers about where technology and its political and economic control are going, when politicians, economists and scientists are at odds about this. I could have argued to some similar conclusions about social values and the subject-teaching in these areas by looking at some differences among feminist theorists about what is to be valued and why (the breaking down of the public and private? a liberatory ethos? the recognition of certain biological necessities? a relativist or non-relativist morality? etc.). Again, I am not trying to suggest that curriculum is or should be a form of propaganda for a certain ideology. But an understanding of what we are valuing and where we want to go must be inherent in the curriculum selection and teaching process.

In the first part of this chapter I argued that we do need in schooling to be acting in ways that are 'friendly' to girls, that value their specific experience. In the second section I have been suggesting that we also need to beware of becoming too caught up in immediate concerns and actions that have immediate pay-offs. We need to do some careful thinking about what type of schooling, in particular what range of content, is a fair, useful and valuable experience in our current era.

Notes

1. Much of the initial activity was associated with the impetus and funding given by the United Nations move to designate 1975 International Women's Year. In Australia, a national report to the Australian Schools Commission, *Girls, School and Society* (1975) was published that year and was followed by various State Committees of Inquiry and further reports in the next four years. A useful discussion of starting points in Britain is Byrne (1978) and the introductions to Deem (1980) and Acker et al. (1984) which both provide some introduction to the initial activity as well as comments on the way in which the issue was largely ignored until the mid-1970s.
2. I could not think of a gender-neutral synonym here, but perhaps the loaded term is appropriate anyway.
3. This is shown in general by the turning to forms of reproduction analysis, see, for example, Young and Whitty (1977), especially the introduction. Even recent, more sensitive and unmechanistic studies

such as Connell *et al.* (1982) are very sketchy and unclear as to what action might follow from their analysis. Some interesting related points are raised in the discussion of the various journals of radical teachers in England by Clark and Davies (1981); and in the discussion of the social location of strategies and analyses of recent years by Wexler (1981).

4. In Australia, VSTA (1971) is a collection of documents from the early period, and Ashenden *et al.* (1984) and, to a lesser extent, Connell *et al.* (1982) an example of where some of those involved have moved. Some interesting analyses of problems with the early emphasis on the relations between students and teachers are Hinkson (1977) and White (1978), and an account by a teacher involved in a community school of changes it has moved through is Freeman (1982). Similar movements can be seen in English writings on the sociology of education from 1971 onwards, for example compare Young (1971) with Young and Whitty (1977). Bernstein (1971; 1975) and Sharp and Green (1975) are accounts which raise with some subtlety ways in which apparently progressive and democratic approaches at school level are not altering the power relations in the ways expected.

5. My analysis here does not adequately reflect the variety of projects taking place in Australia in the last five years, especially differences between states.

6. McRobbie and McCabe (1981) is an exception to this pattern. My comments were based on work in Australia.

7. This is argued in an analysis of the current and future state of the Australian workforce by the man who is now Minister of Science and Technology. See Jones (1982), especially his list of the ten characteristics of future work opportunities, p. 239, *none* of which seem to support the analysis cited in the text.

References

(For further details of Australian references, readers could write to the Victorian Equal Opportunity Resource Centre, c/o Northern Regional Office, Victorian Education Department, Melbourne, Victoria, Australia.)

Acker, S., Megarry, J., Nisbet, S. and Hoyle, E. (eds) (1984) *World Yearbook of Education 1984: Women and Education*, Kogan Page, London.

Allan, M. (1978) 'Talking to some purpose: counter-sexist strategies in school counselling', *Radical Education Dossier*, 6.

Ashenden, D., Blackburn, J., Hannan, B. and White, D. (1984),

'Manifesto for a democratic curriculum', *The Australian Teacher*, 7, 13–20.

Bernstein, B. (1971) 'On the classification and framing of educational knowledge', in Young, M. F. D. (ed.) *Knowledge and Control*, Cassell, Collier & Macmillan, London.

Bernstein, B. (1975) 'Class and Pedagogies: Visible and Invisible', in B. Bernstein, *Class, Codes and Control*, vol. 3, Routledge & Kegan Paul, London.

Blackburn, J. (1982) 'Becoming equally human: girls and secondary curriculum', *VISE News* (Victorian Institute of Secondary Education, 582 St Kilda Road, Melbourne 3004, Australia), 31, 16–22.

Bourdieu, P. and Passeron, J–P. (1977) *Reproduction in Education, Society and Culture*, trans. R. Nice, Sage, London.

Brusec (1982) (Brunswick Secondary Education Committee) *Equal Opportunities Project 1982 Report*, TEAC (Transition Education Advisory Committee), 582 St Kilda Road, Melbourne 3004.

Byrne, E. (1978) *Women and Education*, Tavistock, London.

Clark, M. and Davies, D. (1981) 'Radical education: the pedagogical subtext', in M. Lawn and L. Barton (eds) *Re-thinking Curriculum Studies*, Croom Helm, London.

Connell, R., Ashenden, D., Kessler, S. and Dowsett, G. (1982) *Making the Difference*, Allen & Unwin, Sydney.

Cosin, B. R. (ed.) (1971) *School and Society: A Sociological Reader*, (2nd rev. edn 1977), Routledge & Kegan Paul/Open University, London.

Dale, R., Esland, G. and MacDonald, M. (eds) (1976) *Schooling and Capitalism*, Routledge & Kegan Paul/Open University, London.

D'Cruz, J. V. and Sheehan, P. (eds) (1978) *The Renewal of Australian Schools*, (2nd edn), Australian Council for Educational Research, Melbourne.

Deem, R. (ed.) (1980) *Schooling for Women's Work*, Routledge & Kegan Paul, London.

Dugdale, A. (1983) 'Feminist curriculum vs. non-sexist curriculum', *Bluestocking* (Periodical of the Australian Women's Education Coalition), 44, 1–2.

Earley, P. (1981) 'Girls, school and work: technological change and female entry into non-traditional work areas', *Australian Journal of Education*, 25, (3), 269–87.

Eisenstein, H. (1984) *Contemporary Feminist Thought*, Allen & Unwin, London.

Elshtain, J. B. (1981) *Public Man, Private Women*, Princeton University Press, Princeton N.J.

Foster, V. (1984) *Changing Choices: Girls, School and Work*, Hale & Ironmonger, Sydney.

Fowler, R. (1983) 'Sexually inclusive curriculum', *The Victorian Teacher*, 2, (2), 12–17.

Freeman, G. (1982) *Small School in a State of Change*, Deakin University Press and Victorian Secondary Teacher Association, Geelong.

Gardner, K., Roughead, C., Vale, C. and Borthwick, A. (1984) 'Sexually inclusive curriculum discussion papers from Exhibition High School', *Project Report No. 5*, Transition Education Advisory Committee, 582 St Kilda Road, Melbourne 3004.

Girls, *School and Society* (1975) Report by a Study Group to the Australian Schools Commission, Australian Government Printing Service, Canberra.

Grieve, N. (1981) 'Beyond Sexual Stereotypes. Androgyny: A Model or an Ideal?', in N. Grieve and P. Grimshaw (eds), *Australian Women*, Oxford University Press, Oxford.

Hinkson, J. (1977) 'The emergence of education as therapeutic management of an unconstrained self', unpublished Ph.D. dissertation, Centre for the Study of Innovation in Education, School of Education, La Trobe University, Bundoora, Victoria, Australia.

Jones, A., Reading, D. and Thurgood, P. (1981) 'Transition Education Girls' Project: background information', unpublished mimeo.

Jones, B. (1982) *Sleepers, Wake! Technology and the Future of Work*, Oxford University Press, London.

Kelly, A. (ed.) (1981) *The Missing Half: Girls and Science Education*, Manchester University Press, Manchester.

Lakoff, R. (1975) *Language and Women's Place*, Harper & Row, New York.

McRobbie, A. and McCabe, T. (eds) (1981) *Feminism for Girls: An Adventure Story*, Routledge & Kegan Paul, London.

Ms. *Muffet* (1981) Periodical of the Joint TTUV, VSTA and VTU Elimination of Sexism in Education Project, c/o Victorian Teachers' Union. August, PO Box 456, Camberwell, Victoria 3124, Australia.

O'Brien, M. (1981) *The Politics of Reproduction*, Routledge & Kegan Paul, Boston.

Open University (1971) *School and Society*, Routledge and Kegan Paul/ Open University, London.

Saha, L. (1982) 'Gender, school attainment and occupational plans: determinants of aspirations and expectations among Australian urban school leavers', *Australian Journal of Education*, 26 (3), 247–65.

Sharp, R. and Green, A. (1975) *Education and Social Control*, Routledge & Kegan Paul, London.

Spender, D. (1980) *Man Made Language*, Routledge & Kegan Paul, London.

Spender, D. (1981) 'Education: The Patriarchal Paradigm and the Response to Feminism', in Spender, D. (ed.), *Men's Studies Modified*, Pergamon, Oxford.

Spender, D. and Sarah, E. (eds) (1980) *Learning to Lose*, The Women's Press, London.

Stanley, L. and Wise, S. (1983) *Breaking Out: Feminist Consciousness and Feminist Research*, Routledge & Kegan Paul, London.

Stanworth, M. (1983) *Gender and Schooling*, Hutchinson, London.

Sweet, R. (1980a) 'An analysis of trends in the teenage labour market in NSW 1971–1976', *Research Report*, New South Wales Department of Technical and Further Education, Sydney.

Sweet, R. (1980b) 'The new marginal workers: teenage part-time employment in Australia in the 1970s', *Research Report*, New South Wales Department of Technical and Further Education, Sydney.

Thomas, C. (1980) 'Girls and Counter-school Culture', in D. McCallum and U. Ozolins (eds) *Melbourne Working Papers 1980*, University of Melbourne, Melbourne.

VSTA (Victorian Secondary Teachers' Association) (1971) *Secondary Curriculum*, VSTA, Elizabeth Street, Richmond, Victoria 3121, Australia.

Waugh, P. and Foster, V. (1978) 'Education and the "Down-Girl" Principle', *Refractory Girl*, 16.

Wexler, P. (1981) 'Body and Soul: Sources of Social Change and Strategies of Education', *British Journal of Sociological Education*, 2 (3), October, 247–61.

White, D. (1978) 'Create your own compliance: the Karmel prospect', in J. V. D'Cruz and P. Sheehan (eds) *The Renewal of Australian Schools*, (2nd edn), Australian Council for Educational Research, Melbourne.

Yates, L. (1983) 'The theory and practice of counter-sexist education in schools', *Discourse* (The Australian Journal of Educational Studies), 3(2), 33–44.

Yates, L. (1984) ' "Curriculum becomes our way of contradicting biology and culture" – an outline of some dilemmas for non-sexist education', *Australian Journal of Education*.

Young, M. F. D. (ed.) (1971) *Knowledge and Control*, Cassell, Collier & Macmillan, London.

Young, M. and Whitty, G. (eds) (1977) *Society, State and Schooling*, Falmer Press, Ringmer.

Editorial note

This book started by challenging two myths about schoolgirls: that they are not doing well at school and that their futures will be dominated by an unpaid role as wife and mother. The third section contains a rebuttal of some parallel and equally pervasive myths about women teachers. Women teachers are as well qualified on entry to the profession as men and apply in equal numbers for secondment to take further qualifications. The supposition that the lower status of women in teaching can be ascribed to their domestic responsibilities appears to be a prejudice on the part of male decision makers. Women are penalized for having children, in contrast to men who receive promotion on the grounds that they have children to support.

In Chapter 5 it was argued that girls do not lack interest in science and technology but are simply bored with the limited horizons of these subjects at school. Similarly, Hilda Davidson argues that women are not unambitious for promotion and responsibility, but that their aspirations are depressed by the discrimination, direct or indirect, which they encounter.

A firmer use of legislative powers, as advocated by Lynda Carr, could pioneer the kind of attitude change needed on the part of the gatekeepers of power and responsibility. However, Lesley Kant's comprehensive review of the process by which tribunals arrive at their judgments on sex discrimination shows how pervasively myths about women and double standards applied to the two sexes are undermining the intended force of legislation and dimming the prospects for removal of barriers to female opportunity.

The last chapter of the book analyses how we have now begun to move away from a model of women and girls as deficient males towards a more concrete understanding of the real and ideological barriers confronting them. Yet progress is slow. The failure so far parallels the disappointing results of comprehensivization in reducing class inequalities in educational outcomes. Yates argues that so long as the norms of teaching and the curriculum are still defined in terms of the dominant group (the middle-class, pre-university student; boys), then the subordinate groups (the working class; girls) can never catch up. Equal opportunity, in policy and practice, has been marginalized, and until it is incorporated into mainstream change a genuine shift towards girl friendliness will not take place. Yates concludes that we need a sexually inclusive curriculum, and that current initiatives on classroom dynamics and non-traditional careers should not be allowed to devalue the traditional strengths and achievements of the female sex.

Her argument nevertheless confines the debate to what happens within the walls of the school, and addresses only tangentially the issue of the relative power of women as a group within society. Arguments for persuading more girls into science and technology have rightly been criticized both for employing a deficit model of girls, by implying that the fault lay in their motivation and attitudes, and for the implicit and to some extent unexamined assumption that there are more good jobs available in science and technology, and so women should have a bite at the cherry too.

But these are not the sole arguments for breaking down sexual demarcation in the curriculum. Female exclusion from science and technology debilitates female citizens, cuts them off from significant perspectives for understanding the world we live in, and contributes to their relatively weak presence in political power structures. It is important that full weight be given to the personal and community services that women have traditionally carried out, and to the humanistic values which have resided, more by necessity perhaps than aptitude, with women. But in advanced industrial societies those who understand and develop the technology will continue to wield considerable power. The scenario of women servicing and caring for the weak and helpless by-products of a male dominated technology-led society cannot be an attractive one for feminists. Is it science and technology themselves which are dangerous, or the uses to which they are put by a society skewed towards so-called masculine values? So long as an unequal sexual division of labour continues, the contribution of women, which may prove to be more involved, more humanistic than men's, cannot be engaged for the benefit of society, nor incidentally, can men's different approach, if it proves to be so, to the care of children and old people, be fully utilized. It could be argued that the sacrificial female attitude to caring for others is itself one of the root causes of continuing dependency. If those who have always been dependent and subordinate come to occupy positions of genuine power rather than indirect influence, the relations of power and dependency themselves are bound to change.

Nor should we let an unemployment rate of 15 per cent or more disguise the fact that a great many people are still employed, over 40 per cent of them women. Some women will probably continue to take a break from paid employment while their children are very young, but the average woman will face at least 25 years in the labour market after her youngest child has gone to school. For many single or divorced mothers, the choice of staying at home is not really available. New definitions of women's work imply new relationships between men and women in the home, as well as at work, and there are educational implications for the way we prepare boys for adult life. Girl friendly schooling may be only an interim concept in a programme of educational innovation, subversion or revolution (according to your viewpoint), in which it is to be hoped that schooling will ultimately cease to reproduce the old relations of power and subordination between the sexes.

Bibliography

Acker, S. (1983) 'Women and teaching: A semi-detached sociology of a semi-profession' in Walker, S. and Barton, L. (eds) *Gender, Class and Education*, Falmer Press, Barcombe.

—— (1984) 'Women in Higher Education: what is the problem?' in Acker, S. and Warren Piper, D. (eds) *Is Higher Education Fair to Women?*, SRHE & NFER-Nelson, Slough.

Adams, C. (1984) 'The significance of gender in teacher attitudes towards sex equality: a case study of an in-service course', unpublished MA dissertation, University of London.

Allan, M. (1978) 'Talking to some purpose: counter-sexist strategies in school counselling', *Radical Education Dossier*, 6.

Allsop, T., and Woolnough, B. (1981), 'A technological flavour', *Times Educational Supplement*, 18 Sept.

Ashenden, D., Blackburn, J., Hannan, B. and White, D. (1984) 'Manifesto for a democratic curriculum', *The Australian Teacher*, 7, 13–20.

Association for Science Education (ASE) (1979) *Alternatives for Science Education: A Consultative Document*.

Bernstein, B. (1971) 'On the classification and framing of educational knowledge' in Young, M. F. D. (ed.) *Knowledge and Control*, Cassell, Collier & Macmillan, London.

—— (1975) 'Class and Pedagogies: Visible and Invisible', in B. Bernstein, *Class, Codes and Control*, vol. 3, Routledge & Kegan Paul, London.

Blackburn, J. (1982) 'Becoming equally human: girls and secondary curriculum' *VISE News* (Victorian Institute of Secondary Education 582 St Kilda Road, Melbourne 3004, Australia), 31, 16–22.

Bloomfield, J. (1984) 'Option scheme management for equal opportunity', paper presented at Girl Friendly Schooling Conference, 11–13 Sept, Manchester Polytechnic.

Bourdieu, P. and Passeron, J-P. (1977) *Reproduction in Education, Society and Culture*, trans. R. Nice, Sage, London.

BRUSEC (1982) (Brunswick Secondary Education Committee) *Equal Opportunities Project 1982 Report*, TEAC (Transition Education Advisory Committee), 582 St Kilda Road, Melbourne 3004.

Buchan, L. (1980) 'It's a good job for a girl (but an awful career for a woman!)' in *Learning to Lose: Sexism and Education*, Spender, D. and Sarah, E. (eds) The Women's Press, London.

Byrne, E. (1978) *Women and Education*, Tavistock, London.

Chivers, G. E. and Marshall, P. (1983) 'Attitudes and experiences of some young British women entering engineering education and training courses', paper presented at Girls and Science and Technology Conference, Oslo, Sept.

Clark, M. and Davies, D. (1981) 'Radical education: the pedagogical subtext' in M. Lawn and L. Barton (eds) *Re-thinking Curriculum Studies*, Croom Helm, London.

Clwyd County Council/EOC (1983) *Equal Opportunities and the Secondary School Curriculum*, EOC, Manchester.

Cockcroft, W. H. (Chairman) (1982) *Mathematics Counts: A Report of the Committee of Inquiry into the Teaching of Mathematics in Schools*, HMSO, London.

Cohen, J. (1977) *Statistical Power Analysis for the Behavioral Sciences*, Academic Press, New York.

Connell, R., Ashenden, D., Kessler, S., and Dowsett, G. (1982) *Making the Difference*, Allen & Unwin, Sydney.

Cosin, B. R. (ed) (1971) *School and Society: A Sociological Reader* (2nd rev. edn 1977), Routledge and Kegan Paul/Open University, London.

Cousins, P. (1978) *What's in a Name*, NCCL (National Council for Civil Liberties), London.

Dale, R., Esland, G. and MacDonald, M. (eds) (1976) *Schooling and Capitalism*, Routledge & Kegan Paul/Open University, London.

D'Cruz, J. V. and Sheehan, P. (eds) (1978) *The Renewal of Australian Schools* (2nd edn), Australian Council for Educational Research, Melbourne.

Deem, R. (1978) *Women and Schooling*, Routledge & Kegan Paul, London.

236   *Bibliography*

—— (ed.) (1980) *Schooling for Women's Work*, Routledge & Kegan Paul, London.
DES (Department of Education and Science) (1975) *Education Survey 21: Curricular Differences for Boys and Girls*, HMSO, London.
—— (1976) *Statistics of Education*, HMSO, London.
—— (1978) *Primary Education in England: A Survey by HM Inspectors of Schools*, HMSO, London.
—— (1980) *Statistics of Education*, HMSO, London.
—— (1980) *Girls and Science: HMI Matters for Discussion 13*, HMSO, London.
—— (1981) *Circular 6: The School Curriculum*, HMSO, London.
—— (1981) *Statistics of Teachers in Service in England and Wales*, HMSO, London.
—— (1982) *Science Education in Schools: A Consultative Document*, HMSO, London.
—— (1983) *Circular 8: The School Curriculum*, HMSO, London.
—— (1983) *Statistics of Education*, HMSO, London.
—— (1984) *Assessment of Performance Unit: Science Age 15, Report Number 2*, DES, London.
—— (1984) *Circular 3: Initial Teacher Training: Approval of Courses*, HMSO, London.
—— (1984) *Organisation and Content of the 5–16 Curriculum*, HMSO, London.
—— (1984) *Report by HM Inspectors on the Effects of Local Authority Expenditure Policies on Education Provision in England 1983*, HMSO, London.
—— (1984) *Special Project: A Report on Equal Opportunities*, Coventry LEA, Coventry.
Dugdale, A. (1983) 'Feminist curriculum vs. non-sexist curriculum', *Bluestocking* (periodical of the Australian Women's Education Coalition), 44, 1–2.

Earley, P. (1981) 'Girls, school and work: technological change and female entry into non-traditional work areas', *Australian Journal of Education*, 25(3), 269–87.
Eisenstein, H. (1984) *Contemporary Feminist Thought*, Allen & Unwin, London.
Elshtain, J. B. (1981) *Public Man, Private Women*, Princeton University Press, Princeton, NJ.
EOC (Equal Opportunities Commission) (1978) *Legal Information Bulletin*, 104, January, EOC, Manchester.
——(1979) *Do You Provide Equal Educational Opportunities?* (revised edn EOC 1982).
——(1981) *Education of Girls – A Statistical Analysis*.

—— (1982) *Towards Equality: A Casebook of Decisions on Sex Discrimination and Pay*, EOC, Manchester.

—— (1982) *Proposed Amendments to the Sex Discrimination Act 1975 and the Equal Pay Act 1970 (As amended)*.

—— (1982) *Gender and the Secondary School Curriculum*, Research Bulletin, 6, Spring.

—— (1982) EOC Information Leaflet, *The Case of Gates v. Wirral Borough Council*, December.

—— (1982) EOC Information Leaflet, *The Case of Dick v. University of Dundee*, December.

—— (1983) *Equal Opportunities in Craft, Design and Technology*.

—— (1983) *Girls and Girls' Only Schools: A Review of the Evidence*.

—— (1983) *Information Technology in Schools, The London Borough of Croydon*.

—— (1983) *Report of the formal investigation into Sidney Stringer School and Community College*.

—— (1984) *Report of the formal investigation into Ebbw Vale College*.

—— (1985) EOC Information Leaflet, *The Case of Hay v. Lothian Reg. Council*.

—— (1985) *Equal Opportunities and the School Governor*.

—— (1985) *Equal Opportunities and the Woman Teacher*.

Equals (1983) *Publications to Promote the Participation of Girls and Women in Mathematics, Science and Technology*, Lawrence Hall of Science, University of California, Berkeley.

Foster, V. (1984) *Changing Choices: Girls, School and Work*, Hale & Ironmonger, Sydney.

Fowler, R. (1983) 'Sexually inclusive curriculum' *The Victorian Teacher*, 2 (2), 12–17.

Freeman, G. (1982) *Small School in a State of Change*, Deakin University Press and Victorian Secondary Teachers' Association, Geelong.

Gardner, K., Roughead, C., Vale, C. and Borthwick, A. (1984) 'Sexually inclusive curriculum discussion papers from Exhibition High School', *Project Report No. 5*, Transition Education Advisory Committee, 582 St Kilda Road, Melbourne 3004.

Gardner, P. L. (1984) 'Summary and cross evaluation of national reports', presented at IPN/UNESCO International Symposium on Interests in Science and Technology Education, Kiel, W. Germany April 2–6.

Girls, School and Society (1975) Report by a Study Group to the Australian Schools Commission, Australian Government Printing Service, Canberra.

Grieve, N. (1981) 'Beyond Sexual Stereotypes. Androgyny: A Model or an Ideal?' in N. Grieve and P. Grimshaw (eds), *Australian Women*, Oxford University Press, Oxford.

Griffith, J. A. G. (1977) *The Politics of the Judiciary*, Fontana, London.

Hinkson, J. (1977) 'The emergence of education as therapeutic management of an unconstrained self', unpublished Ph.D. Dissertation, Centre for the Study of Innovation in Education, School of Education, La Trobe University, Bundoora, Victoria, Australia.

HMI (Her Majesty's Inspectorate) (1982) *Technology in Schools*, HMSO, London.

Home Office (1975) *A Guide to the Sex Discrimination Act 1975*, HMSO, London.

—— (1975) White Paper *Equality for Women*, HMSO, London.

Humberside County Council Education Department (1983) *Equal Opportunities and Sex Discrimination*, Humberside County Council, Beverley.

ILEA (Inner London Education Authority) (1982) *Sex Differences in Educational Achievement*: ILEA *Research and Statistics Reports 823/82*, London.

—— (1984) *Women's Careers in Teaching*, ILEA, London.

Jackson, M. (1983) 'More LEAS may join the technical revolution', *Times Educational Supplement*, 4 Feb.

Jackson, S. (1984) 'The Paternal Instinct' in the *Guardian*, 10 July.

Jones, A., Reading, D. and Thurgood, P. (1981) '*Transition Education Girls' Project: Background Information*', unpublished mimeo.

Jones, B., (1982) *Sleepers, Wake! Technology and the Future of Work*, Harvester Press, Brighton.

Kelly, A. (1978) 'Sex differences in science enrolments: Reasons and remedies', *Collaborative Research Newsletters 3 and 4*, Centre for Educational Sociology, University of Edinburgh.

—— (1981) *The Missing Half: Girls and Science Education*, Manchester University Press.

—— (1984) 'The construction of masculine science', submitted to *British Journal of Sociology of Education*, August.

Kelly, A., Whyte, J. and Smail, B. (1984) *Girls into Science and Technology: Final Report*, GIST, Department of Sociology, University of Manchester.

Lakoff, R. (1975) *Language and Women's Place*, Harper & Row, New York.

Lester, A. and Bindman, G. (1972) *Race and Law*, Penguin, Harmonds-worth.

Lippitt, R. O. (1974) 'Identifying, documenting, evaluating and shar-ing innovative classroom practices' *Final Report to the Office of Health Education & Welfare*, USA, cited in Zaltman *et al.*, for which see p. 243.

MacDonald, M. (1980) 'Schooling and the reproduction of class and gender relations' in Barton, L., Meighan, R., and Walker, S. (eds) *Schooling, Ideology and the Curriculum*, Falmer Press, Barcombe.
—— (1980) 'Socio-cultural reproduction and women's education' in Deem, R. (ed.) *Schooling and Women's Work*, Routledge & Kegan Paul, London.

McMullen, J. (1978) *Your Rights at Work; Workers' Guide to Employment Law*, Pluto Press, London.

McRobbie, A. and McCabe, T. (eds) (1981) *Feminism for Girls: An Adventure Story*, Routledge & Kegan Paul, London.

May, N. and Rudduck, J. (1983) *Sex Stereotyping and the Early Years of Schooling*, Centre for Applied Research in Education, University of East Anglia, Norwich.

Millman, V. (1984) *Teaching Technology to Girls*, Coventry LEA.

Ms. Muffet (1981) periodical of the Joint TTUV, VSTA and WTU Elimina-tion of Sexism in Education Project, c/o Victorian Teachers' Union, August, PO Box 456, Camberwell, Victoria 3124, Australia.

MSC (Manpower Services Commission) (1984) *TVEI: Annual Review 1984*, MSC, Sheffield.

Nash, M., Allsop, T. and Woolnough, B. (1984) 'Factors affecting pupil uptake of technology at 14+', *Research in Science and Technological Education*, 2 (1) 5–19.

NATFHE (National Association of Teachers in Further and Higher Education) (1980) *The Education, Training and Employment of Women and Girls*, NATFHE, London.

Newton, P. (1981) 'Who says girls can't be engineers?' in Kelly, A. (ed.) *The Missing Half: Girls and Science Education*, Manchester University Press, Manchester.

NUT (National Union of Teachers) (1980) *Promotion and the Woman Teacher*, NUT/EOC, London.
—— (1983) *TVEI – Extension of pilot scheme*, NUT Circular 392/83, London.

Oakley, A. (1981) 'Interviewing Women: A Contradiction in Terms', in Roberts, H. (ed.) *Doing Feminist Research*, Routledge & Kegan Paul, London.

240   Bibliography

O'Brien, M. (1981) *The Politics of Reproduction*, Routledge & Kegan Paul, Boston.
O'Connor, M. (1982) 'Preparing for the real world outside', *Guardian*, 23 Nov.
Ormerod, M. B. (1971) 'The Social Implications Factor in Attitudes to Science', *British Journal of Educational Psychology*, 41 (3) 335–8.
—— (1975) 'Subject preference and choice in co-educational and single sex secondary schools', *British Journal of Educational Psychology*, 45, November, 257–67.
—— and Duckworth, D., (1975) *Pupils' Attitudes to Science: A Review of Research*, NFER, Slough.

Partington, G. (1976) *Women Teachers in the 20th Century*, NFER-Nelson, Slough.
Payne, G., Cuff, E. and Hustler, D. (1984) 'GIST or PIST: teacher perceptions of the project "Girls Into Science and Technology"', mimeo, Manchester Polytechnic.
Pratt, J., Bloomfield, J. and Seale, C. (1984) *Option Choice: A Question of Equal Opportunity*, NFER-Nelson, Slough.

Rendel, M. (1976) 'Law as an Instrument of Oppression or Reform', *The Sociology of Law*, University of Keele, Keele.
Rendel, M. (1980) 'How many women academics 1912–1976?' in Deem, R. (ed.) *Schooling for Women's Work*, Routledge & Kegan Paul, London.
Rendel, M. (1984) 'Women academics in the seventies' in Acker, S. and Warren Piper, D. (eds) *Is Higher Education Fair to Women?* SRHE & NFER-Nelson, Slough.
Richardson, E. (1973) *The Teacher, the School and the Task of Management*, Heinemann, London.
Roberts, H. (1984) 'A feminist perspective on affirmative action' in Acker, S. and Warren Piper, D. (eds) *Is Higher Education Fair to Women?*, SRHE & NFER-Nelson, Slough.
Rudduck, J. (1981) *Making the Most of the Short In-Service Course*, Methuen, London.
Rutter, M., Maughan, B., Mortimore, P. and Ouston, J. (1979) *Fifteen Thousand Hours: Secondary Schools and Their Effects on Children*, Open Books, London.
Ryrie, A. C., Furst A. and Lauder M. (1979) *Choices and Chances*, Hodder & Stoughton: SCRE.

Sachs, A. and Wilson, J. (1979) *Sexism and the Law*, Free Press, New York.
Saha, L. (1982) 'Gender, school attainment and occupational plans:

determinants of aspirations and expectations among Australian urban school leavers', *Australian Journal of Education*, 26 (3), 247–65.

Sharp, R. and Green, A. (1975) *Education and Social Control*, Routledge & Kegan Paul, London.

Simpson, L. A. (1969) 'Attitudes of higher education employment agents towards academic women', *comment* Wayne State University, Michigan, 12, 1, 41–6.

Slade, P. and Jenner, F. A. (1978) 'Questionnaire measuring attitudes to females' social roles', *Psychological Reports*, 43, 351–4.

Smail, B. (1983) 'Getting Science Right for Girls,' paper presented to the second International Conference on Girls and Science and Technology, Oslo, Norway.

—— (1984) *Girl Friendly Science: Avoiding Sex Bias in the Curriculum*, Longman for the Schools Council, London.

Smail, B., Whyte, J. and Kelly, A. (1982) Girls into Science and Technology: the first two years, *School Science Review* 63, 620–30; *South Australian Science Teachers Association Journal*, (1981), 813, 3–10; EOC Research Bulletin (1982), 6, Spring.

Spear, M. (1984) 'Sex bias in science teachers' ratings of work and pupil characteristics', *European Journal of Science Education*, 6 (4), 369–77

Spender, D. (1980) *Man Made Language*, Routledge & Kegan Paul, London.

—— (1981) 'Education: The Patriarchal Paradigm and the Response to Feminism', in Spender, D. (ed.) *Men's Studies Modified*, Pergamon, Oxford.

Spender, D. and Sarah, E. (eds) (1980) *Learning to Lose: Sexism and Education*, The Women's Press, London.

Stanley, L. and Wise, S. (1983) *Breaking out: Feminist Consciousness and Feminist Research*, Routledge & Kegan Paul, London.

Stantonbury Campus Sexism in Education Group (1984) 'The realities of mixed schooling' in Deem, R. (ed.) *Co-education Reconsidered*, Open University Press, Milton Keynes.

Stanworth, M. (1981) *Gender and Schooling: A Study of Sexual Divisons in the Classroom*, Women's Research and Resources Centre, London. (Revised edn (1983) Hutchinson, London.)

Steedman, J. (1983) *Examination Results in Mixed and Single-Sex Schools: Findings from the National Child Development Study*, EOC, Manchester.

Stenhouse, L. (1975) *An Introduction to Curriculum Research and Development*, Heinemann, London.

Sweet, R. (1980) 'An analysis of trends in the teenage labour markets in N.S.W. 1971–76, (*Research Report*) New South Wales Department of Technical and Further Education, Sydney.

—— (1980) 'The new marginal workers : teenage part-time employment in Australia in the 1970's', *Research Report*, New South Wales Department of Technical and Further Education, Sydney.

Thomas, C. (1980) 'Girls and Counter-school Culture' in D. McCallum and U. Ozolins (eds) *Melbourne Working Papers 1980*, University of Melbourne, Melbourne.

Venning, P. (1983) 'From MSC dream to curriculum reality', *Times Educational Supplement* 14 Oct.
—— (1984) 'And now for something completely different', *Times Educational Supplement* 27 Jan.
Vlemmiks, J. (1983) 'Girls in the Technology Club', *School Technology*, 17(2), 10–11.
VSTA (Victorian Secondary Teachers' Association) (1971) *Secondary Curriculum*, VSTA, Elizabeth Street, Richmond, Victoria 3121, Australia.

Walters, P., Allen, A. J. and Fogarty, M. (1971) *Women in Top Jobs*, Allen & Unwin, London.
Waugh, P. and Foster, V. (1978). 'Education and the "Down-Girl" Principle' *Refractory Girl*, 16.
Wexler, P. (1981) 'Body and Soul: Sources of Social Changes and Strategies of Education', *British Journal of Sociological Education*, 2(3), October, 247–61.
White, D. (1978) 'Create your own compliance: the Karmel prospect', in J. V. D'Cruz and P. Sheehan (eds) *The Renewal of Australian Schools*, (2nd edn) Australian Council for Educational Research, Melbourne.
Whyld, J. (1983) *Sexism in the Secondary Curriculum*. Harper & Row, London.
Whyte, J. (1983) 'Non-sexist teachers: evaluating what teachers can do to help girls opt into science and technology', *Proceedings of the 2nd International GASAT Conference*, Gran, Norway.
—— (1984) 'Observing sex stereotypes and interactions in the school lab and workshop', *Educational Review* 36(1).
—— (in press) *Girls in Science and Technology*, Routledge & Kegan Paul, London.
Wilce, H. (1983) 'TVEI may foster sex differences', *Times Educational Supplement*, 25 Nov.
—— (1984) 'Professor speaks out for sex equality', *Times Educational Supplement*, 30 March.
Witcher, H. (1984) 'Responses to gender typification in the primary classroom', unpublished M. Ed. thesis, University of Stirling.

Womens National Commission (1984) *Interim Report of ad hoc Working Group on Training Opportunities for Women*, WNC, London.

Yates, L. (1983) 'The theory and practice of counter-sexist education in schools', *Discourse* (The Australian Journal of Educational Studies), 3(2), 33–44.

—— (1984) ' "Curriculum becomes our way of contradicting biology and culture" – an outline of some dilemmas for non-sexist education', *Australian Journal of Education*.

Young, M. F. D. (1971) *Knowledge and Control*, Cassell, Collier–Macmillan, London.

Young, M. and Whitty, G. (eds) (1977) *Society, State and Schooling*, Falmer Press, Ringmer.

Zaltman, G., Florio, D. H. and Sikorski, L. A. (1977) *Dynamic Educational Change: models, strategies, tactics and management*, Free Press, New York and Collier-Macmillan, London.

Index

schools – *cont.*
 xiii; head teachers of 109–10;
 more difficult to implement
 equal opportunities in 150–1;
 women teachers in 168);
 science in 17; secondary
 schools xvi, 19, 108 (in Brent
 109; women teachers in 168;
 whole school co-ordinators for
 equal opportunities in 153–4);
 whole school policy 20, 121,
 123, 150, 152, 155; *see also*
 boys' schools, girls' schools
Schools Council 12, 133
School Curriculum Development
 Committee (SCDC) 12
science: departments of 19, 194;
 girls and, *see* girls; girl friendly,
 description of 79–81;
 masculinity of 81–3; pupils'
 interests in 80, 83
Scotland 93
Scottish teachers 74, 93, 96
secondary schools *see* schools
Secondary Science Curriculum
 Review (SSCR) 15
sex bias in books and resources
 19, 81, 114–15, 152
sex differences: in examination
 entries 7–8; in performance on
 APU tests 13; in science
 interests 80–1; in subject
 choice 3; *see also* teachers'
 attitudes, on equal
 opportunities, effects of gender
 on
Sex Discrimination Act (1975) 7,
 18, 24, 159ff., 166ff., 171,
 187, 188; amendments to 161;
 complaints under 167; guide to
 163; provisions of 167;
 weakness in 160–1, 183–6
Sex Disqualification Removal Act
 (1919) 184

sex roles: discussion with pupils of
 17, 88–9, 98–9, 102, 112
sexual harassment 55, 214–15,
 217
sexually inclusive curriculum
 215–16
Sheffield LEA xviii
single sex: crafts clubs 81, 88;
 education, advantages or
 otherwise for girls in 18; groups
 and classes xvii, 80, 122, 123;
 on INSET courses 122, 129;
 science teaching 82–3, 88
strategies 8, 62, 67, 75, 149, 164,
 213, 219; anti-sexist 96, 98,
 100, 102, 106, 124, 134,
 143–4; classroom 100;
 evaluation of 67, 209–26;
 implications of 216–17; for
 intervention, in the GIST
 project 79–83; in the 1970s
 209–10

teachers: of CDT 4; of English,
 project in Brent of 113–14;
 GIST teachers 84–7; of history
 119; included in attitude survey
 on girls and technology 37;
 influence of on girls' choices
 42–3; of physical science 4;
 primary teachers, project in
 Brent of 114; reluctance to
 admit to change of 79, 86–7;
 resistance to change of 123; of
 science 5; Scottish infant 96; of
 secretarial studies 174; of social
 studies 5, 119; of technology 5;
 see also men teachers, teachers'
 attitudes, women teachers
teachers' attitudes xviii, 129, 191;
 attempts to change 86–7;
 biology teachers 26, 27; on
 compulsory physical science 29;
 on co-operative working 126;